100 Years of Rock Climbing in the Lake District

Napes Needle.   *Abraham Collection*

100 YEARS OF ROCK CLIMBING IN THE LAKE DISTRICT

Edited by A. G. Cram

ROCK CLIMBER
1986 STYLE

FELL AND ROCK JOURNAL 1986

David Roberts, President 1984-86.   *Ken Grassick*

THE
FELL AND ROCK
JOURNAL

Edited by A.G. Cram

VOLUME XXIV (2)
No. 70

Published by
THE FELL AND ROCK CLIMBING CLUB
OF THE ENGLISH LAKE DISTRICT
1986

Editor

A.G. Cram
23 Kingsley Avenue
Adel
Leeds 16

Librarian/Reviews

Mrs. M.J. Parker
University Library
Bailrigg
Lancaster

New Climbs

D. Miller
31 Bosburn Drive
Mellor Brook
Blackburn
Lancashire

Photographs/Adverts

R.J. Kenyon
30 Wordsworth Street
Penrith

Obituaries

R. Brotherton
Silver Birch
Fell Lane
Penrith
Cumbria

The editor would like to thank Jean Cram, Muriel & Bobby Files, Ron Kenyon and Peter Hodgkiss for their extra help, as well as all those who have sent articles and photographs, and Jill Aldersley, who provided the excellent sketches.

Only 1000 copies of this issue are for sale.

The Abbot Hall Gallery, Kendal is the custodian of the FRCC collection of Abraham photographs.

Produced by The Ernest Press, Glasgow.

100 years of rock climbing in the Lake District.—
(Fell and Rock Climbing Club journals; no. 70)
1. Rock climbing—England—Lake District—History
I. Cram, Alan Geoffrey II. Fell and Rock
Climbing Club of the English Lake District
III. Series
796.5'223'094278   GV199.44.G72L34
ISBN 0-85028-023-0

CONTENTS

	Page
Editor's Notes .... *Geoff Cram*	1
The First Ascent of Napes Needle .... *W.P.Haskett Smith*	3
A Short History of Lakeland Climbing, Part I .... *H.M.Kelly & J.H.Doughty*	9
A Short History of Lakeland Climbing, Part II .... *John Wilkinson*	39
A Short History of Lakeland Climbing, Part III .... *Pete Whillance*	67
A Short History of Lakeland Climbing, Part IV ...... *Ron Kenyon & Al Murray*	87
The North-East Spur of the Droites .... *Geoff Oliver*	109
Rock Climbing in Northern Italy .... *Al Churcher*	115
13 Miles from the Equator .... *Ray Cassidy*	121
All Out .... *W.Heaton Cooper*	125
The Abraham Collection of Mountaineering Photographs .... *June Parker*	129
The Wasdale Climbing Book................................ *Muriel Files*	139
Scafell Central Buttress .... *G.S.Sansom*	143
More of C.B... *Bill Birkett*	148
Climbing in the Middle Ages .... *Tony Greenbank*	151
The Man Who Broke the Needle .... *Graham Sutton*	155
The Old Man at Stoer .... *Ed Grindley*	160
The Modern Icarus .... *Ed Cleasby*	163
Climbing is more a Dancing Thing .... *Angela Soper*	167
The Well-Oiled Machine — Twelve Months On .... *Tony Burnell*	170
A Ski Mountaineering Jubilee .... *A.Harry Griffin*	175
Way Out West .... *Tom Price*	181
The Day I Broke the Needle .... *Stan Thompson*	187
Winter First Ascent Photographs........................... *Al Phizacklea*	188
Scotland .... *P.A.A.*	190
The Year with the Club .... *Jim Sutcliffe*	191
New Climbs and Notes .... *Alan Murray & Phil Rigby*	196
In Memoriam	213
Reviews..	215
Club Officers and Meets....................................	224

EDITOR'S NOTES

Geoff Cram

In June 1886, W.P. Haskett Smith made the first ascent of Napes Needle, solo, and left his white handkerchief on top 'fluttering in the breeze', an event widely regarded as the beginning of the sport of rock climbing. This year, then, we are celebrating 100 years of rock climbing in the Lake District with a Centenary Meet at Wasdale Head, an exhibition of photographs and a special issue of the *Journal*.

This number of the *Journal* reprints the famous accounts of the first ascents of Napes Needle and Central Buttress and includes a continuous history of rock climbing in the Lake District in four parts. Part I, 1802 to 1934, by Doughty and Kelly, originally appeared in the 1936-37 *Journal*. Part II, by John Wilkinson, covers 1935-59. Part III by Pete Whillance, covers the period from 1960-69. Part IV, by Ron Kenyon and Al Murray, was written at short notice and covers 1970-86.

This special issue has a substantial number of photographs, including many by the Abraham brothers — famous photographers and early members of the Club. Also included is a reflection of the modern rock climbing trend on limestone and on the continent.

It is fifty years since the first sod was cut for the Club hut at Brackenclose. There is considerable enthusiasm at present for the purchase of a suitable hut in Scotland. This would undoubtedly expand the Club's rock, ice, skiing and Munro-bagging activities.

The Fell and Rock Climbing Club has always been closely associated with the development of rock climbing in the Lake District, especially in the production of a continuing series of definitive rock climbing Guides. It is good to see that, with the evolution of 'high-tech' rock climbing, the discovery of large numbers of new climbs continues on high crags and far-flung outcrops. Long may this continue.

1986 is the Year of the Tiger. It is definitely the year to celebrate and enjoy rock climbing in the Lake District.

171   George à cheval on the Arete, Scafell Pinnacle, with Gaspard above. *Abraham Collection*

THE FIRST ASCENT OF NAPES NEEDLE

W.P.Haskett Smith

Reprinted from the FRCC Journal, No.8, 1914

The task of finding anything either new or interesting to say on the subject of the Napes Needle is one which is vastly easier for a light-hearted editor to set than for an unhappy contributor to perform.

Ever since its bold outlines began to stare at us on every railway platform and the newspapers realised that however poorly reproduced its form could never be mistaken for anything else, the British public has been open to listen to the little that can be said about it, and consequently that little has been said over and over again.

However, as was observed by some philosopher whose system made no allowance for trifles like radium and marconigrams: "There is nothing New except the Very Old" — and my only chance will be to dive back into the dark ages, the dim and distant days when the Needle had never been climbed, or even noticed.

One day in the early eighties the weather was beginning to clear after two or three days of southerly gale. Masses of cloud surged up the valley, but after a forenoon of heavy rain were driven from the centre of the dale and clung tightly to the sides of the hills. After luncheon we ventured on a walk to the neighbourhood of Piers Gill, believing that the shelter of Lingmell would give us less wind and less cloud there.

Above Burnthwaite we lingered awhile, watching a curious cloud-eddy at the entrance of Mosedale causing that valley, though sheltered from the wind, to become tightly packed with the backwash at the very time when the main valley was gradually clearing.

As we mounted into the great recess of Greta Force we were almost free from the drift and even got an occasional gleam of sunshine, but across the path to Sty Head only the lower screes were visible and Great Gable was completely concealed. Suddenly, however, the mist grew thinner, and it became just possible to locate the Napes. Then they were swallowed up again, but a moment later the outermost curtain of mist seemed to be drawn aside and one of the fitful gleams of sunshine fell on a slender pinnacle of rock, standing out against the background of cloud without a sign of any other rock near it and appearing to shoot up for 200-300 feet.

The vision did not last more than a minute or two and we all thought that our eyes had been tricked, as indeed to a certain extent they had been, but resolved to take an early opportunity of hunting down the mysterious rock.

In those days climbers had never really looked at the Napes. The vast slopes of cruel scree below them not only kept explorers away, but gave the impression that the whole mass was dangerously rotten.

W.P.Haskett Smith, 1936. *Roland Brown*

The fine cairn built by the brothers Westmoreland to mark a point of view led people to imagine that they had put it up to mark a climb of great severity and it was further supposed that the cliff below that cairn was the only piece of sound rock on that side of the mountain.

We made one attempt a few days later to find our rock and did in fact get to it, but it was a dreadfully thick, dark day, and we were by no means sure of its identity or of its precise position.

I did not return to Wastdale till 1884, and one of my pleasantest memories of the Needle hangs on the fact that my next sight of it was enjoyed in the company of John Robinson and during the very first climb that he and I ever had together.

Petty had made a remarkable recovery from his terrible accident on Mickledore a fortnight before and was considered well enough to be taken home. It was no easy job, however, to get him down from Burnthwaite to the road where the carriage was waiting for him below the inn.

Robinson, good fellow that he was, walked over from Lorton to help and, by means of a rough handbarrow, he and I carried the invalid the whole way. To me it seemed terribly hard work, but the sturdy dalesman's hornier hands stood the strain very much better than mine and, as soon as our farewells had been said and Petty started down the valley, the next question was: where should we go for a climb?

Mr. Bowring, who had been the means of bringing us together, wanted for some reason to take the direction of Sty Head and it was arranged that we should all three go together as far as the great scree funnel at the east end of the Napes known as Hell Gate, though I believe that the maps call it Deep Gill. Here there was at that time a curiosity in the way of climbs. From the stream of scree rises a small island of rock forming a very narrow ridge. The actual crest of this ridge then consisted of a line of sharp triangular blocks all severed from the mother rock but resting pretty firmly on it, owing to their bases being flat though extremely narrow. The problem of passing along them from end to end (which could only be done astride) was delicate enough, but when it came to crossing the gap left by the only block which had fallen, without pulling over either the block you were leaving or that to which you were seeking to transfer your weight, it made all ordinary conjuring tricks seem clumsy by comparison.

After many struggles Robinson had to confess defeat by stepping into the gap; but the next man I brought there did far worse, for he pulled two of the tallest blocks over and at my last visit nothing remained of that once exciting problem.

Our next business was to hunt for my elusive pinnacle and make an examination of the Napes as we went. With this object we climbed up at once and then began a traverse across the face, keeping a rough level of perhaps 100 feet above the foot of the rocks. It was a jolly climb and before long we came rather suddenly into full view of the rock which we were seeking. Robinson's delight was unbounded, and he eagerly inquired whether any Swiss guide would be ready to tackle such a thing.

We did not go down to it, but continued our course to the gap between it and the main rock, turned up the Needle Ridge for a few yards, and crossed it into the Needle Gully, which we followed to the top.

Two years later some friends who had been climbing with me were to leave by way of Drigg and we arranged to start a couple of hours earlier than would otherwise have been needful in order that I might help them along with their sacks, have a farewell climb with them on Buckbarrow, and then return to Tyson's. We rose very early, but some of the party were slow in getting off and we had to hurry. The result was that the long walk in a hot sun left me with a headache by the time I got back to the Inn. The afternoon was cooler, and it occurred to me to stroll over into the head of Ennerdale and have a look at the cliffs on that face of Gable. These had never been climbed at any point, though Cookson and I had made a horizontal route across them about half-way up.

The marks of a recent stonefall drew my attention to a part of the cliff where I found a very fine gully and climbed it, not without difficulty, being impeded by a long fell-pole. Coming out on the top of the mountain I thought of the ridge beside which Robinson and I had come up two years before and made for it, intending to follow the edge down as strictly as might be. This proved to be quite feasible, though at one point my pole gave me a lot of trouble by dropping down a deep and narrow crevice. However, the ridge was so steep at that spot that some 20 feet below, on peering into the crack, I espied my stick stuck upright, and by thrusting my arm in was at length able to reach it with my finger-tips and finally to draw it out.

Continuing down into the gap and now warmed by exertion, I forgot my headache and began to examine the Needle itself. A deep crack offered a very obvious route for the first stage, but the middle portion of this crack was decidedly difficult, being at that time blocked with stones and turf, all of which has since been cleared away. Many capable climbers were afterwards turned back when trying to make the second ascent not by the sensational upper part but by this lower and (under present conditions) very simple piece.

From the top of the crack there is no trouble to reach the shoulder, whence the final stage may be studied at ease. The summit is near, being as they say in Transatlantic cities "only two blocks away," but those same blocks are set one upon the other and the stability of the top one looks very doubtful. My first care was to get two or three stones and test the flatness of the summit by seeing whether anything thrown-up could be induced to lodge. If it did, that would be an indication of a moderatley flat top, and would hold out hopes of the edge being found not too much rounded to afford a good grip for the fingers. Out of three missiles one consented to stay, and thereby encouraged me to start, feeling as small as a mouse climbing a milestone.

Between the upper and lower blocks, about five feet up, there is a ragged horizontal chink large enough to admit the toes, but the trouble is to raise the body without intermediate footholds. It seemed best to work up at the extreme right, where the corner projects a little, though the fact that you are hanging over the deep gap makes it rather a "nervy" proceeding. For anyone in a standing position at the corner it is easy to shuffle the feet sideways to the other end of the chink, where it is found that the side of the top block facing outwards is decidedly less vertical. Moreover, at the foot of this side there appeared to my great joy a protuberance which, being covered with a lichenous growth, looked as if it might prove slippery, but was placed in the precise spot where it would be most useful in shortening the formidable stretch up to the top edge. Gently and cautiously transferring my weight, I reached up with my right hand and at last was able to feel the edge and prove it to be, not smooth and rounded as it might have been, but a flat and satisfactory grip. My first thought on reaching the top was one of regret that my friends should have missed by a few hours such a day's climbing, three new things, and all good; my next was one of wonder whether getting down again would not prove far more awkward than getting up!

Hanging by the hands and feeling with the toes for the protuberance provided an anxious moment, but the rest went easily enough, though it must be confessed that it was an undoubted satisfaction to stand once more on solid ground below and look up at my handkerchief fluttering in the breeze.

Climbers on the Needle and Needle Ridge.   *Abraham Collection*   176

A SHORT HISTORY
OF LAKELAND CLIMBING
PART I (1802 - 1934)

H.M.Kelly & J.H.Doughty

Reprinted from the FRCC Journal, Lakeland Number, 1936-37

Introduction

Climbing history, like the climber's rope, is made up˙of three interwoven strands, which we may designate as the rocks, the climbers, and the sport. It is our aim to trace the development of climbing in its broader technical aspects, but the tale must perforce be told largely in terms of men and routes. It is not proposed to mention all the first ascents made or the persons participating in them. A full knowledge of these can be had from the lists of First Ascents in the new Fell and Rock Club Guides. But as names will have to be mentioned, only those considered to have made some contribution to climbing history and technique will be used. Naturally any references to individuals will be concerned mainly with the leaders of climbs; but it must not be thought that, even if the praises of seconds and other supporters on a climb are left unsung, they have been ignored in our study of the subject: space alone prevents their inclusion. An interesting article could be written on 'Famous Seconds.' Such a one was Morley Wood, who became known as 'the perfect second', whose unambitious mind and general self-effacement always led him to take second place, but did not stop him on occasion from taking greater risks than the leader of the party himself in order that success should crown the efforts of the party. Then there were men like G.S. Sansom and C.F Holland, who, owing to their own aptitude for leadership, were a source of inspiration in their seconding of first ascents. Their climbing with others was in this respect a real partnership and not merely a case of providing morale to the leader by being tied on to the same rope.

Regarding the development of climbing on its technical side, we can distinguish four main phases—*(a)* the period of the Easy Way, no matter what kind of technical problem presented itself, *(b)* the Gully and Chimney period, *(c)* the Ridge and Arête (Rib) period, and *(d)* the Slab and Wall period. It is difficult to assign precise dates to these, as there is considerable overlapping. Perhaps the best course is to recognise this and label them as follows—*(a)* up to 1880, *(b)* 1880 to 1900, *(c)* 1890 to 1905, *(d)* 1905 to date. Apart from this overlapping there have been also, as in all evolutionary processes, the usual anticipations and reversions, such as Eagle's Nest Direct, a *(c)* climb done in the *(b)* period, and Smuggler's Chimney, a *(b)* climb done in the *(d)* period. The accompanying time chart, and still more the list of first ascents at the end of this article, will indicate broadly the scheme of classification and the reasons for it.

Combined tactics on Tophet Arete, the Napes. *Abraham Collection*

One other point calls for mention here. In order to avoid scrappiness, and in the interests of a coherent and comprehensive story we have found ourselves concentrating almost inevitably on the best known climbing grounds and paying scant attention to work on the less frequented outlying crags. This is true both of the history and the accompanying lists of climbs. We should like to state emphatically that it does not betoken any lack of appreciation for this work; and to all who might feel themselves to have suffered disparagement by implication we beg to offer this explanation and our respectful apologies.

THE TIME CHART

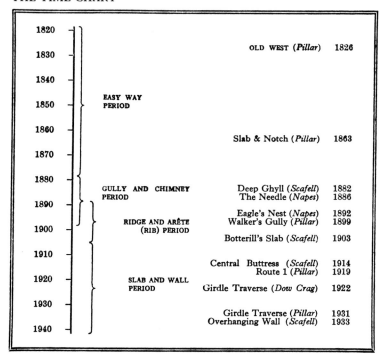

1820		
1830	OLD WEST (*Pillar*)	1826
1840		
1850	EASY WAY PERIOD	
1860		
1870	Slab & Notch (*Pillar*)	1863
1880		
	GULLY AND CHIMNEY PERIOD	Deep Ghyll (*Scafell*) 1882
1890		The Needle (*Napes*) 1886
	RIDGE AND ARÊTE (RIB) PERIOD	Eagle's Nest (*Napes*) 1892
1900		Walker's Gully (*Pillar*) 1899
		Botterill's Slab (*Scafell*) 1903
1910		
		Central Buttress (*Scafell*) 1914
1920	SLAB AND WALL PERIOD	Route 1 (*Pillar*) 1919
		Girdle Traverse (*Dow Crag*) 1922
1930		Girdle Traverse (*Pillar*) 1931
1940		Overhanging Wall (*Scafell*) 1933

The Pioneers

(From the earliest beginnings to the ascent of the Napes Needle)

The history of rock-climbing in the Lake District may be said to have started soon after 1880; for it was in the beginning of the last century that the thoughts of those who frequented these hills began to turn towards the crags which flanked the mountains they climbed. These cliffs must always have held some sort of interest for those who passed them by; but as the summit of the mountain was the object in view, and the grassy slopes seemed to offer the easiest line of ascent, the buttresses and pinnacles encountered en route presented little more than an awful spectacle for aesthetic contemplation.

The first rock-climb of which we have any trace is an undated and uncertain ascent of Broad Stand* alleged to have been made by the poet Coleridge, who was presumably aiming for the summit of Scafell, and took this as the easiest way he could find from Mickledore—the only evident breach in that long line of forbidding cliffs that appeared to extend from Eskdale nearly to Wasdale. Coleridge, who was a keen mountaineer, influenced Wordsworth in the same direction; and the latter must have helped even though unwittingly, to produce the change in men's minds, for it was his reference to Pillar Rock in his poem 'The Brothers' that gave general publicity to its existence. It is true that Green and other earlier Guide writers, had mentioned the Pillar Stone as one of the sights for the tourist to see as he wended his way up Ennerdale; but to them it was just a striking distant view, whilst Wordsworth's reference was of the morbid kind which always attracts closer and greater attention. It is not claimed that climbing had its genesis in morbid curiosity. All that Wordsworth did was to focus attention on the Rock, and its isolation naturally became a challenge to those who visited it; so that we may fairly assert that Atkinson's ascent of it in 1826 was the inauguration of rock-climbing as we know it today. Could it have begun in a more alluring spot!

Up to now, all that the mountaineer had been concerned with was the summit and the view he could see therefrom. A new element arose when Atkinson got to the top of Pillar Rock—the lure of the inaccessible. Yet it is interesting to note that the idea of reaching the summit of some kind remained for many years (as is still remains in countries where summits difficult of access are more plentiful) a controlling influence. The idea of a climb without some obvious top in view was a plant of very slow growth, and definite points such as Pillar Rock, Scafell Pinnacle, and Napes Needle were for long the main centres of attraction. Indeed, it was not until the late 'sixties, by which time nearly thirty people had followed in Atkinson's footsteps, that any crag other than the Pillar attracted attention from climbers at all, and by 1872 no less than four distinct routes to its summit had been discovered, the Old West Route, the Old Wall Route, the Slab and Notch Climb, and the Pendlebury Traverse.

* Actually a descent, 5 August 1802; see FRCC *Journal* 1985, p55.

Despite this concentration on Pillar, Scafell had not passed unnoticed, for this was the crag which, in the 'sixties, provided an alternative climbing ground. Here three routes had been worked out—Petty's Rift, the North Climb, and Mickledore Chimney. The motive behind these ascents is an interesting subject for conjecture. Was it climbing for climbing's sake, or were they prompted by a desire to avoid the awkward Broad Stand route to Scafell summit? Even as late as 1881 we find Jenkinson writing in his *Practical Guide to the English Lakes* 'To cross the Mickledore Chasm from Scawfell Pike to Scawfell, without making a detour, is considered, next to the dangerous ascent of Pillar Rock, as the most difficult bit of mountaineering work in the Lake Country.'

However, with the beginning of the Gully and Chimney period all doubt as to motive was set at rest. Rock-climbing as a sport in itself was definitely established. The Alpinist was to some extent responsible for this. Winter climbing in Switzerland at this time was not generally, if at all, thought of as a possibility; and the Alpinist's need to be on some mountain or other drove him to consider whether his own lesser hills might not fill this winter hiatus. Moreover, there was always the possibility of winter conditions at home approximating to summer conditions abroad. His home mountains, too, would keep him fit for his beloved Alps. So he went to the gullies and wide chimneys which he might hope to find filled with snow and thus get some practice for the greater couloirs. That he did not always find them so—much to the benefit of his rock technique—did not stop him from treating British hills as small alps, and so his conquest followed Alpine tradition. Because of this training and mental outlook, he was rather inclined to frown upon anything savouring of what he dubbed 'rock-gymnastics.' Nevertheless, and despite the fact that his prejudices died very hard (for they were in evidence up to 1914, if not later), it cannot be gainsaid that he played a considerable part in the development of cragsmanship.

It was W.P. Haskett-Smith who showed the real possibilities of the sport as a thing to be enjoyed for itself alone, and during the decade of the 'eighties he set his mark for all time on British Cragsmanship. No other man has wielded anything like the same influence. It is no exaggeration to call him the Father of British rock-climbing. The impossible became at once a target for his skill and natural ability, and his successes were many and varied. At one end of the scale is the Napes Needle, while at the other is the long and successful siege of the North Climb on Pillar Rock. He made the Needle his very own, and his lone ascent of it was the second landmark in climbing history. He laid all the great crags under contribution, as a glance at the List of First Ascents will show. But it was the ascent of the Needle which had the greatest import. As an example of this, it is said that a photograph of it in a London shop turned O.G. Jones's thoughts to the possibilities of Lake District climbing, and there can be no doubt about the role *he* played in its development.

A constant companion of Haskett-Smith was John W. Robinson who

Near the summit of Scafell Pinnacle; John Wilson Robinson, W. Blunt and V. Blake.   182
Abraham Collection

lived at Lorton, near Cockermouth. He probably introduced the former to the Needle for he had an early acquaintance with it as the following will show. Seatree, in an obituary notice, writes: 'John told me of his father so far back as 1828 discovering and sketching the Gable Needle on one of his youthful excursions across the Wasdale face of that mountain.' Naturally with breeding such as this, Robinson acquired an extensive knowledge of fells and crags which he placed at the disposal of Haskett-Smith and others. He was a great walker and rock-climber and was endowed with extraordinary endurance and strength. For example, 'when living at Lorton he frequently rose at 4 a.m. walked to Wasdale Head to join a party of climbers, completed a hard day's climbing, and then tramped home apparently as fresh and vigorous as when he started.' In fact Lorton was almost invariably his headquarters for any day's climbing. Such enthusiasm was a great inspiration to others and it is not difficult to measure his contribution to the sport. The memorial notice to him in the first issue of this Journal gives a fuller insight into the character of this great-hearted mountaineer than is possible here.

Another prominent figure of this period was George Seatree, a native of Penrith. He was first attracted to the sport by the fame of Pillar Rock and made an ascent of it in 1875. Although he did not neglect the other crags, it was his first love which claimed most of his attention and he treated the Rock as a sort of shrine. Many were the parties which he conducted to the sanctuary on the top. His devotion was whole-hearted and the greater part of our knowledge of the early history of Pillar is due to the care and foresight with which he collected every scrap of information relating to his beloved crag. Perhaps this concentrated devotion was the reason why his name does not appear in First Ascents, for he was a skilful climber and a great friend of Robinson's with whom he did a great deal of climbing. Both being 'natives' they had much in common apart from their genuine love for the fells.

The Master Builders

Naturally, with this new-born enthusiasm, new ascents were quickly discovered. First came the easy gullies, such as those on Great End, in the early 'eighties, followed by such climbs as the shorter routes on Pillar Rock (Central Jordan, Great Chimney, etc.). There were, however, bigger fish to be fried, and the conquest of Moss Ghyll by J. Collier, G. Hastings, and J.W. Robinson in 1892, clearly received its inspiration from the wonderful victory over the north side of Pillar Rock in 1891 by W.P. Haskett-Smith, G. Hastings and W.C. Slingsby. Haskett-Smith with various companions had roamed up and down the north face of Pillar on and off for ten years, always to be defeated by that steepening of the cliff which extends from the north-west angle of Low Man eastward to the Nose overhanging Savage Gully. Did they turn down Savage

A.E. Field on the Collie Step, Moss Ghyll, Scafell.   *Abraham Collection*   184

Savage Gully in despair of ever climbing the Nose? It is strange nowadays to think of the hero of the Napes Needle being defeated by the severity of the Nose. The cause could not have been isolation or altitude—one would have thought the exposure was about equal in both cases. Possibly what is now a clean landing on sound bare rock may have been an earth-covered ledge heaped with scree from Stony Gully above. Howbeit, the problem was solved in the following year by the Hand Traverse, a much more strenuous and exposed route than the Nose itself. After this the Nose seems to have lost its terrors for it was climbed in the following year.

Haskett-Smith collected another scalp in the shape of a short climb on to Scafell Pinnacle from Jordan Gap (another place which was probably earth-covered), and this naturally led to the frontal attacks on the Pinnacle by Steep Ghyll in the same year, and the Slingsby's Chimney route in 1888.

The leading figures during this time were Haskett-Smith, Robinson, Hastings, Slingsby, Collie, and Collier, and gullies and chimneys were falling right and left to their assaults. Noteworthy feats were the overthrow of the Great Gully of the Screes under the leadership of G. Hastings, and the conquest of Moss Ghyll in the same year (1892) by a party led by J.N. Collie. Moss Ghyll proved a most popular addition and along with the North Climb on Pillar has remained a classic to this day.

It was a little outside this period, however, when O.G. Jones sealed the Gully Period by his magnificent achievement, on a cold January day in 1899, over Walker's Gully, a truly noble cleft, as Laycock remarks, and in most respects our finest gully climb this side of the Scottish border. Though Savage Gully was done in 1901 it belongs, by its very character, to a later phase, combining as it does all the qualities of the Gully-Chimney cum Slab and Wall Period.

It would seem that up to now the climber demanded from his climb some sort of enclosing protection for his body, and as the wide gullies were gradually vanquished, it was naturally to the remaining—and narrower—fissures that he looked for further routes. These, though often only wide enough for the insertion of an arm and leg, still gave some degree of the sense of security, and so it came about that a host of chimneys of varying widths were added to the growing list of climbs. Amongst these might be mentioned Gwynne's Chimney, Oblique Chimney, Kern Knotts Chimney, Shamrock Chimneys, and Hopkinson's Crack. Thus the climber was gradually squeezed out on to the faces of the cliffs in order to increase, and give variety to, his climbing.

He was however, still reluctant to take undue risks and in consequence he turned to the edges or ribs of the crags, for these by the very nature of their structure would give frequent halting places, as well as afford more opportunity for anchorage than the more exposed walls and slabs. It should be recalled that a forestate of this was experienced in the middle 'eighties, for the Needle Ridge was ascended by then. Still, it was not until the late 'nineties that serious attention was paid to them, and bearing this in mind it still seems an outstanding feat on G.A. Solly's part to have led a party up the direct route of Eagle's Nest Ridge in 1892, two days before the West Chimney was first done, the latter a reversion to the Gully Period and very much in the nature of an anti-climax. The Arrowhead Ridge (Ordinary Way) followed suit the same day as the West Chimney under the leadership of Slingsby. Other climbs of this character were Pisgah Buttress, Shamrock Buttress, Bowfell Buttress, C. Buttress, Abbey Buttress, and Gordon and Craig Route. O.G. Jones, however, was now on the scene and had weighed up the possibility of scaling the Pinnacle of Scafell via Low Man from Deep Ghyll, a programme which he brought to fruition in 1896; this was a combination of crack, face, and perpendicular arête (rib) climbing. A later, but more wonderful achievement than this was his forcing of a way up the front of the Pinnacle Face in 1898, a feat ranking with that of Solly's effort on Eagle's Nest. It was, however, not a ridge climb but a great forerunner of the Slab and Wall Period.

With the turn of the century we enter upon a new phase of British Climbing. The great fissures and ridge routes had all been conquered, and the climber desirous of fresh triumphs was forced out on to the open faces; the Slab and Wall Period had begun. Jones's stupendous performance on the Pinnacle Face of Scafell had already pointed the way, and whilst this climb was not itself to be repeated until 1912, the new decade gave birth to a number of climbs of similar character. Some of these took place on Gimmer Crag, hitherto unexplored but now yielding to the efforts of some bold pioneers, among whom E. Rigby and H.B. Lyon were especially prominent. There was also considerable activity on Dow Crag, in which the brothers Abraham, the brothers Broadrick, and the brothers Woodhouse played leading parts. But the most remarkable developments were due to that wayward genius, Fred Botterill, who startled the climbing world in 1903 by his *tour de force* on the famous slab of Scafell that bears his name, and followed this up three years later by his first ascent of the North-West Climb on Pillar Rock. Both were climbs of great severity and exposure which were looked at askance for some years. Like Jones's route, they were before their time both in character and quality, setting an entirely new standard.

Things were really beginning to move. Haskett-Smith had published in 1894 his small but charming guide to climbing in England and Wales, and O.G. Jones produced in 1897 his classic *Rock Climbing in the English Lake District*, in which he introduced a classification of climbs prevailing to this day. The written word was not wasted on the desert air, for we find 'two enthusiasts' in 1906 making for Dow Crag 'every Sunday for fell rambling and first essays in rock-climbing, for they had read Owen Glynne Jones, and so knew all about it.' Obviously the thing could not rest there and they looked round for kindred spirits, discovered three in the persons of Charles Grayson, G.H. Charter, and S.H.Gordon, and decided that they were good enough to form a climbing club with. Thus started in 1906 the Fell and Rock Club of the English Lake District.

It was by the shores of Goat's Water that it was born, and whilst the majestic Pillar of Ennerdale and the mighty cliffs of Scafell were magnetising men's minds and bodies, it was left to the humbler outpost, Dow Crag, to have the greatest influence of all. Little did Owen Glynne Jones, when his love for the Lakeland crags inspired him to write his book, and Alan Craig and E. Scantlebury when they devoured his words, realise what they were starting. An extract from the first membership ticket will not be out of place here:

'This Club was founded in November, 1906, with the sole object of fostering a love of mountaineering and the pastime of rock-climbing in the English Lake District, and to provide such facilities for its members as to enable them to meet together in order to participate in this sport in one another's company; also to enable lovers of this branch of athletics to become acquainted with one another; and further, to provide information and advice on matters pertaining to local mountaineering and rock-climbing.'

The Club commenced with a library of one book, naturally Jones's 'and one-100 ft rope for use in case of emergency,' the last a cryptic phrase which possibly means if a member turns up without a rope of his own. This question of the rope is of interest, for it must be borne in mind that the general use of the rope—if any at all— probably did not start till about 1880. When George Seatree 'met my old friend J.W. Robinson in 1886' he was surprised to find that the latter had brought a climbing rope with him, which caused Seatree to write later: 'I then found how vast had been the progress made in the art and sport of rock-climbing in Lakeland. A multitude of ascents had been achieved.' It will be noticed that Seatree refers to his 'old friend' (elsewhere he states that he met Robinson in 1874). One surmises from this that Robinson had had the use of the rope recently introduced to him, by whom we cannot say. Probably some of the Alpinists were responsible. Anyhow, its introduction gave the climber greater confidence, with the result mentioned by Seatree.

Coming back to the Fell and Rock Club, its growth was mushroom like, for it at once attracted a host of men interested in the sport, among whom were the brothers George and Ashley Abraham, who by their literary enterprise, and their skill alike in cragsmanship and photography, have left their mark on British climbing.

Earlier mention has been made of the difficulty of assigning any particular date to any particular phase or type of climbing; but there is no doubt that about 1910 exposure was less and less considered a bar to route-finding, in consequence of which the technique of the sport developed in a surprising degree. Hitherto one might claim that the race was to the strong, if not necessarily of the Sandow type, but now it was found that delicacy of balance and good nerve could be put to considerable service in the cause. At the same time the climber was gaining a wider acquaintance with the cliff faces he frequented through the increase in the number of climbs, and increased geographical knowledge inspired further exploration.

PIONEERS OF THE FELL AND ROCK CLUB.
(S. H. Gordon, E. H. P. Scantlebury, A. Craig, R. Goodier, C. Grayson).

Various factors contributed towards the new outlook; but it undoubtedly derived its chief impetus from the advent into the climbing world of S.W.Herford, G.S.Sansom, J.Laycock, A.R.Thomson, and their companions. The names of Laycock and Thomson must be mentioned, because although they were not in the big things the other two did, their knowledge of climbing was extensive, and their association with Herford was of real importance. From 1910 to 1912, while Herford was still an undergraduate at Manchester University, these three spent most of the week-ends, when time could not be spared for visits to the Lakes or Snowdonia, on the gritstone crags of Derbyshire. The repercussions of this fact, indeed, the general influence of the gritstone training ground on the modern development of our sport, are perhaps imperfectly appreciated. Gritstone climbs are short; but they have a high standard of severity and exposure; and the exiguous nature of their holds tends to produce a balance technique which is precisely what is required for face climbing of the delicate order. One need only cite the names of a few men who have had their early training and experience on gritstone—Botterill, Herford, Kelly, Frankland, Pigott, Linnell, A.T. Hargreaves—to drive home the point. Haskett-Smith would probably have led the Nose on Pillar at the first attempt if he had had any gritstone experience at that time. Laycock's little book *Some Gritstone Climbs* has had a much bigger influence than its size and subject would indicate; and those acquainted with the climbs he describes will admit that it is not a far cry from The Crack at Castle Naze to the Pinnacle Face of Scafell; so that when Herford in 1912 carried his superfine technique to the greater cliffs, it is not surprising that these huge challenging slabs claimed his early attention. Their upper reaches had been explored by C. Hopkinson in 1893 and the lower part had been climbed by Jones in 1898, as already described. But Jones's Route had never been repeated, and the disastrously abortive attempt to link up the two sections in 1903 had only succeeded in investing climbers with an almost superstitious dread of the awful face, which even the brilliant exploits of Botterill did nothing to dispel. And now came a veritable Siegfried, to whom its legendary inaccessibility was as little daunting as Loge's encircling fires had been to his namesake of the ancient story. In April, 1912, Herford repeated Jones's climb, and before the year was out had not only climbed the face from bottom to top but had forced a way up Hopkinson's Gully, both climbs being done in company with G.S. Sansom. A year later, the same brilliant partners worked out the magnificent Girdle Traverse of Scafell, and it is perhaps not too fanciful to ascribe the novel development once more to the gritstone influence. When rocks are less than a hundred feet in height, the climbers are led to the idea of traversing in order to gain a respectable length, and we know that girdle traverses on at least two of the gritstone cliffs had been made prior to this date. The apogee of the Herford-Sansom combination was reached in 1914 when the hitherto impregnable Central Buttress of Scafell was vanquished. Despite the plethora and severity of more modern discoveries it can still hold its place with the hardest of them, and will continue to do so, for most parties attempting it have still to adopt the combined tactics invented by the first leaders to overcome the Great Flake. Undoubtedly it stamped climbing with yet a new hallmark, and the inspiration due to it is not yet exhausted: all the great modern climbs in the British Isles are its lineal descendants. These men, too, gave evidence of the new spirit that had entered into the sport—the feeling that rock-climbing was an art in itself and could be pursued for its own sake and enjoyment. Unlike Jones and others of his day, they hadn't one foot on Scafell and the other on the Matterhorn. There was, indeed, something like an inversion of values; men began to measure the routes in the Alps against their own climbs. The former were certainly not technically more difficult; as far as rock work was concerned it was mainly a matter of more stamina. The self-reliance engendered at home may also have influenced guideless climbing abroad. The Central Buttress was first climbed in April, 1914. A few months later its conqueror was serving as a private in France, the prescience of the War Office having failed to discern in him sufficient evidence of powers of leadership to warrant the granting of the commission he applied for. In January, 1916, he fell in action.

The Inheritors

(Post-war climbing)

With the close of hostilities in 1918 a great renaissance in climbing was naturally to be expected. For four long years the big majority of active climbers had been able to pay but brief, fugitive visits to their happy hunting grounds; and now they returned with an avidity sharpened by the lengthy period of rock-starvation, and the spirit of adventure which the searing experiences of the war had intensified rather than dulled. Yet an observer of those days might well have had misgivings as to the outcome. Had Herford been a solitary genius to whom no heir could be expected, whose vitalising influence had expired with his own demise? Were there indeed the opportunities for further explorations of this order? Even so shrewd a judge as Laycock had expressed some doubts. 'From 1911 onwards it has been no easy matter to discover good new climbs in England and Wales.' Thus we find him writing in 1916. It is true that a few lines later he continues, with characteristic generosity and breadth of view: '....a new tradition has arisen. But all Herford's friends will be, as he himself would have been, the first to welcome the arrival of a greater climber still.'

All doubts were soon laid to rest. It would be rash to assert that a greater climber arose, or has since arisen; but this much can be said with confidence—that within a few brief years of the post-war era a new harvest had been garnered, far surpassing in quantity anything accomplished hitherto in a comparable period of time, and much of it at least worthy of the new tradition in its quality.

The first blow of the new campaign may be said to have been struck by G.S.Bower in his ascent of Route D on Gimmer Crag in May, 1919; but all other doings of that vintage year were eclipsed by the performances of that remarkable triumvirate, C.G.Crawford, C.F.Holland and H.M.Kelly. Of these, Holland formed a direct link with pre-war climbing: he had been with Herford and Sansom on their exploration of the Central Buttress. A great climber, an even greater inspirer, he has probably exerted more influence on ambitious youth in the climbing world than any other man of our time. His knowledge of the crags was extensive, his courage boundless, his temperament ideal. Holland's eye for a route, Crawford's cheery optimism in conjunction with his remarkable aptitude for the sport, and Kelly's technical skill in leadership formed an irresistible combination when these three got together. They first swept clean the face of Scafell Pinnacle, climbing every route already known upon it, and making numerous variations of great merit. They next transferred their attentions to the west face of Pillar Rock, which has had a curious history. Although the Rock had proved a focus of attraction for more than half a century, exploration was for a long time concentrated on the northern, southern, and eastern sides, and Atkinson's original route in 1826 remained in solitary splendour on the western face until 1901, when the brothers Abraham worked out their ingenious and entertaining New West Climb. Then in 1911, H.R.Pope led the South-West Climb, a delicate face route of high standard. Thus we had three climbs spread over nearly a century. Within a fortnight the number was more than doubled; on 27th July they repeated Pope's climb and improved it by a direct finish. Two days later Holland led them up the Rib and Slab Climb, and Kelly made a new route up the West Wall of Low Man. Crawford and Holland now turned back to Scafell, while Kelly went off to Gable with R.E.W.Pritchard, and added three first-class routes to the four previously known on Kern Knotts. On 9th August he was back at Pillar, and along with Holland made two further routes of superlative difficulty up the west wall of High Man. It was truly a wonderful year, and before closing its account we must mention the ascent of the Great Central Route on Dow Crag by J.I.Roper and G.S.Bower. Though not a climb of great length, this was of the super-severe standard which the climbing world was now for the first time coming to take as a matter of course, and it had for its own crag much the same detonating effect that climbs like the Central Buttress and Routes I and II on Pillar had in other fields.

The story of the next year is largely concerned with the exploits of G.S.Bower. Besides accompanying Kelly and Pritchard on two notable routes on opposite sides of Deep Ghyll, he was himself responsible for quite a number of additions to the climbs on Gimmer, Pavey Ark, and Dow Crag, and broke entirely new ground by his climb on Esk Buttress, a course giving 400 feet of severe climbing.

It was now becoming clear that climbing had entered upon a fundamentally new phase. What had been regarded a few years before as the unapproachable plane of performance attainable by occasional gifted geniuses like Jones, Botterill, Herford, was now looked upon rather as the norm by which our leading climbers measured their own achievements. Virgin rock was approached in a new spirit of confidence and enterprise. It was not that the best men were any better than the giants of the past, but they were more numerous, while the standard of ability among climbers in general had increased enormously. The quickened interest in climbing and the rapid growth in technical skill were stimulated by the timely appearance of two books, H. Raeburn's *Mountaineering Art*, and G.Winthrop Young's monumental *Mountain Craft*, in which the problems of climbing technique were handled with a fullness and clarity unapproached hitherto.

The first wave of post-war activity had by no means spent its force in the achievements of 1919-20 which have already been detailed; and although there was nothing later which quite matched those wonder-years in splendour, first ascents, continued to pour in for a good many years in a fairly steady stream. It is impossible within the limits of this account to particularise more than a few of these, and the basis of selection is perhaps a little arbitrary, so that the reader may take it that for every climb mentioned there are at least two or three more of approximately equal merit. Among the major crags, attention was chiefly focussed on Dow Crag, Gimmer, and the Napes. The last named cliff was pretty thoroughly combed by various enthusiasts among whom C.D.Frankland and Fergus Graham were prominent. Further east, Kelly and Bower added to their respective successes Tophet Wall and the repulsive (looking) Innominate Crack on Kern Knotts. Meanwhile Bower was continuing his explorations of the more holdless sections of Gimmer and Dow Crags, and in connection with these climbing grounds especially the name of H.S.Gross became increasingly prominent. His successive Eliminate Routes conformed to the best standards of contemporary severity, whilst the magnificent Girdle Traverse of Dow Crag was worthy to rank with its famous counterpart on Scafell.

After the great successes of 1919, it is not surprising that we have little fresh to record on Scafell Crag. The second and third ascents of Central Buttress were made in 1921, 1922 by C.D.Frankland and A.S.Pigott respectively. In 1925 the enterprise of Fergus Graham in forcing a direct route to Moss Ledge showed that even the Pinnacle Face was not quite exhausted, and in the following year Kelly found a new route up the Central Buttress by way of the Moss Ghyll Grooves.

We have said that it is impossible to detail all the new climbs made at this period; but some mention must be made of those enterprising explorers who collected not merely new climbs, but new crags. They included, among others, Mosedale Buttresses (F.Graham), Boat Howe Crags (G.Basterfield and G.Graham Brown), Green Gable Crags (G.G.Macphee), and Black Crag, Ennerdale (the Wood-Johnson brothers). In this class also may be mentioned the

WEST FACE OF HIGH MAN.

R².—ROUTE 2.   R¹.—ROUTE 1.   R.S.—RIB AND SLAB CLIMB.
N.W.—NEW WEST CLIMB.   S.W.—SOUTH WEST CLIMB.
W.J.G.—WEST JORDAN GULLY.   P.—PISGAH WEST RIDGE.

opening up of the southern end of Pikes Crag by Kelly and Holland in 1924.

Yet another noteworthy feature of this period was the rapid growth in the art of descent. Herford's famous article, 'The Doctrine of Descent' in the 1914 *Journal*, coupled with the increasing influence of gritstone-trained climbers to whom the descent of severe courses was all in the day's work, produced a marked effect and classic routes like Savage Gully and Botterill's Slab were now descended for the first time. Nowadays few first ascents of importance go for very long before a first descent is also made.

Toward the end of the first decade of post-war climbing a kind of lassitude set in. It seemed as if the great wave of exploration started by Herford and so brilliantly ridden by his immediate followers had spent its force at last.

But it surged up again in 1928 when the temporary association of H.G.Knight and H.M.Kelly produced new climbs on Pillar, the Napes, and Kern Knotts—the Kern Knotts Chain, another girdle traverse, being a climb of quite exceptional severity. After that it seemed for a time to be almost in danger of subsiding altogether; and it must be confessed that about this period the centre of gravity of British climbing had shifted to another part of our island.

The history of Welsh climbing is, of course, beyond the purview of this article. The restriction is the less regrettable since developments in Snowdonia have followed courses roughly parallel to those in our own district, a fact which is not so remarkable when we consider that, apart from a few conspicuous exceptions, the same leading figures have been responsible for exploration in both regions. The post-war renaissance in North Wales lagged a little behind that in the Lakes; it was just about reaching its full force as the great wave further north was beginning to die down, and it obtained especial impetus from the ascent by A.S.Pigott in 1927 of the East Buttress of Clogwyn du'r Arddu. The particular importance of this climb lay in the fact that it opened up the possibilities of a crag of major proportions, which had hitherto been regarded as invulnerable. It therefore set men thinking along new lines, much as the ascent of Central Buttress and the great 1919 campaign on Pillar had done. A year later the companion West Buttress fell, this time to J.L.Longland, with the original conqueror Pigott in the party. Thenceforward the exploration of the crag proceeded apace, chiefly through the enterprise of C.F.Kirkus, one of a band of brilliant young members of the Climbers' Club, who were specially active in Wales about this time.

The two years 1929-30 were comparatively barren in the Lake District, but the next year saw the making of two first-class routes in which the Clogwyn du'r Arddu influence was plainly discernible. There was no virgin crag in Lakeland to compare with this mighty cliff, but the nearest approach to it was undoubtedly the East Buttress of Scafell. Though not on so large a scale as Clogwyn, its steepness, severity, and reputed inaccessibility were quite comparable; whilst in some respects, such as the relative absence of vegetation, it might claim a slight superiority. In 1931 Kirkus tried it at its northern end (an

attempt on this out of Mickledore Chimney had been started but abandoned by Kelly some years earlier) and made the first ascent by the Mickledore Grooves.

The other great climb of this year was due to the inspiration of an equally brilliant young cragsman, Maurice Linnell, whose untimely loss in 1934 was a disaster to British climbing only to be compared with the death of Herford. Linnell had climbed a great deal with Kirkus and was himself responsible for one of the hardest of all the hard Clogwyn du'r Arddu climbs. And now in conjunction with A.B. Hargreaves and A.W. Bridge (who must be reckoned joint leader) he made the first Girdle Traverse of Pillar Rock. At this point we may summarise the intervening and subsequent history of the famous Stone, which was last mentioned in connection with the great campaign of 1919. In 1920 and 1923 Kelly made further climbs on the West Wall of Low Man, and in 1928, in company with H.G. Knight, yet another route, this time on the west wall of Walker's Gully. The Girdle Traverse opened the eyes of climbers to the possibilities of the last inviolate section of Pillar—the formidable stretch between the North and North-West climbs, and A.T. Hargreaves made two new routes here in 1932 and 1933, the Nor'-Nor'-West Climb and Hadrian's Wall, which are among the hardest of the Pillar climbs.

Meanwhile, Linnell had turned his attention to the East Buttress of Scafell and in the summers of 1932 and 1933 (the last summer, alas! in which he was to climb) launched a series of great attacks with the result that this supremely formidable face, which three years before had been unclimbed, now possessed several magnificent routes. Two of these, it must be mentioned, were led by A.W. Bridge and A.T. Hargreaves respectively, but Linnell was in at both and was himself responsible for the remainder.

Summary

With this series of splendid leads our tale of first ascents may fitly close. If it has been too much a tale of first ascents, we can only plead that these, like specific advances or battles in military history are the obvious, convenient pegs on which to hang the skein. But we have tried to indicate throughout the broad background of general development that lies behind these glittering fires of individual performance; and the present is a convenient stage at which to review a few of the more general aspects which have received too scant attention.

We have seen how British climbing, originally—like Alpinism—a pursuit of summits, and for long regarded even on its technical side as a humble handmaid of Alpinism, gradually established itself as an independent sport, in which the route is followed for its own sake. We have seen, too, how the early climbers, ever prone to seek the deeper recesses of the crags for their big routes, were gradually driven into the narrower fissures, and finally forced out on to the ridges and open faces.

Concurrently with this may be observed certain technical developments in the art of climbing. The main tendency here, as we have already noted, has been away from mere strength and toward delicate balance work. This is not to disparage the older climbers, especially the best of them. There can have been nothing seriously amiss with the technique that took Haskett-Smith up the Needle, Solly up Eagle's Nest Ridge, or Jones across the Pinnacle Face. Nevertheless, it cannot be denied that a concentration on fissure climbing tends to develop a kind of 'all in' technique which lacks the delicacy and precision in the use of holds which are called for by the more difficult face routes so common today. In some of the older books the novice was enjoined to practice exercises which would develop his muscles, especially his arm muscles—such as pulling up and down twenty times in succession on a horizontal bar. In *Mountain Craft*, Geoffrey Winthrop Young recommends him to take up dancing.

Of course the comparison is not all to the advantage of one side. Some brilliant face-climbers of the younger generation are relatively clumsy in cracks and chimneys. Even the psychological situation may become inverted. Whereas the older climbers sought the rifts for the comforting suggestion of security afforded by their retaining walls, one may find nowadays an occasional cragsman who, whilst perfectly at home on the slenderest of airy stances, seems to suffer from a paralysing claustrophobia when immersed in the depths of a gully. On the whole, however it must be admitted that the average modern climber has a much completer technical equipment than his predecessors; and there can be no doubt that there has been since the war, a substantial increase not only in the average standard of climbing, but also in the rapidity with which beginners learn their craft. In early days the neophyte was expected to begin on the easiest climbs and work his way upwards methodically through the moderates and difficults. If he was sufficiently gifted, he might hope, after some years of this patient apprenticeship, to lead a severe—and that (if he was a conscientious member of the F. & R.C.C.) only under conditions carefully prescribed by the Committee. (*FRCC Journal no. 3*, p.318) Our young men of today would laugh at such elaboration. They start their training on difficults and expect to be leading severes within a year or two; after two or three years the best of them will be hankering after Central Buttress or something near that class. And whilst at times this speeding up may be overdone—to the learner's ultimate detriment—it is as unnecessary as it would be futile to demand a return to the more pedestrian methods of the past.

One notable result of the lessened importance of muscular effort in climbing technique has been a marked increase of interest in the sport by women. There have been some women climbers almost from the earliest days, but for long they worked under serious handicaps. The great demands on strength made by some of the early climbs (at least as climbed by the early methods) and the unsuitability of the garb prescribed by convention: these were bad enough, but they were as nothing compared to the supreme psychological handicap imposed by the general relationship between the sexes. Women were still regarded very much as objects of male protection. Once the idea of their climbing at all had been accepted, the protective attitude was marked, and it is amusing to read some of the older accounts of climbs with a woman in the party (she was, of course, never referred to as a 'woman'—always a 'lady'). When the climb is finally accomplished the 'lady' invariably comes in for a special meed of praise; but one feels behind it all the implication that the plaudits should really be reserved for the gallant fellows who had cheerfully accepted the unwonted burden and risen so nobly to the occasion. And of course, one great difficulty in combating this attitude was that too many of the women climbers were prepared to accept it. The more independent revolted, naturally; but it was not until 1921 that this revolt showed itself openly in the formation of an independent women's climbing club. The term 'revolt' is perhaps a little strong here, and certainly the setting up of the new organisation implied no sort of antagonism with the Fell and Rock Club, which had admitted women from the start. But 'Pat' Kelly, the founder of the Pinnacle Club, believed, and rightly so, that women could not hope to develop fully their climbing potentialities under the conditions of that time unless they did some at least of their climbing quite independently of men. Her own remarkable powers (at that time she was probably in a class by herself among British women climbers) she willingly placed at the service of this cause; and it is profoundly to be regretted that she did not live to see the full fruition of her venture. The new club was an immediate success and has had a continuous growth, with precisely those beneficial effects on women's climbing that the founder foresaw. If we have yet to wait for outstanding pioneer work by a woman climber, it can at least be said today that the best of them are very near to the best of the men.

Another outstanding feature of post-war climbing is the enormous increase in the number of participants, an increase which brings various knotty problems in its train. Firstly, there is a social problem. In former days we had among climbers a preponderance of the more fortunate people endowed with a certain limited degree of means and leisure. Never what would be called a rich man's sport, it was not a poor man's either. Nowadays all that is largely changed. The general movement towards outdoor exercise and more frequent holidays, increased facilities of transport, and various other factors have combined to produce a large influx of climbers of more limited means. That many of them do not find a natural and congenial home in the old-established climbing clubs is not in itself, perhaps, a matter of great moment. But the organisations towards which they tend to gravitate lack the historical background and perspective of the older clubs. These latter are the repositories of the great traditions of our craft, and it seems a pity that the young aspirants should not enjoy more directly the benefits of that valuable store.

One of the less fortunate results of this great influx of new climbers who are not directly in touch with the main tradition is a tendency to the growth of slipshod methods, especially in rope management. The use of the rope has evolved gradually from its first tentative introduction, when it was almost more of a menace than an aid at times, to the present-day elaboration in which great care is devoted to its texture, storage, testing, method of attachment both to bodies and rocks, handling in use, and a score of other details. For if the novices are inclined to carelessness, it can truly be said of experienced climbers that never in the history of the sport was more concentrated attention given to this subject than at present.

There is one type of climber to whom the art of rope management is a matter of secondary importance, that is, the solitary climber. There are probably few, if any, who addict themselves to solo climbing exclusively; but it has always had a fascination for certain minds. Whether because it has sometimes been frowned on by those in authority, or for other reasons, solitary climbing is but scantily documented; so that we must content ourselves with referring to its existence and mentioning that its devotees have included many of the most distinguished climbers at all times.

It was not our intention, for we did not feel that it came within the scope of this article, to deal with equipment, but as the rope has been mentioned a word or two about footgear might not be out of place especially, as in one respect, a change in it had considerable influence on the development of climbing. It is not easy to trace the introduction of the climbing nail into the boot and the various changes that have taken place in the composition and shape of it. No doubt climbers were first content with the strong type of boot such as was worn by the dalesman until the need for something affording greater friction started the various fashions in the projecting nail. But regarding the introduction of the rubber shoe there is less uncertainty, for gritstone climbing was chiefly responsible for it. Like most innovations this did not come about at once and at first problems demanding footgear of this kind were usually overcome by discarding the boot for the stockinged-foot; as Jones did on the final pitch of Walker's Gully, and Herford and Sansom on the Central Buttress. But when this method was applied to gritstone—and it was more applicable to this type of climbing than any other—the abrasive nature of the rock demanded something more durable than wool, and ultimately the rubber-shoe was adopted as the most suitable medium for the purpose. Its durability, together with its better 'feel' and greater flexibility than the boot, brought it into favour for the bigger crags, and a pair of rubbers were naturally stored into the rucksack before starting out for them.

One of two features which have distinguished British from Continental climbing should also be mentioned here. One is the almost complete refusal of our own climbers to resort to artificial aids, apart from the rope. The continental climber, with his armoury of pitons (wall-hooks), hammer, and carabineers (sic) (snap-rings), has no counterpart in this country. Of course, our home crags offer a fair supply of natural belays, and do not call so imperatively

for the piton (wall-hook), etc., as do the rocks of the Eastern Alps. And if the German and Austrian have perhaps been over-ready to rely on these adventitious aids, they have been led thereby to the development of new technical methods, enabling them to make attacks on smooth faces that could be surmounted by no other means. We may yet see such methods introduced in Lakeland as the supply of new routes gives out, but they will have to encounter the resistance of strong prejudice.

Another point of difference is the almost complete absence, until quite recently, of the professional element in British climbing. Before the war there was often to be found at Wasdale Head in winter a Dauphiné guide, but it can hardly be said that he was taken very seriously; and in the real climbing season he was always back in his native land. After the war, this practice was not revived; but about ten years ago J.E.B. Wright started an organisation known as the Lakeland Mountain Guides, and published a fixed tariff for various Lakeland climbs. His example has since been followed by others, and there are now quite a few professionals available. The mere fact that the Guides have grown in numbers may be taken as evidence that they are a need, but whilst they include among them some first-class cragsmen, it cannot be said that they have yet played much part in shaping climbing history.

And what of the future? It is no use saying that the crags are exhausted. That has been said too often, and too often falsified. What new forms climbing may take is an interesting subject for speculation. Here is a fragment, hitherto unpublished, which was written some fifteen years ago by a well-known climber:

'Some time ago there passed away in London a great painter, little known to the world of those days. For the last few years he had lived in obscurity. He had lost interest in everything except his art, his wordly affairs being managed by a few close friends, including those who had been directly interested in his productions. He would take up his brush before his easel and endeavour to transmit his ideas into form and outline on the canvas. The picture always remained unfinished, idea after idea would be painted over each other until the canvas became nothing but a glowing mass of colour. Colour became the supreme thing—he would toy with dyed wools and silks; all the ranges of the modern dyer's colours expressed in these mediums attracted him.

'I think of rock-climbing. Routes jostle and spill over each other. Today there is definition and form in rock-climbing—gullies, chimneys, cracks—but it is fast losing this, and the cause of it is slab-climbing. The caterpillar form of movement demanded by the former type of climbing is giving way to the flowing movement of the latter; one might say one twinkles up a slab. It is on slabs that one enjoys the real delight of rock-climbing. And the trend of all this is that the rock climber of the future will view a face of rock from a new aspect—his climbing will be of the whole and not part only. Defined routes will be crossed and re-crossed, lines of movement will take him up and down, diagonally and otherwise, in every direction. Holds will be just caressed and passed by for others, a veritable flirtation will be carried on until he almost becomes a rock-climbing Don Juan. Think, for example, of wandering at will over Deep Ghyll Slabs. As the mind's eye follows the ramifications of one's movements, an exhilaration will ensure such as to fill the imagination with a sense of riotous feeling, analogous to the passion for colour of the great departed painter.'

Stanley Watson leading Innominate Crack.   *Abraham Collection*

There you have an ideal: it seems to envisage solitary climbing, a complete casting aside of the shackles of the rope. Others, differently minded, may see in the future an eager embracing of the rope and kindred aids, tending to the development of a highly mechanised form of climbing which will satisfy a different kind of aspiration. Whether the climbing of the future will take on either or both of these forms, or perhaps develop along entirely different lines as yet undreamt of we cannot say. Enough for us that there is as yet no sign of diminution in interest in the sport. And if after another fifty years the Fell and Rock Club decides to celebrate the centenary of the first ascent of the Needle by another special number of the Journal, there seems no reason why the historian chosen to record the doings of those intervening years should not have at least as rich and varied a story to relate as that which we have tried to tell.

LIST OF FIRST ASCENTS IN CHRONOLOGICAL ORDER

Year	Name of Climb	Classification	Crag	Leader
1826	*Broad Stand*	M	SCAFELL	Not known
	Old West Route	E	PILLAR ROCK	J. Atkinson
1850	*Old Wall Route (?)*	E	PILLAR ROCK	C.A.O. Baumgartner
1850	*Corner above the Slab*	—	PILLAR ROCK	—. Whitehead
1863	*Slab and Notch Climb*	E	PILLAR ROCK	J.W.E. Conybeare
1869	*North or Penrith Climb*	M	SCAFELL	Major Ponsonby
1869	*Mickledore Chimney*	M	SCAFELL	C.W. Dymond
1872	*Pendlebury Traverse*	M	PILLAR ROCK	F. Gardiner
1882	*Deep Ghyll (descent in snow)*	M	SCAFELL	A.L. Mumm
1882	*Deep Ghyll*	M	SCAFELL	W.P. Haskett-Smith
	Central Gully	M	GREAT END	W.P. Haskett-Smith
	South-East Gully	M	GREAT END	W.P. Haskett-Smith
	Central Jordan Climb	D	PILLAR ROCK	W.P. Haskett-Smith
	West Jordan Climb	D	PILLAR ROCK	W.P. Haskett-Smith
	Great Gully	D	PAVEY ARK	W.P. Haskett-Smith
	Western Gully	—	GIMMER CRAG	W.P. Haskett-Smith
1884	*High Man from Jordan Gap*	M	SCAFELL	W.P. Haskett-Smith
	Steep Ghyll	S	SCAFELL	W.P. Haskett-Smith
1886	*The Needle*	D	THE NAPES	W.P. Haskett-Smith
	Needle Ridge	D	THE NAPES	W.P. Haskett-Smith
1887	*Great Chimney*	D	PILLAR ROCK	W.P. Haskett-Smith
	The Arête	M	PILLAR ROCK	W.P. Haskett-Smith
	The Curtain	D	PILLAR ROCK	W.P. Haskett-Smith
1888	*Great Gully*	D	DOW CRAG	G. Hastings
	Slingsby's Chimney	D	SCAFELL	W. Cecil Slingsby
1889	*Green Crag Gully*	M	BUTTERMERE	J.W. Robinson
1890	*Shamrock Gully*	S	PILLAR ROCK	G. Hastings
1891	*North Climb*	D	PILLAR ROCK	W.P. Haskett-Smith

1892	Moss Ghyll	VD	SCAFELL	J.N. Collie
	Great Gully	S	THE SCREES	G. Hastings
1892	Eagle's Nest Ridge			
	Direct	S	THE NAPES	Godfrey A. Solly
	Gwynne's Chimney	D	PAVEY ARK	H.A. Gwynne
	Arrowhead Ridge	D	THE NAPES	W. Cecil Slingsby
	Oblique Chimney	D	GABLE CRAG	J. Collier
1893	Hopkinson and Tribe's			
	Route	D	SCAFELL	C. Hopkinson
1893	Collier's Climb	VS	SCAFELL	J. Collier
	Pier's Ghyll	S	LINGMELL	J. Collier
	Sergeant Crag Gully	D	LANGSTRATH	O.G. Jones
	Kern Knott's Chimney	D	KERN KNOTTS	O.G. Jones
1894	Shamrock Chimneys	VD	PILLAR ROCK	R.S. Robinson
1895	Intermediate Gully	S	DOW CRAG	E.A. Hopkinson
	Hopkinson's Crack	S	DOW CRAG	C. Hopkinson
1896	Jones's Route from Deep			
	Ghyll	S	SCAFELL	O.G. Jones
	Doctor's Chimney	D	GABLE CRAG	C.W. Patchell
1897	C Gully	S	THE SCREES	O.G. Jones
	Central Chimney	S	DOW CRAG	O.G. Jones
	Kern Knotts West			
	Chimney	D	KERN KNOTTS	O.G. Jones
	Kern Knotts Crack	S	KERN KNOTTS	O.G. Jones
	Keswick Brothers' Climb	VD	SCAFELL	G.D. Abraham
1898	Jones's Route Direct			
	from Lord's Rake	S	SCAFELL	O.G. Jones
	Jones and Collier's			
	Climb	VD	SCAFELL	O.G. Jones
	Pisgah Buttress	VD	SCAFELL	O.G. Jones
	West Jordan Gully	S	PILLAR ROCK	W.P. McCulloch
	West Wall Climb	D	SCAFELL	J.W. Robinson
	Rake End Chimney	D	PAVEY ARK	C.W. Barton
1899	Ling Chimney	VD	THE NAPES	W.N. Ling
	Walker's Gully	S	PILLAR ROCK	O.G. Jones
	Broadrick's Route	S	DOW CRAG	H.C. Broadrick
	Engineer's Chimney	S	GABLE CRAG	G.T. Glover
1901	New West Climb	D	PILLAR ROCK	G.D. Abraham
	Savage Gully	VS	PILLAR ROCK	C.W. Barton
1902	Shamrock Buttress			
	Route 1	M	PILLAR ROCK	G.D. Abraham
	Bowfell Buttress	D	BOWFELL	T. Shaw
	Broadrick's Crack	S	DOW CRAG	R.W. Broadrick
	South-East Chimney	D	GIMMER CRAG	E. Rigby
1903	Abraham's Route	S	DOW CRAG	G.D. Abraham
	A Route	S	GIMMER CRAG	E. Rigby
	Botterill's Slab	VS	SCAFELL	F.W. Botterill
	Birkness Chimney	S	BIRKNESS COOMB	N. Sheldon
1904	C Buttress	D	DOW CRAG	G.F. Woodhouse
1905	Woodhouse's Route	D	DOW CRAG	G.F. Woodhouse
1906	North-West Climb	VS	PILLAR ROCK	F.W. Botterill
1907	B Route	S	GIMMER CRAG	H.B. Lyon

	Woodhead's Climb	S	SCAFELL	A.G. Woodhead
1909	*Giant's Crawl*	D	DOW CRAG	E.T.W. Addyman
	Abbey Buttress	VD	THE NAPES	F. Botterill
	Smuggler's Chimney	S	GABLE CRAG	J.S. Sloane
	Shamrock Buttress			
	Route 2	VD	PILLAR ROCK	H.B. Gibson
	Gordon and Craig Route	D	DOW CRAG	S.H. Gordon
1910	*Arête, Chimney and*			
	Crack	S	DOW CRAG	T.C. Ormiston-Chant
	Various	—	ELLIPTICAL CRAG	H.B. Lyon
1911	*South-West Climb*	VS	PILLAR ROCK	H.R. Pope
1912	*Kern Knotts West*			
	Buttress	VS	KERN KNOTTS	G.S. Sansom
	North-East Climb	VD	PILLAR ROCK	G.D. Abraham
	Direct from Lord's Rake			
	to Hopkinson's Cairn	S	SCAFELL	S.W. Herford
	Gillercombe Buttress	S	GILLERCOMBE	H.B. Lyon
	Hopkinson's Gully	S	SCAFELL	S.W. Herford
	Girdle Traverse	S	SCAFELL	S.W. Herford and
				G.S. Sansom
1913	*Wayfarer's Crack*	S	GREAT END	S.W. Herford
1914	*Central Buttress*	VS	SCAFELL	S.W. Herford and
				G.S. Sansom
1918	*Murray's Route*	S	DOW CRAG	D.G. Murray
	C Route	S	GIMMER CRAG	A.P. Wilson
1919	*D Route*	S	GIMMER CRAG	G.S. Bower
	Tophet Bastion	S	THE NAPES	H.M. Kelly
	Rib and Slab Climb	S	PILLAR ROCK	C.F. Holland
	West Wall Climb	VD	PILLAR ROCK	H.M. Kelly
	East Jordan Wall	VS	PILLAR ROCK	C.G. Crawford
	Jordan Bastion	S	PILLAR ROCK	C.G. Crawford
	Route 1	VS	PILLAR ROCK	H.M. Kelly
	Route 2	VS	PILLAR ROCK	H.M. Kelly
1919	*Kern Knotts Buttress*	VS	KERN KNOTTS	H.M. Kelly
	Central Climb	S	KERN KNOTTS	H.M. Kelly
	Flake Climb	VS	KERN KNOTTS	H.M. Kelly
	Great Central Route	VS	DOW CRAG	J.I. Roper
1920	*Esk Buttress Route 1*	S	SCAFELL PIKE	G.S. Bower
	Upper Deep Ghyll			
	Buttress	VS	SCAFELL	H.M. Kelly
	North Wall Climb	S	DOW CRAG	G.S. Bower
	Black Wall Route	VS	DOW CRAG	J.I. Roper
	Ash Tree Slabs	S	GIMMER CRAG	G.S. Bower
	Central Route, Deep			
	Ghyll Slabs	S	SCAFELL	H.M. Kelly
	Nook and Wall Climb	S	PILLAR ROCK	H.M. Kelly
	Trident Route	S	DOW CRAG	G.S. Bower
1921	*Innominate Crack*	VS	KERN KNOTTS	G.S. Bower
1922	*Eliminate C*	VS	DOW CRAG	H.S. Gross
	Eliminate B	VS	DOW CRAG	H.S. Gross
	Girdle Traverse	VS	DOW CRAG	H.S. Gross and
				G. Basterfield

1923	Tophet Wall	S	THE NAPES	H.M. Kelly
	The Appian Way	S	PILLAR ROCK	H.M. Kelly
	Bracket and Slab	S	GIMMER CRAG	H.B. Lyon
	Chimney Buttress	S	GIMMER CRAG	H.B. Lyon
1924	Various	VD	PIKE'S CRAG	H.M. Kelly and C.F. Holland
	Right-hand Wall	VS	BOWFELL	M. de Selincourt
	Gimmer Traverse	S	GIMMER CRAG	M. de Selincourt
1925	Various	—	BOAT HOWE	G. Basterfield
	Tower Buttress	S	SCAFELL	H.M. Kelly
	Moss Ledge Direct	VS	SCAFELL	F. Graham
	Eagle's Corner	S	THE NAPES	C.D. Frankland
	Tricouni Rib	S	THE NAPES	C.D. Frankland
1926	Diphthong	VS	GIMMER CRAG	Morley Wood
	Moss Ghyll Grooves	S	SCAFELL	H.M. Kelly
1927	Hiatus	VS	GIMMER CRAG	G.S. Bower
1928	Grooved Wall	VS	PILLAR ROCK	H.M. Kelly
1928	Long John	VS	THE NAPES	H.G. Knight
	Kern Knotts Chain	VS	KERN KNOTTS	H.M. Kelly and H.G. Knight
1929	Various	—	BLACK CRAG	E. Wood-Johnson
1930	Sepulchre	VS	KERN KNOTTS	J.A. Musgrave
1931	Girdle Traverse	VS	PILLAR ROCK	M. Linnell and A.W. Bridge
	Mickledore Grooves	VS	SCAFELL	C.F. Kirkus
1932	Nor'-Nor'-West Climb	VS	PILLAR ROCK	A.T. Hargreaves
	Esk Buttress Route 2	S	SCAFELL PIKE	A.W. Bridge
	Great Eastern Route	VS	SCAFELL	M. Linnell
1933	Hadrian's Wall	VS	PILLAR ROCK	A.T. Hargreaves
	Overhanging Wall	VS	SCAFELL	M. Linnell
	Morning Wall	VS	SCAFELL	A.T. Hargreaves
	G.E.R. (Yellow Slab Variation)	VS	SCAFELL	M. Linnell
	O.W. (White Slab Variation)	VS	SCAFELL	M. Linnell
1934	Engineer's Slab	VS	GABLE CRAG	F.G. Balcombe
	*Buttonhole Route (sic)	VS	KERN KNOTTS	F.G. Balcombe

*Buttonhook Route Ed.

A SHORT HISTORY OF
LAKELAND CLIMBING
PART II (1935-1959)

John Wilkinson

An Earlier Review

The 50th anniversary of the first ascent of the Napes Needle in 1886 by Haskett Smith was commemorated by the publication of the Lakeland number of the *Fell and Rock Journal* (Vol X1, Nos. 30 and 31, 1936 and 1937), which contained a major contribution by H.M.Kelly and J.H.Doughty entitled 'A Short History of Lakeland Climbing'. The development of rock climbing in the Lakes was surveyed from the earliest recorded climb, a descent of Broad Stand on Scafell by the poet Samuel Coleridge in 1802, until the end of 1934. They showed how the sport of rock climbing, where ascents were made purely for the enjoyment of climbing and not merely as a means of getting to the top of something for a view, began with Haskett Smith's explorations of 1882 and was firmly established by his ascent of the Needle in 1886. In a masterly exposition they showed how the early climbers, who initially demanded the security of deep clefts in the hills, were, as the gullies ran out, gradually driven first into the narrower chimneys and cracks, and finally forced out on to the ridges and open faces. They also demonstrated how the rising standard of climbing paralleled the introduction of new techniques and equipment. This fascinating tale was told largely in terms of the climbers and routes they made mainly on the well-established major crags; Scafell, Pillar, Gable, Dow and Gimmer, although minor (and today highly unfashionable) crags such as Elliptical Crag in Mosedale, Black Crag in Wind Gap, Green Gable and Boat Howe were mentioned. However, lacking the gift of clairvoyance, Kelly and Doughty were not able to appreciate the impact which was to be made on Lakeland climbing by some ascents on other 'minor' crags during this period, and which were omitted from their account. I refer in particular to early ascents in White Ghyll (The Chimney and two Slab Routes), Deer Bield (Deer Bield Crack), Castle Rock of Triermain (The Direct Route, and Scoop and Crack), Raven Crag Langdale (The Original Route), Pavey Ark (Stoat's Crack, and Crescent Wall), Black Crag in Borrowdale (Troutdale Pinnacle), and various routes on Grey Crag and Eagle Crag in Birkness Combe. Kelly and Doughty were not to know of course that, purely in terms of popularity, the low-lying crags of Borrowdale, Langdale and the Eastern Fells were destined to surpass the old established crags on Gable, Pillar, Dow, and even the majestic Scafell. Kelly and Doughty drew up a chronological list of first ascents, and it is amazing to see how many routes were omitted. In addition to the routes on the 'minor' crags mentioned

Eliminate A on Dow Crag.

Chris Bonington

above, other important routes also went unrecorded; The Crack, Joas and Asterisk on Gimmer, Sinister Slabs on Bowfell, Eliminate 'A' on Dow, and many others. These omissions are quite inexplicable, as some of them constitute important milestones in the development of the sport of rock climbing in the Lakes. The list ended in 1934 with two brilliant routes by that meteor of the climbing world, F.G.Balcombe; Buttonhook on Kern Knotts, which was possibly the most technically hard climb at that time, and Engineer's Slab on Gable Crag, an uncompromising steep face lacking in belays, a route which went unrepeated for around twenty years. No mention was made of Balcombe's equally important Direct Finish to Central Buttress on Scafell however.

Thus Kelly and Doughty left the history of Lakeland climbing at a time when, to quote the prophetic words of C.F.Holland in the 1936 Scafell guide, 'the future is bright with the possibility of great developments, a time when there is no danger of the call of Ichabod, a time when we may feel that the best is yet to come'. Kelly and Doughty ended their masterly review with the hope that 'if the Fell and Rock Club decides to celebrate the centenary of the first ascent of the Needle by another special number of the Journal, there seems no reason why the historian chosen to record the doings of those intervening years should not have at least as rich and varied a story to relate as that which we have tried to tell'.

The rate of exploration in the Lakes has increased almost exponentially since 1934 with the result that whilst Kelly and Doughty could encompass the first one hundred and fifty years of climbing in a relatively short review, justice can only be done to the following half-century by splitting the history into three sections.

The 1930's: The Great Aid Debate Commences.

By the end of 1934, the foundations of modern rock climbing had already been laid. The hard-won technique of the gritstone-trained climbers Botterill, Herford, Kelly, Frankland, Piggott, Linnell and A.T.Hargreaves had resulted in a great advance in standards, and the renaissance of Welsh climbing, particularly the early development of Clogwyn du'r Arddu, had a pronounced effect on Lakeland climbing by encouraging the exploration of crags which had previously been declared unclimbable. The opening up of the East Buttress of Scafell was a direct result. The use of a piton to accomplish a difficult ascent (Overhanging Wall on Scafell, 1933), an event which was regarded with disfavour by many climbers at that time, triggered-off a debate on the use of aid which has continued unabated ever since. That superb climber Maurice Linnell must have had reservations about planting the piton when he threw out a challenge in the *Rucksack Club Journal* of 1934: 'those who prefer to climb the place unaided are cordially invited to remove the piton and do so'. Generations of climbers did not appear to have either the inclination or ability to take up this generous offer, and some forty years were to elapse before the second pitch was de-pegged and climbed unaided, thereby increasing the standard by a full grade to HVS. Kelly and Doughty referred to 'features which have distinguished British from Continental climbing, one of which is the refusal of our own climbers to resort to artificial aids, apart from the rope', and G.R.Speaker in the 1933 *Fell and Rock Journal* reflected the main body of opinion of the time when he wrote ....'At a time when rock and ice climbers abroad have adopted new engineering tactics and are climbing more and more with the aid of pitons, the admirable restraint shown by leaders on the more severe of our courses is as commendable as it is reassuring. To a great many of us the general introduction of mechanised climbing would rob this wonderful and noble pursuit of ours of a great deal of the force of its appeal and of its charm.' It is significant that the sentiments so ably expressed by Speaker have been heeded only comparatively recently, and the use of aid in any form is now condemned by most modern cragsmen. A somewhat more realistic approach to the use of aid was taken by Colin Kirkus, one of the best rock climbers of his time, in his article 'The Ethics of Ironmongery' (*Wayfarers Journal, No 6, 1939*) '....nobody has the right to climb with pitons a route which is conceivably possible without. If he does he will be depriving a more worthy contender of the honour of the first ascent. But some day the human limit must be reached. Are men of that generation, then, to be deprived of all the thrills of pioneer exploration? Obviously this cannot be so; they will take the law into their own hands ....be it a matter of years or decades piton climbing will come to be a recognized practice in this country'. Indeed, as Kirkus foresaw, many first ascents in the quarter-century beginning in 1950 used pitons, or later, nuts and wedges, for direct aid.

In later years, the 1970's in particular, it was a point of contention in many climbing circles whether this route or that would still be unclimbed had it not first been climbed with aid, which in almost every case was eliminated later. There is no doubt, however, that had Kirkus's strictures been heeded, there would have been rich pickings for the highly trained rock athletes of later years.

By the mid 1930's, the great wave of exploration had almost completely died away both in the Lakes and Wales. The great innovators of the previous decade had either aged or given up exploration (Kelly and Kirkus); had been killed whilst climbing (Frankland on Gable, Linnell on Ben Nevis); or had turned their attention to other sports (Balcombe took up pot-holing where he made an outstanding contribution as one of the original pioneers of cave diving). The creative ability of top climbers rarely extends beyond a few years.

New men were slow in coming forward, but by the end of the decade great strides were being made once more, principally due to the efforts of a local quarryman, Jim Birkett, who subsequently became a legend in his own lifetime. Scafell was, yet again, the scene of the main action when, on May 1st 1938, Birkett, at the instigation of Charlie Wilson, turned his attention to the expanse of overhanging rock on the East Buttress between Mickledore Grooves and

Overhanging Wall. Birkett must have had Linnell's example on the latter route very much in mind when he launched himself on to the steep, almost holdless and unprotected slab carrying a pocketful of pitons manufactured by Charlie's blacksmith uncle: two were used for protection together with a shoulder for aid, and a third constituted the belay at the top of the first pitch. This pitch, climbed without aid, is currently graded at 5b, the whole climb being HVS: it was without doubt the hardest climb in the Lakes at that time, and was to remain so for over a decade. Birkett's use of pitons on Mayday, as he aptly named the route, proved to be a unique event for him, for over the next twelve years during which he recorded forty-six new climbs in the Lakes, most of them VS or harder, pitons were never employed again. Birkett reinforced his grip on the East Buttress when, in the same year, he girdled a substantial section of the crag, incorporating some of the best bits of earlier routes, notably the White and Yellow Slabs. These splendid climbs were not long in receiving further ascents, and Alf Mullen set a precedent for aid removal when he made the third ascent of Mayday; this was made without the benefit of a shoulder, which was perhaps as well as he was wearing tricouni-nailed boots at the time! Mullen, like Birkett, was a superb nail climber, and the same year climbed Tricouni Slab, parallel to Botterill's Slab. His assessment that 'it is doubtful whether clinkers or rubbers would be any use on this climb' was subsequently proved to be faulty on both counts. Mullen also led a Direct Start to Central Buttress, thereby completing the work so ably begun by Herford in 1914, and extended by Balcombe's Direct Finish, thus providing what is still one of the most satisfying climbs in the District at a continuous HVS standard.

Other crags in the Lakes were also receiving attention; on Gimmer, Mullen linked Asterisk and 'D' (Hyphen), and Sid Cross made the first of several excellent contributions by leading Citadel, VS, a pleasant route containing a fine crack up the centre of Pike's Crag. The old established crags of Dow and Gable received surprisingly little attention during this period, although a visit to Pillar by yet another gritstone expert, Arthur Birtwhistle, resulted in South-West-by-West, VS, a belated companion to Pope's South-West, made in 1912.

However, one of the most important developments of the decade, which was to influence progress for many years to come, took place in the Eastern Fells, an area largely neglected hitherto, when the previously unscaled North Crag of Castle Rock of Triermain and the impending Dove Crag were breached by Jim Birkett and Jim Haggas respectively. Birkett's efforts were rewarded by the ascents of the splendid Overhanging Bastion, VS, and Zig-Zag, VS, events well recorded by the press at that time. Overhanging Bastion, the crux of which took the line of a narrow gangway slanting across the main face and sandwiched between overhangs, was impressively exposed, sensational, and lacking in protection. Birkett showed how far ahead of the times he was regarding the use of protection when, on one of the lower pitches, he inserted pebbles in a crack and threaded them with thin line to provide a running belay of sorts. (The line

was Jones's Gold Seal, sold at threepence a foot. Birkett once remarked 'I wouldn't trust my mother's washing on it.') Haggas's route Hangover, VS, took the easiest line up one of the most impressive pieces of virgin rock in the whole of the Lakes. Indeed, Hangover made such an impression on later climbers that Arthur Dolphin, one of the greatest climbers of his day, wrote (*Fell and Rock Journal, 1948*) that 'Haggas's route, perhaps with minor variations, follows the only possible line of ascent, and must rank as one of the purest climbs in the country'. These routes were all destined to become classics.

Sadly, the climbing scene was shortly to be overtaken by more stirring events on an international scale and, as in 1914, the commencement of a world war effectively retarded the great wave of exploration that had just broken.

The 1940's — The Austere Years

The war years were a quiet time on the fells and climbers were rarely seen on the crags. During this period, leave from the forces was sparse and much of the exploration was in the hands of a few local men employed in essential industry.

1940 was notable in that it marked the opening up of important new climbing areas and resulted in a number of excellent routes. Bill Peascod began his comprehensive development of the Buttermere area, a task which continued without hindrance over a ten-year period, and which yielded many fine ascents. On Eagle Crag in Birkness Combe, five VS routes were climbed in 1940 alone including the classic Eagle Front, Fifth Avenue, and the Girdle Traverse. On Boat Howe, that rarely visited crag overlooking the head of Ennerdale and described by its original explorer, T.Graham Brown, as resembling the stern of a ship, Sid Cross climbed a remarkably hard and direct line up the centre of the crag, which was misnamed as the Prow of the Boat, HVS. In Borrowdale, the foundations of a great climbing area were being laid almost single-handedly by Beetham who, over the war years, meticulously surveyed the whole area and produced a veritable mountain of debris gardened from a score of crags. But undoubtedly one of the greatest feats of the period was the opening up of the formidable area of rock on White Ghyll Crag, to the right of the Chimney. Not surprisingly, this major break-through was engineered by the man who had done the same for Dove Crag the previous year, Jim Haggas. A gripping account of his first ascent of Gordian Knot, VS, appeared in the 1941 *Fell and Rock Journal* , and the thoughtful choice of the climb's name set a precedent for the names of many climbs to be made in the Ghyll over several decades.

Some of the well-established crags still had secrets to divulge, and in 1940 Birkett discovered two excellent routes on the Napes: Eagle's Crack, VS, which

which split the wall above the Dress Circle and combined strenuous and delicate climbing, and the excellent Tophet Grooves, HVS, the hardest route on the Napes at that time on one of the steeper sections of the wall looming over the Great Hell Gate, a wall which, with its bulging overhangs, resembles a smaller version of Scafell's East Buttress. It was not repeated for seven years. Gimmer too was not forgotten as Birkett climbed North West Arête, MVS, the ridge to the right of Asterisk, and Sid Thompson, a powerful gritstone climber, led the technical Crow's Nest Direct, VS. Tragically, Sid, like that other great climber, Colin Kirkus, was not to survive his service in the Royal Air Force.

As the war dragged on, steady progress continued to be made, particularly in Buttermere where Peascod took the whole area by the throat, and in Langdale where Birkett celebrated his imminent nuptials by climbing Bachelor's Crack and the tremendous classic crack of 'F' Route, VS, on Gimmer. Another notable milestone was the ascent of Bilberry Buttress, VS, on Raven Crag, an event which drew attention to the good climbing to be had on the long line of crags above the O.D.G.

It may well have been the scent of victory in the air which stimulated the great burst of activity in 1944 and 1945. The principal contender was again Jim Birkett, who first turned his attention to Esk Buttress, that lofty, lonely crag overlooking upper Eskdale, which had last seen action when Alf Bridge climbed his classic route a dozen years earlier. The result was nine new routes of which the best, Great Central Climb, VS, provided over 500 feet of good climbing and is a tribute to Birkett's unerring eye for a classic line. He then returned to the scene of his earlier triumphs on the East Buttress of Scafell to open up the previously undeveloped eastern wing of the crag: Gremlin's Groove, VS, and the hard, but seldom climbed South Chimney, HVS, where Tom Hill led the top pitch, was the result. For good measure, he crossed Mickledore and found Steep Ghyll Grooves, VS, on the Pisgah wall of the ghyll.

1944 was also marked by the emergence of a climber who, over the following decade, was destined to make a lasting impact on Lakeland climbing. Arthur Dolphin, Yorkshire born and bred, was a student of metallurgy at Leeds University and, since his early teens, had trained religiously on his local gritstone crags of Ilkley and Almscliffe, developing his technical skills and surprising strength. Much of his holidays was spent in the Lakes and, after a hesitant debut on Gable Crag (Windy Ridge, S, a route named after its location, not the condition of the leader), he crossed to the opposite side of the mountain where the climbing of Demon Wall, VS, pointed the way to the excellent Girdle of Tophet Wall, MVS.

The end of the war was celebrated in fine style by Arnold Carsten's ascent of Rake End Wall, VS, on Pavey Ark, which drew attention to one of the largest areas of unclimbed rock in the whole District. The immediate post-war period was, despite the great increase in the number of climbers on the crags, a time when the exploration of Lakeland was almost exclusively in the hands of four

men: Birkett, Peascod, Dolphin and Beetham. Beetham's largely solo efforts continued to yield routes on a large scale in Borrowdale, albeit of a relatively low standard, which had the effect of attracting other harder climbers on to the newly-gardened expanses of rock. This was also the time when H.M.Kelly began the process of up-dating the Rock Climbing Guides to the English Lake District, published by the Fell and Rock Climbing Club.* The previous four-volume Second Series had begun with Pillar in 1935, and ended with Dow Crag, Langdale and Outlying Climbs, a composite volume published in 1938. The proliferation of new routes, particularly in Borrowdale, Buttermere, the Eastern Fells and Langdale now necessitated separate guides for each of these areas, with the result that the Third Series of F.R.C.C. guides was expanded to eight volumes. In the course of guide-book writing operations, the writers invariably become so familiar with their areas that new routes are discovered, and it is no surprise to find the writers' names pre-eminent in the list of first ascents. Jim Birkett, who climbed all over the Lakes, was a notable exception to this rule, not being a member of the F.R.C.C., but Peascod (Buttermere), Beetham (Borrowdale), Drasdo (Eastern Fells), and Dolphin (Langdale and Scafell) all wrote guides to the areas where they themselves had made a great contribution. The format of the Third Series of guides was identical to that invented by Kelly for the earlier series, and climbs were listed in order of increasing difficulty (the sub-division of the grades did not take place until the Fourth Series in 1967, and the technical grading of pitches in 1979). So the only way in which it was possible to ascertain the difficulty of a route was to look at its position in the graded list, not always too reliable a method when the VS category was open-ended.

When guide books were not forthcoming at short and regular intervals, much information required by the young hard climber had to be gleaned from various hut books and logs located in certain pubs, or by word of mouth, a situation somewhat different from today when many guide supplements and climbing journals are readily available.

In Buttermere, Peascod's energies were unabated and many excellent climbs were recorded: Buckstone Howe, that steep chunk of slaty rock overlooking Honister Pass, was opened up by the ascent of the pleasant Honister Wall, S, and the more testing Sinister Grooves, VS, Groove II, VS, and the Girdle, VS, culminating in 1949 with the splendid Cleopatra, VS. On the other side of the hill, the ascent of Dale Head Pillar, MVS, opened up yet another new crag in Newlands, a valley well endowed with small crags, which were being investigated by G.Rushworth ably assisted by Peascod.

In Borrowdale too, exploration proceeded steadily. Some forty new routes were discovered, mainly by Beetham. Several proved to be excellent, particularly Monolith Crack, MVS, and Shepherd's Gully, MVS, both on Shepherd's Crag. However, the greatest contribution in the area was made by

*F.R.C.C. Guides: 1st series 1922-26 (Red Guides); 2nd series 1935-38; 3rd series 1949-59. Kelly called the 49-59 edition 2nd series (*his* second).

Peascod who opened up yet another new crag, Eagle Crag, the buttress prominent on the spur separating Langstrath from Greenup. Three excellent climbs resulted; Postern Gate, MVS, Great Stair, MVS, and the splendidly strenuous Falconer's Crack, VS.

Birkett was active all over the Lakes, and in 1947 paid a rare visit to Dow Crag to climb the bold Leopard's Crawl, HVS, a delicate route on 'B' Buttress, and the first new route on the crag since his own excursion up the exposed North Wall of 'A' Buttress, VS, in 1940. He also returned to Castle Rock and climbed the strenuous May Day Cracks, VS, on the North Crag, and by way of contrast the pleasant Chapel Cracks, MVS, on the South Crag. But undoubtedly his big effort came in 1949, when he put up what was probably one of the hardest routes in the Lakes at that time, the strenuous Harlot Face. This splendid climb was traditionally regarded as the first climb in the Lakes to warrant the grade of Extremely Severe, although in the current guidebook it has been downgraded to HVS. On Esk Buttress, Birkett was obliged to share the honours with Dolphin who climbed Gargoyle Groove, VS, and the excellent Medusa Wall, VS, leaving Square Chimney, VS, for Birkett. Birkett's last new route on Scafell was the beautifully delicate Slab and Groove, VS, a parallel though more difficult companion to Moss Ghyll Grooves.

It was in Langdale, however, where the principal action of the decade occurred, and from 1946 to 1949 over fifty new routes were discovered, many of them of excellent quality at a high standard. The main honours were shared more or less equally between Birkett, who was resident in Little Langdale, and Dolphin who, based on the new Fell and Rock hut, Raw Head, was engaged on the guide writing project. Birkett essentially made White Ghyll his own, and over the four-year period, he was on the first ascent of eleven new routes, nine of which he led. The best of these were White Ghyll Wall, MVS, the easiest line up the great central mass of the crag; Slip Knot, MVS, an equally popular climb; Haste Not, VS, a more difficult companion to Haggas's Gordian Knot; and the most exposed and impressive of all, Perhaps Not, HVS, the first route to break through the barrier of overhangs below White Ghyll Wall, a route which only yielded after several determined attempts. However, the hardest pitch in the ghyll, and arguably the first Extremely Severe route in the Lakes, was to fall in October 1949 to Ken Heaton, a frequent companion of Dolphin at that time. After previous inspection on a rope Dolphin failed to lead the pitch, and it was led without runners by Heaton at 5b to complete the superb climb Do Not, E1. Birkett had climbed the top pitch, 5a, a few months earlier as a variation finish to Slip Not. Several 5b pitches had been climbed even earlier, although with the exception of Maurice Linnell's bold lead of the Bayonet-shaped crack on C.B.,1932, aid in some form or other was employed: the Great Flake of C.B.,1914, (combined tactics); the Bandstand Wall of Great Central Route, 1919, (leader's feet held on); and Mayday, 1938, (shoulder used on the first pitch). By the mid 1950's Heaton, like that other superb technician before him,

Balcombe, forsook rock climbing for another sport where he made an equally impressive contribution as a fell runner, becoming in 1961 the holder of the Lakeland 24-Hour Record (51 tops in 22 hours 13 minutes, covering 82 miles and 31,000 feet of ascent). Whilst Birkett was cleaning up White Ghyll, Dolphin was attempting to forestall other first ascentionists by scouring the whole area for new crags and new routes; Raven Crag Walthwaite, Side Pike, Raven Crag, and East Raven all yielded spoils of which the painfully-named Kneewrecker Chimney, HVS, was the best. However, it was on the high crags that Dolphin discovered the choicest routes. On Pavey Ark, the large expanse of rock to the right of Crescent Slabs attracted his attention: after a series of meanderings on the face, the pleasantly delicate Alph, VS, resulted, aptly named after the wandering sacred river. (Dolphin frequently spent almost as much time devising a suitable name for a climb as he had spent climbing it). The previously untouched East Wall of Pavey Ark was also explored, and the most obvious line, Hobson's Choice climbed, an impressive route for its grade of Hard Severe following 'what appears to be the only route' *(Fell and Rock Journal 1948)*.

But it was on Gimmer that, in 1948, Dolphin demonstrated his inventiveness by climbing his most famous, if not his hardest route. The previous season had seen him exploring the impressive and unclimbed section of the crag between the West and North-West Faces, an area which had also excited the interest of Birkett, who had spotted the same line. This culminated in his lead of Kipling Groove, HVS, (so named because it was Ruddy 'ard), a route which along with Birkett's Harlot Face was considered at the time to be harder than anything else in the Lakes. Lacking the protection which was available in later years, and unwilling to plant a piton, Dolphin elected to top-rope the crux twice before leading it. There were of course precedents for top-roping; new routes on grit were often top-roped at that time, and the adjacent Crack and Hiatus had both been top-roped before being led. Dolphin's last runner was in the crack well below the crux, and a fall on a single hemp rope was unthinkable. It was left to Joe Brown on the third ascent to render the climb safe for a generation of leaders by planting a piton just before the crux moves. The following year, the superb Gimmer Girdle, HVS, was worked out, and a very technical pitch, Grooves Superdirect, HVS, 5b, gave yet another finish to Hiatus.

The 1940's — A Technical Summary

It is significant to note that, despite the great increase in the number of climbers on the crags, the 1940's did not yield appreciably more very hard routes (Hard Very Severe and above) than earlier decades, although the overall number of routes, and routes in the Very Severe grade were considerably greater.

Up to the end of 1919 there were three routes currently graded at HVS; 1920-1929 five routes; 1930-1939 seven routes; 1940-1949 eleven routes. This is

Gimmer Crack and Kipling Groove.   *Malcolm Grout*   220

hardly surprising, when during the whole of this period, the only real development in climbing technology resulting in a marked increase in standards had been the replacement of the nailed boot by the rubber-soled gym shoe, an innovation attributed to H.M.Kelly and introduced about 1915. The introduction of the karabiner for the use of Alpine mountaineers made virtually no impact on the pre-World War II British climber, and running belays were seldom used despite the lead given by Herford in 1914 when he threaded his rope through a loop of rope tied round the chockstone in the Flake Crack of Central Buttress, and Birkett's use of jammed pebbles on Overhanging Bastion. During the second world war, climbing equipment of any kind was almost impossible to come by, and all manner of rubbish was in use on the crags; cotton or sisal ropes, window sash cord, and home-made tricounis, ice-axes, karabiners, and so on. Even the post-war introduction of the vibram-soled boot, invented in Italy and tested by that great mountaineer Gervasutti, did not affect standards of climbing in Britain since hard routes were invariably climbed in rubbers anyway. In the immediate post-war years, however, more climbers were beginning to realize the value of the running belay for protection, and karabiners were at last becoming available. The ex-War Department karabiners proved of doubtful value as they had a tendency to open up under strain, but karabiners of improved quality imported from Europe were gradually becoming available. Even by the end of the decade, however, leaders were still carrying only a pitifully small number of slings and karabiners. Most climbers were reluctant to use pitons, and their single hemp ropes had inadequate strength, so it is scarcely surprising that the number of high standard routes climbed during this period did not rise appreciably: the leader simply could not afford a fall. Indeed it is a remarkable tribute to the ability and courage of climbers of the period up to 1950 that so many hard routes were made with such poor protection.

Until the 4th Series of F.R.C.C. guides (1967) all hard climbs were graded Very Severe, and the VS section of the graded list of climbs, in which routes were listed in order of difficulty, embraced the grades currently known as Mild VS, VS, Hard VS, and Extremely Severe; in 1978 the XS grade was sub-divided E1 to E5, and in 1979 pitches were given numerical gradings to indicate their technical difficulty, 4a, 4b, 4c, 5a, 5b, 5c, 6a, 6b. The grading of routes is not a precise science, and guide writers and other climbers frequently differ in their assessment of difficulty. (Currently climbs are graded for guidebook purposes only after canvassing the opinions of many climbers).

It is interesting to look at a typical graded list of this period, for example that in the 1950 edition of the Langdale guide by Dolphin and Cook, and to compare their gradings with those in the most recent guide, the 1980 edition by Mortimer. Most of the climbs near the bottom of the VS section of the 1950 guide are now down-graded to Hard Severe (Asterisk, Samaritan Corner, Diphthong, Bachelor Crack and Sinister Slabs), and those at the top of the list are now Hard Very Severe (Deer Bield Crack 4c, Kneewrecker Chimney 5a, Perhaps Not 5a, Gimmer Girdle 5a, Grooves Superdirect 5b), with Kipling Groove 5a, as the hardest climb: Do Not, the second hardest climb in the list, is now graded E1 5b. Do Not would appear to be the first E1 in the Lakes, since Harlot Face (1949), which was an Extreme in the 1969 edition of the Eastern Fells guide, has now been downgraded to HVS in the 1979 edition. It is clear, however, that by the end of the 1940's there were a number of routes on the borderline of HVS/E1, with pitches of 5a and 5b.

It is, perhaps, an overgeneralization to suggest that increased climbing standards were solely due to improvements in equipment and technique. Training and attitude of mind were also of great importance, and there have always been a few exceptional climbers around to whom lack of protection or the use of rudimentary equipment made little or no difference to their high standard of performance. Indeed, from the earliest days of the sport when Haskett Smith set a precedent with his solo first ascent of the Needle, there have always been a few bold individuals who were prepared to solo some of the hardest climbs of the day, although there is no record of a solo first ascent of a hard route during this period, and even today such solo ascents are uncommon. Ronnie Jackson on his fleeting trips to the Lakes in the late 1930's was soloing, in nails, routes such as Eliminate 'B', Great Central Route, and Black Wall, all currently graded HVS: and in the mid 1940's Joe Griffin began a programme of soloing hard routes which has continued virtually uninterrupted for (so far) forty years. Also many climbs were led virtually without protection, and to all intents and purposes constituted solo ascents: for example Ken Heaton's runnerless lead of the first pitch of Do Not.

Of the eleven hard (HVS and E1) climbs put up during this period, of which six were in Langdale and were climbed in 1948 and 1949, nine were climbed by either Birkett or Dolphin, the honours being almost equally shared.

The 1950's — A Climbing Explosion

The austerity of the war years was fast becoming an unpleasant memory, and large numbers of people were taking to the hills at weekends and holidays mainly as a result of a more affluent and car-owning society. There were more climbers than ever before, and more of them were climbing hard routes. Whilst the exploration of the 1940's was mainly in the hands of four men, well over a dozen participated in the discovery of new routes in the following decade.

Perhaps the most surprising feature of the 1950's was that whole areas of the Lakes were still neglected and even several of the major crags received scant attention. Whilst Langdale, Borrowdale, the Eastern Fells and Scafell were all extensively explored, in Buttermere and Newlands, the scene of such frantic activity in the 1940's, there appeared little enthusiasm for new routes after Peascod's departure for Australia: Dow was left severely alone, and it was the end of the decade before new climbs were to appear on Pillar and Gable. This neglect is quite inexplicable in view of the extensive developments which were to take place later.

The early years of the decade were essentially those of Arthur Dolphin, and it was in Langdale that the real action began. Having got the manuscript of the Langdale Guide off to the printers, Dolphin swiftly girdled Pavey Ark, HVS, then, in 1951, changed into a higher gear and solidly confirmed the new grade of climbing, which was subsequently named Extremely Severe. It is interesting to note that at the time Dolphin was consolidating the new standard in the Lakes, Joe Brown was doing precisely the same in Wales. After a determined siege, Deer Bield Buttress, E1, became the first of Dolphin's climbs in the new hard grade and the first route of consequence on that superb, steep little crag since A.T.Hargreaves led the magnificent Deer Bield Crack over twenty years earlier. Having made the break-through, equally difficult routes followed; Rubicon Groove, E1, another well-named climb, the first on Bowfell for almost a decade, and, the following year, the classic Sword of Damocles, E1, of which Dolphin led the crux and Peter Greenwood the remainder. Dolphin's exploratory interests were wide ranging and hard routes were put up in White Ghyll, where a flimsy holly guarded the entrance to a steep groove, Shivering Timber, VS; on Deer Bield, with Peter Greenwood, a companion crack to the famous Deer Bield Crack was climbed to its left (Dunmail Cracks, HVS); in the Eatern Fells, a visit to the repulsive Iron Crag produced the terrifying loose Ferrous Buttress, VS; and on Esk Buttress, the great groove line crossed by Birkett's Great Central Climb yielded the splendid Trespasser Groove, HVS. However, apart from Langdale, it was on Scafell that Dolphin made his greatest contribution. Having been asked to write the new Scafell guide, he set about it in the traditional fashion by trying to forestall others and make easy work of guide writing by climbing as many unclimbed lines as he could find. There was a big gap between Morning Wall and Gremlin's Groove on the imposing left wing of the East Buttress, and it was here, in May 1952, that Dolphin made two of his greatest contributions to Lakeland climbing, the ascents of Pegasus, HVS, and Hell's Groove, HVS. On the second pitch of Pegasus, a long diagonal line parallel to Morning Wall, Dolphin arranged a long sling from a piton to enable a delicate move into a groove to be made, thereby enabling a generation of leaders to enjoy the route: almost thirty years later, aid was dispensed with. To the left of Pegasus, a short overhanging crack barred the way to a huge corner. Peter Greenwood, a short, tough gritstone climber and a frequent companion of Dolphin on new routes, was the first to solve this awkward problem, leaving the big corner to Dolphin; the superb Hell's Groove. These splendid climbs, together with his crop of new hard routes in Langdale, were sadly his last contribution to Lakeland climbing, as he was killed in July 1953 whilst descending solo from the Dent du Géant. Having raised the standard of climbing in the Lakes there is no doubt that Dolphin, then in his prime, would

have radically transformed the climbing scene in the District. The death of a great innovator had a profound effect on many of his contemporaries, and the pace of exploration slowed, as indeed it had during an earlier decade after Linnell's death.

Rock climbing in Britain as a whole was, for the rest of the decade, dominated to a considerable degree by the members of the Rock and Ice Club, though their impact on Wales was immensely greater than on the Lakes. Nevertheless, the contributions made by Joe Brown, Don Whillans, and Ron Moseley in particular were formidable. In 1953 Moseley prepared his first route by abseiling down the steep wall left of Dunmail Cracks on Deer Bield Crag and planting a piton, which was subsequently lassooed to create Pendulum, first climbed free in 1977 at E2: and on Gimmer, he led the steep wall from the Bower on Gimmer Crack to produce Dight, E1. Whillans made a hard Girdle of Deer Bield, E2, and in White Ghyll, Brown led the magnificent corner-crack of Laugh Not, HVS, which involved a tension traverse under the overhang, and later, in 1957, returned to force a direct passage up to, and through the roof of Perhaps Not, giving Eliminot, E2, using one point of aid.

On Scafell, the East Buttress was once more under attack, and in 1955 Whillans discovered the excellent crack line of Trinity, HVS, whilst Moseley, two years later, put up Phoenix, E1, an exposed and strenuous route climbed with one point of aid and one of the hardest climbs in the whole District at that time.

The potential of the Eastern Fells did not pass unnoticed either, once Harold Drasdo had pointed the way with his superb routes on the North Crag of Castle Rock of Triermain; Barbican, MVS, in 1951, and the very hard North Crag Eliminate, E1, in 1952. Whillans and Brown followed swiftly with the very strenuous Triermain Eliminate, E1, in 1953. The following year, having got himself into the right frame of mind by emerging triumphant from a punch-up in Keswick, Whillans made a brilliant lead up the great expanse of steep unclimbed rock to the left of Hangover on Dove Crag to produce the strenuous Dovedale Groove, E1, climbed with one point of aid, the first route on the crag for fourteen years. The Eastern Fells were well endowed with new crags ripe for exploitation, and the early 1950's saw the opening up of Hutaple Crag, a big grassy cliff, and the steep and compact Scrubby Crag, both in the remote Deepdale, and the steep and impressive Raven Crag, Thirlmere, where Drasdo, Greenwood and Dolphin had all made excellent contributions. Drasdo's Grendel, MVS, on Scrubby and Dolphin's Communist Convert, VS, on Raven, both made in 1953, subsequently achieved well-deserved popularity. In 1954 Birkett climbed his last new route, Kestrel Wall on Eagle Crag, Grisedale, a pleasant Severe, to end a brilliant climbing career.

As the familiar faces faded away, new ones were appearing on the crags. One in particular, the diminutive, boyish Paul Ross from Keswick, was just beginning to make his mark. The Thirlmere area and Borrowdale were his

227 Al Beatty and Phil Rigby on Eliminot, White Ghyll.   *Ron Kenyon*

backyard, and during the rest of the decade and well into the next, Ross's name was to feature prominently in the first ascent lists. The strenuous Thirlmere Eliminate, E1, climbed with Pete Greenwood in 1955, was to usher in a whole spate of new routes, particularly in Borrowdale where the crags laid bare by Bentley Beetham in earlier years were ripe for exploitation. Shepherd's Crag was a popular venue, although Pat Vaughan's Fool's Paradise, VS, on Gowder Crag was to prove to be one of the best climbs of its standard in the valley. 1954 saw Ross's début on Black Crag, where the Super Direct, HVS, was a splendid addition to a fine crag. The big left wing of Black Crag proved an irresistible attraction, and several long and difficult climbs were made: Obituary Groove, VS, in 1955, the Shroud, VS, in 1958, together with an aid climb, Vertigo, not climbed free at E2 until 1977. Eagle Crag also yielded some hard routes; in 1956, Post Mortem, which had previously repulsed Don Whillans, was led by Ross using a sling for aid, and became the first E2 in the Lakes. In 1959, the crag was girdled at HVS, and the Cleft was climbed using five points of aid, a pitch which was clearly too hard for the time, and would have been better left for future development: sixteen years later, the Cleft was led without aid by Pete Botterill at E3. Perhaps the most notable feature of Ross's campaign was the brilliant development of the impressive crags overlooking Derwentwater, crags to which attention had been drawn by Dr. John Brown in a letter published in 1770 describing the vale and lake of Keswick. 'On the opposite shore (of Derwentwater) you will find rocks and cliffs of stupendous height, hanging broken over the lake in horrible grandeur, some of them a thousand feet high, the woods climbing up their steep shaggy sides, where mortal foot never yet approached'. The intrepid Ross was not overawed, and made a determined assault on Falcon Crags where the Lower Crag yielded seven very impressive hard climbs, although the Upper Crag required three pitons for aid on the top pitch of Route 1, a route which was not de-pegged and climbed free until 1975, at E2.

The year after Ross's début, another remarkable climber appeared, the portly, bespectacled Allan (Tubby) Austin, a Yorkshireman whose appearance belied a determined and powerful climber. His training on gritstone had given him the essential equipment for the task ahead, that of making Langdale essentially his own.

Over the period 1956-1974, Austin discovered some thirty-eight new routes in Langdale alone, most of them of a high standard, and effectively transformed the area. Indeed, his contribution to Lakeland climbing was unequalled even by Birkett, Dolphin and Ross, and throughout his brilliant climbing career, he adopted a rigorously purist approach, eschewing aid in any form. Indeed, in his 1973 Langdale guide he refused to include some routes which others had climbed with aid, being convinced that in the not too distant future they would be climbed free, which they were. Crags such as Pavey Ark which had been somewhat neglected in the past were now to prove a treasure trove yielding,

Top:- Jim Birkett; Bert Beck and Bill Peascod, 1940.   228
Bottom:- Paul Ross, 1954; Allan Austin.

after considerable gardening, many superb long climbs of great technical interest. The assault began at the foot of Jack's Rake, where Stickle Grooves, HVS, took a line up the exposed edge of the crag where the East Buttress bends round to become the East Wall. The following year, he ventured on to the East Wall itself, where Dolphin's Hobson's Choice was the only route, to climb the superb steep slabs of Cascade, HVS.

1958 proved to be a vintage year for Lakeland climbing, with great developments all over the District. In Langdale, Austin discovered five excellent routes on Pavey Ark, of which the delightfully delicate Golden Slipper, HVS, took pride of place; this incredibly rough slab above the upper part of Jack's Rake has, over the years, proved to be one of the best slab climbs in the District. Heron Crag, that steep face overlooking the Esk, was first climbed in 1955 as a result of the explorations of the Outward Bound Mountain School in Eskdale, but the true potential of the crag was not realized until three years later when the main face was breached by O.R.D. Pritchard, who climbed Bellerophon, VS, and laid the foundations for many notable ascents in the following decade. 1958 was also notable for a superb day's work by Robin Smith, one of Scotland's finest moutaineers: on one of his rare visits to the Lakes, he ventured on to the East Buttress of Scafell to discover two excellent new routes in the vicinity of Mickledore Grooves; Chartreuse, E1, a brilliant combination of delicate and strenuous climbing, and Leverage, HVS, (named for his second, Derek Lever), a strenuous line to its left. Sadly, these, together with pitch 3 of Whit's End on Gimmer, were to be his only contributions to Lakeland climbing, as he was killed in the Pamirs in 1962: however, his first ascents north of the border, including Shibboleth, E2, and July Crack, two of the his best and hardest routes which were made only a few weeks after his visit to Scafell, remain a fitting memorial to one of Scotland's greatest climbers. The decade ended with a flurry of activity all over the District, and was marked by the appearance of several newcomers, all of whom were destined to play a major part in the future development of Lakeland climbing; Les Brown, who was well-placed by his work at Windscale, Geoff Oliver from the North East, and Jack Soper, a geologist from Sheffield University. In 1959, all made their first contributions, the forerunners of many. Although Ross and Austin were still very active in their respective areas, this did not deter the newcomers who picked excellent plums in the Eastern Fells and Langdale; Oliver led the superb wall climb Agony, HVS, on Castle Rock, Moss Wall, VS, in White Ghyll, and the short but serious Virgo, HVS, on the Neckband Crag of Bowfell; and on Gimmer, Brown found Inertia, HVS, an excursion up the steep ground to the left of the Crack.

It was away from the now-popular areas of Langdale, Borrowdale and the Eastern Fells that the most important developments took place, particularly on Scafell, on Pillar, which had last received a first ascent eighteen years previously, and in Buttermere, which had also been largely neglected since

Peascod's departure. The summer of 1959 marked the beginning of a campaign of exploration by Les Brown which took him all over the District to climb many classic lines on the great crags, and also to discover new ones. On Buckstone Howe, his route Caesar, HVS, was an excellent companion to Cleopatra, climbed ten years earlier by Peascod; and on Scafell, the wall above the West Wall Traverse was breached by Xerxes, HVS. But it was on the East Buttress that the main action took place: 1959 was a phenomenally dry summer, and the central section of the crag, which often resembles a waterfall, was at last dry enough for Brown to climb Moonday, E2, a splendid climb which broke through the bulging wall to the left of Overhanging Wall. The exposed edge between Mickledore Chimney and Mickledore Grooves was also climbed by Geoff Oliver, and named Pernod, VS, to conform with the other aperitifs on the wall of the Chimney. Oliver also climbed the great corner above the second pitch of Mayday, which is normally a watercourse; Mayday Direct is now climbed free at E2, although a piton was used for aid on the first ascent. Hugh Banner discovered yet another slab parallel to Moss Ghyll Grooves, the well-named Narrow Stand, HVS, also a fine crack line up the front of Pisgah, Bos'n's Buttress, VS, which had been inviting attention for years.

On an incredible June day, Pillar finally received its just deserts when the West Face of both Low Man and High Man yielded excellent climbs. To the left of Appian Way, climbed by Kelly in his hey-day, there is a very steep and exposed wall, and it was here that Maurice de St. Jarre climbed the exacting Goth, HVS. Between Kelly's classics Sodom and Gomorrah, Oliver turned the big overhang to climb the pleasant crack line of Vandal, HVS.

All in all, 1959 was a brilliant end to a superb decade's climbing, with new climbing grounds being well exploited by a number of highly competent leaders, who were clearly destined to make names for themselves in the succeeding years.

The 1950's — A Technical Summary

The 1950's were notable for a new breed of climber who had not, as Kelly and Doughty envisaged, 'taken advantage of the perspective and historical backgrounds of the older clubs the repositories of the great traditions of our craft'. Fortunately, the lack of enthusiasm shown by these new young climbers for the old well-established clubs did not result, as feared by Kelly and Doughty, in 'a tendency to the growth of slipshod methods, especially in rope management'. In fact, the situation was quite the reverse. The rock techniques and safety standards developed by these young men, mainly gritstone trained, transformed the sport as their predecessors from Herford to Linnell had done in previous decades.

Scores of small climbing clubs sprang up all over the country, and the contribution to rock climbing made by their members soon outstripped that being made by the older clubs, which were now having great difficulty in recruiting young active climbers. Prominent amongst the clubs formed at that time was the Rock and Ice Club whose members, particularly Joe Brown and Don Whillans, made a lasting and outstanding contribution to the development of the sport of rock climbing, and pushed up standards to heights previously unattained.

The great explosion of standards in the 1950's was due not only to the larger number of climbers, but more significantly to the introduction of new climbing techniques and equipment, which resulted in vastly improved safety measures. Nylon ropes, which during the war had been used for towing gliders, now began to make their appearance on the crags; they were much stronger than the manilla ropes used earlier and, more importantly, they stretched instead of snapping. Running belays were now used whenever possible, and manufactured where necessary, using first knotted slings, and later artificial chockstones inserted into cracks. (Joe Brown used to carry a selection of small stones tucked into his balaclava). Greater protection meant that climbers were now able to push themselves further without the risk of a catastrophic fall. Forgotten was the unwritten law that the leader must never fall, and many leaders now began to press themselves to the limit and even beyond it. There is no doubt that the increased use of protection in the post-war years has substantially reduced the death rate from climbing accidents *(Fell and Rock Journal* 1981, pp 135-148). One effect of the improved protection was the phasing-out of top roping of new climbs practised by some leaders, although it did encourage others to be over-indulgent in the use of pitons and slings on chockstones for aid. This was particularly noticeable in Borrowdale, where Ross and his contemporaries attacked many imposing lines previously regarded as unclimbable. They refused to be thwarted by technical difficulty, and if a climb did not yield, aid was used without qualm. This practice encouraged others, and the excessive use of aid was destined to continue for a number of years all over the District, despite the lead given by Allan Austin and other purists. However, aid removal was to provide considerable sport for the technically gifted climbers of later years.

One of the most important technical innovations, which had a profound effect on the whole future of hard rock climbing, occurred in 1958 when a new form of footwear became generally available. The introduction of the special light-weight rock boot known as the P.A. (after Pierre Allain, one of the best French rock climbers) made as big an impact on British climbing standards as did the replacement of the nailed boot by the soft-soled rubber gym shoe, first used by Kelly about 1915. Whilst the gym shoe had excellent adhesive properties on purely friction holds, it had the great disadvantage that, being flexible and soft-soled, it was extremely difficult to use on very small sharp holds. The P.A. was originally designed for use on the difficult sandstone boulders at Fontainebleau, the practice crag for Parisian climbers. It had a much more rigid sole than the gym shoe, thereby enabling the climber to stand on small sharp holds with a far greater degree of comfort and security. The few British climbers who, in the mid-1950's found themselves at Fontainebleau were so impressed by the revolutionary rock boots that they took some home to try out on the British crags. The word soon spread that the new boots had magical qualities, and by 1958, climbing shops were importing them from France, although it was some time before they were universally adopted. Over the years, various manufacturers have produced their own versions of the P.A., and, a quarter of a century on, although many climbers still use the P.A. (now known as the E.B. after the manufacturer Edouard Bourdeneau, the name of Pierre Allain having been transferred to the climbing boot manufacturer Galibier in 1970), others, particularly the top performers, have switched their allegiance to similar but superior models such as Canyons, Hanwags, Contacts, Cragratz and so on.

The new techniques and equipment produced an immediate increase in both standards and the numbers of hard routes. Whilst the whole period up to 1949 had only yielded a total of twenty-six routes in the grade which we now call Hard Very Severe (eleven of them in the years 1940-1949), the 1950's produced a total of fifty routes of this standard, or above: of these, fifteen were subsequently graded Extremely Severe in the 4th Series of F.R.C.C. Guides, which commenced in 1967. It is interesting to note that, during the 1950's, no hard climbs (HVS or XS) were made on Dow or Gable: the new developments were principally in Langdale (20 routes), Borrowdale (8 routes), Eastern Fells (9 routes) and Scafell (10 routes), with only two on Pillar and one in Buttermere.

Summary (1935-1959)

During the quarter-century covered by this review, great advances were made in the sport of rock climbing. Despite the retardation of exploration caused by the war, the number of new climbs made in the Lakes in the period 1935-1959 (655) was almost double the total number climbed from the beginning of the sport in 1882 up to 1934 (393). Furthermore, the number of hard routes (228 at VS and above) climbed during this later period amounted to over one third of all new climbs. Standards, which had remained more or less static since Central Buttress was climbed in 1914, began to rise dramatically with the increasing number of well-trained climbers on the crags, and with the introduction of new equipment and techniques. From 1949, when the first climb currently graded Extremely Severe was climbed unaided, the number of routes in this grade has increased steadily year by year. The other great feature of the period was the discovery and development of extensive new climbing grounds, particularly the low-lying, fast-drying and easily accessible crags of Langdale, Borrowdale and the Eastern Fells. Scores of new crags were rigorously explored during this period, contrasting with the sparse attention received by some of the majestic high crags, Dow and Pillar in particular, which had been in the forefront of development of the sport in earlier years.

With the opening up of the new crags, and the fact that there were now many good climbers armed with improved skills and equipment, the stage was set for future great developments.

Thanks are due to Pete Whillance for helpful suggestions.

Scafell Crags — Jill M. Aldersley

A SHORT HISTORY OF LAKELAND CLIMBING PART III (1960-1969)

Pete Whillance

This article is not intended as a definitive history. It is more an outline of the major events that occurred and my personal interpretation of the course that important developments followed.

I have not confined myself to a chronological list of the facts, but rather attempted to examine how the trends, attitudes and approaches of individuals and groups (as well as more obvious influences such as weather and equipment), have affected progress and developments in climbing, during this period.

Such an approach is inevitably controversial as it involves selective opinions and personal interpretations, but if this article does go some way towards achieving my objectives of discovering how and why events happened as they did; it will be worth suffering the potential wrath of those who disagree.

1960 — A Golden Year

By any standards, 1960 was an exceptional year in the annals of Lakeland climbing history. Indeed, there are many who feel, with some justification, that in terms of quality new climbs produced, it represented *the* Golden Year of the whole 100 years of climbing development in the region. Whether or not one agrees, there can be little doubt that routes of the calibre of Ichabod, Extol, Gormenghast, Astra, Sidewalk and Centaur will continue to rank amongst the top all-time classics of the District.

In retrospect, the forging of so many outstanding climbs in that year might almost have been predicted. The drought of 1959 had already witnessed the production of a remarkable quota of excellent routes. Paul Ross was firmly established as the dominant and most prolific pioneer in the Borrowdale and Thirlmere areas, whilst Allan Austin was gradually emerging as the primary driving force behind Langdale developments. Into this arena stepped the new talents of Les Brown and Geoff Oliver, their arrival on the scene being signalled by an impressive list of achievements during 1959. (Oliver — Pernod, Mayday Direct, Agony, Vandal, Virgo and Moss Wall. Brown — Xerxes, Moonday, Inertia and Caesar.)

In addition to this wealth of local potential was the constant threat from 'Welsh Activists'. Don Whillans in particular had made evident his interest in the area with numerous forays during the late fifties resulting in climbs such as Trinity and Delphinus.

Thus it may be argued that the ingredients were all present. When the hot dry weather of 1959 recurred in 1960, the stage was clearly set for some further dramatic developments.

Pitch 1, Centaur, Scafell East Buttress. *I. Roper*

Les Brown

John Lagoe's article 'Some Eskdale Rock Climbs' and the accompanying photographs in the FRCC *Journal* of 1959, had well advertised the potential of the relatively new find of Heron Crag in Eskdale:-

'Beyond doubt the best is yet to be. The main nose with a remarkable flake half way up, seen in profile on the way from Taw House, and the whole right wing of the crag, overhanging by several feet at the bottom, remain untouched, waiting for some V.S. pioneers.'

The main nose was indeed a superb prize and it didn't have to wait long for a pioneer. Les Brown confounded his opposition by completing the first ascent of Gormenghast by the end of March 1960. Brown was ideally placed for snatching this particular gem, as he was working at nearby Windscale, but he was rapidly acquiring a reputation for quietly picking off outstanding routes over the length and breadth of the Lakes.

Typically, in less than a month he had established three more notable new routes on crags as widely spread as Dow, Scafell and Bowfell. His ascent of the excellent and improbable looking Sidewalk on Dow's 'A' Buttress was a significant breakthrough on a crag which had seen no important developments for some thirteen years. The crucial first pitch requires a bold approach to gain access to the upper buttress and Brown took the unusual and precarious step of employing a hand-placed piton for resting.

Brown's next foray produced Armageddon, a difficult line on Scafell's East Buttress which he had doubtless spotted the previous year whilst making the first ascent of the adjacent Moonday. Three points of aid were used to tackle some of the most impressive ground so far attempted on this crag. However, the climb was seldom to be found dry, and it did not achieve the instant classic status normally associated with Les Brown's creations.

Two days later Brown ascended the obvious groove line left of Sword of Damocles on Bowfell's North Buttress to gain Gnomon.

Later in the year Brown returned to Scafell's East Buttress to take on the huge area of unclimbed rock to the right of Great Eastern. By a superb piece of route finding he succeeded where others had failed and produced a magnificent climb at the remarkably reasonable grade of HVS. Centaur remains one of the best and longest routes on the crag but even this fine achievement was overshadowed by the efforts of that other relative newcomer to the scene, Geoff Oliver.

Geoff Oliver

Oliver and his Newcastle companions had made a considerable impact on the Lakeland cliffs during the summer of 1959, and further successes followed in the autumn of that year in the shape of repeat ascents of many of the top Rock and Ice Extremes in North Wales.

1960 began quietly with his ascent of two obvious crack lines on the Napes. Although Alligator Crawl and Crocodile Crack are both good routes they have never gained the popularity they deserve.

As the sunny weather continued into May, Oliver moved up to the East Buttress of Scafell to attempt one of the last great natural lines left on the cliff. The hair-raising ascent that followed is described by Geoff in his article 'Recent Developments on Scafell' (FRCC *Journal* 1962) and the resulting Ichabod is one of the very best classic climbs that the Lake District has to offer. It says much about the unassuming nature of this man that as co-writer of the 1967 Scafell Guide, he chose not to mention his own contributions, including Ichabod, in the historical section of that publication.

The very next day Oliver teamed up with Paul Ross to produce two new routes on Castle Rock. By alternating leads, the pair completed a new girdle on the crag in one and a half hours. Eliminate Girdle takes in many of the finest pitches of the crag and made Jim Birkett's Gossard largely redundant. To round off the day, Ross took revenge for his previous fall on a line at the right hand end of the crag and established Drag, a short yet surprisingly difficult problem. (See 'Castle Rock of Triermain' by Ross, FRCC *Journal*, 1961).

Don Whillans

In the new 1959 Eastern Crags guide, Harold Drasdo somewhat rashly said of Dove Crag that 'the central part of the main cliff presents a challenge unanswerable by unaided climbing'. Furthermore his article 'Extremes and Excesses' in the FRCC *Journal* of 1960 stated that 'It is not for want of trying that only one new route has appeared on Dove Crag in the last 20 years, and this route, Dovedale Groove by Whillans and Brown, indicates at what level the next ones will be carried out. I have not seen a more impressive piece of igneous rock, of similar size, anywhere. All one can say is that we have failed; others can try.'

The ink could barely have dried on the paper before the challenge had been met. In the spring of 1960, Don Whillans, the man most likely to succeed, forced Extol, a ferocious line straight up the centre of the crag. Colin Mortlock's account of the first ascent ('Entity', *C.C. Journal* 1961) had all the hallmarks we have come to expect of a Whillansian route; wet conditions, unrelenting difficulty and a high level of seriousness which included at one point both leader and second climbing extreme rock simultaneously.

In a year in which local climbers did so much to redress the balance with Wales and establish hard classic routes comparable with many of the Rock and Ice finer achievements on Cloggy and the Llanberis cliffs, it is perhaps ironic that Whillans' Extol was probably the most outstanding accomplishment of 1960.

Allan Austin

Although Austin had been producing new climbs in the Langdale area for several years, it was not until 1960 that he really showed his metal and thus began a long campaign which was to make him the most outstanding Lakeland pioneer of the decade.

Austin's primary ambitions around this time lay in the development of Pavey Ark, a huge rambling cliff which still remained largely untouched by modern climbers of the day. His additions that year included Rectangular Slab, Astra and Red Groove. Astra is a magnificent and bold lead which was for many years considered to be the hardest undertaking in the area, and today it is still one of the finest climbs in the Lake Disctrict. Both Astra and Red Groove were significantly harder than any of Austin's previous routes and opened up areas of the East Wall, which had previously been considered unclimbable.

Two other climbs are worthy of mention in 1960 as each in its own way had a bearing on future developments in the Lakes. Paul Ross and others who operated mainly in the Northern Lakes area were developing a different philosophy towards the use of pegs and aid climbing from their contemporaries in Langdale and the South. Ross's artificial route If on Gimmer Crag caused a good deal of controversy among the Langdale devotees. Ross explained in 1974: 'We did If as a totally provocative route, up an incredible piece of rock..... Greenwood provoked me into it. I got Geoff Oliver interested in turn and he tried it twice before I did it. He was a little bit that way, trying to provoke people, but he never pulled it off, he was a nice guy.' (*Leeds University C.C. Journal 1974*)

Also in that year Pete Crew, still a relative unknown, who had just begun to cut his teeth on the Black Cliff of Clogwyn D'ur Arddu, made a rare visit to the Lakes and climbed a new route on Pillar Rock. Although Odin was not an outstanding route the ascent was instrumental in awakening local climbers to the potential of the cliff and gave due warning of the interests of a man shortly to become one of Britain's leading climbers.

All in all, 1960 was a magnificent year which arguably produced proportionally more truly great Lakeland classic routes than any other before or since. Equally significant however was the fact that most of these climbs attacked areas of cliff previously thought impregnable and thus opened many eyes to possibilities for the future.

1961-1962

After the phenomenally dry summers of '59 and '60 it was hardly surprising that 1961 turned out to be something of a wash-out. In terms of quantity of new climbs produced, it was certainly one of the worst on record and the only developments of any importance occurred on the fast drying Heron Crag.

Brown's route Gormenghast attracted much attention and became instantly popular, with Austin adding a direct start and Whillans a direct finish. Austin was impressed by the vast scope of the mossy right wing and returned to establish two very good climbs, Spec Crack (HVS) and Flanker (HVS). Both

On Central Pillar, Esk Buttress.   *I. Roper*   240

routes acquired a somewhat inflated reputation and were not repeated for seven years. Ian Roper wrote in 1967; 'Spec Crack and Flanker continue to resist all attempts at second ascents, despite many assaults, particularly on the former. It might well be that Spec Crack is one of the hardest half-dozen routes on Scafell.' (Lakeland Letter in *New Climbs*, 1967)

In 1962, the pace of development picked up again. Les Brown returned to Dow Crag's 'A' Buttress to climb a very good pitch which was later linked by Dave Miller to Unfinished Symphony to give today's Isengard. Miller himself added the excellent Nimrod to 'B' Buttress, a sustained piece of wall climbing which proved to be the hardest route on the crag.

The Race For The Pillar

Much of the main activity during 1962, however, centred on Esk Buttress. Allan Austin began the year by ascending Right Hand Route on the Buttress, before returning to his exploration of Pavey Ark and the discovery of another superb route in the form of Arcturus. A Carlisle team led by Dennis English also visited Esk Buttress and climbed the very fine Gargoyle Direct, but the best was yet to come.

During 1961 and 1962, Pete Crew had been establishing himself at the forefront of Welsh climbing in the company of Jack Soper, with a string of impressive new routes on Cloggy which culminated in his ascent of the Great Wall. Crew took time off from his beloved Cloggy in June to visit Dove Crag. Here he succeeded where others had failed in ascending the brilliant line of Hiraeth, and pressed home the point further by making the second ascents of Dovedale Groove and Extol. 'The Big Three' as they were later to become known had all been pioneered by climbers primarily associated with Wales.

A week later Crew returned to deal another blow to the pride of Lakeland activisits. The great outstanding problem of Esk Buttress's Central Pillar had received a number of attempts, which were ultimately repulsed by the existence of a crucial pile of loose blocks. Jack Soper finally abseiled down and removed these, but he did not finish the climb. Thus it was that, one Sunday morning, two rival teams raced for the prize of the Central Pillar. When Soper arrived with Austin and Metcalf he found Crew's party already established having made a dawn start from Langdale.

Austin and his party compensated for their loss with admirable first ascents of their own, the appropriately named Black Sunday and the bold and elegant Red Edge. As a final gesture Crew returned to the Lakes in September to climb the best pitch on Buckstone How, Alexas.

Other important ascents in the Northern Lakes that year included High Crag Buttress in Buttermere by J.J.S. Allison and L. Kendall and further developments on Falcon Crags in Borrowdale. Ado Liddell and Ray McHaffie made their first appearance on the new climbs scene that year with three very good routes on Lower Falcon Crag — Interloper, The Niche and The Girdle Traverse, all of which required pegs for aid. The Niche, which is still regarded as the best route on this overhanging crag, caused a certain amount of controversy at the time due to the liberal use of pegs to assist gardening. Both McHaffie and Liddell in different ways went on to exert a considerable influence on the future of climbing in this valley. The other important ascent on the same crag that year was Plagiarism, by the new names of Paul Nunn and Oliver Woolcock, soon to be found gracing the first ascent credits of many new routes in this area.

The Divided Kingdom (1963-1967)

There has perhaps always been an inclination by climbing pioneers to concentrate their efforts on specific areas. Even when transport improved, factors such as social gathering centres, peer group influences, ease of limited access, favourite locations, familiar ground and local knowledge, continued to polarise the activities of many groups of climbers into well defined areas. In the Lake Distrct, geographical lay-out and lack of road systems across the central massif has tended to accentuate this effect.

Polarisation of climbing groups towards exploration of specific valleys or areas became particulary noticeable during the mid-sixties and with it came the development of localised ethics, approaches and codes of practice. This may be an over-simplification of what occurred, but hopefully it will help to explain the course that Lakeland climbing followed during the mid and late sixties and its repercussions during the seventies.

The North — 'The Borrowdale Piton Image'

Paul Ross was easily the most prolific and influential climber operating in Borrowdale and Thirlmere from 1954 to his departure for Canada in 1966. Most of his new routes were confined to the Borrowdale valley and by 1959 his systematic development of Shepherds, Falcon, Walla and Black Crags had yielded around thirty new routes. Some excellent and very hard routes were climbed with a minimal use of aid (Post Mortem and Eagle Girdle) whilst others were criticised for the over-use of pegs (Vertigo, The Cleft, Rigor Mortis).

Ross and his companions developed a different philosophy and felt justified in using pegs on climbs which were often dirtier, looser and more vegetated than elsewhere in the Lakes. Their attitudes were far different from those of today: 'If you'd thought that in twenty years time Ken Wilson was going to play hell with you, you wouldn't have done some routes with pegs, they would have been done without.' (Paul Ross interview in *Leeds University C.C. Journal* 1974)

Ross's own article 'Castle Rock of Triermain' (F.R.C.C. *Journal* 1961) has a description of the first ascent of Rigor Mortis which included the use of pegs for aid and the chipping out of three separate spikes for use with aid slings.

Ironically, the Editor's Notes in the same *Journal* state: '....at last, in this number, we are fortunate in having an account of the climbing there (Castle Rock) from the pioneer of so many recent outstanding routes.

At the other end of the scale one hears of misguided enterprise — hand holds chipped from a Moderate......a piton hammer is certainly a menace in the hands of irresponsible people!'

In the sixties Ross was joined by fresh talent in the shape of Liddell, McHaffie, Nunn, Woolcock, Henderson, Clark, Thompson and Toole. Many new crags were explored in Borrowdale and the local attitude towards pegs continued to be somewhat more liberal than elsewhere. Manufactured nut-runners were now becoming generally available, but many of the teams operating in Borrowdale preferred the security of pegs for protection and saw no ethical differences between pegs and nuts when direct aid was required.

Few top quality routes were climbed during 1963-64 but aid proliferated, resulting in a number of purely artificial climbs (Exclamation, The Dangler, Via Roof Route, Hells Wall, The Technician, Joke, D,T.'s etc.) During the next two years, however, some fifty new routes were added to Borrowdale. Paul Nunn and Paul Ross climbed a number of excellent routes on Eagle Crag, the best of which was Daedalus (although this also used substantial aid.)

The attitude of South Lakes climbers was expressed by Dave Miller's comments in the F.R.C.C. *Journal* 1965-66 'New Climbs and Notes.'

'Surprisingly, Eagle Crag had a spate of routes which are said to be good and of a high standard of difficulty. It would appear from the descriptions, however, that they are more likely to be enjoyed by enthusiasts of peg and sling dangling.'

The long overdue guidebook to Borrowdale was scheduled for 1967/8, so Ross and Thompson in protest produced their own private guide within six weeks. Many of the routes were overgraded but the guide did serve as a useful stop-gap measure and the use of asterisks to denote climbs of quality was a futuristic concept.

The major climbing event of 1965 and 1966 was the discovery and development of Goat Crag. Until 1964, its northern face was so heavily vegetated that few had considered it worth climbing upon. Yet again, it was Les Brown's eye for a great route that led him to spend a whole winter, in total secrecy, gardening his chosen line. In the spring of 1965, just as local climbers were starting to get wind of his operations, Brown moved in to make the first ascent of Praying Mantis; a magnificent route which was destined to become one of the best and most popular in the Lakes. Brown's route triggered off such a spate of activity from the valley's regular climbers, that it resembled a modern day gold rush! None of the routes that followed managed to match the quality of Praying Mantis, but several excellent routes materialised from beneath the carpets of grass. In less than two years Goat Crag was transformed from an obscure vegetated hillside into a major crag that boasted twenty-eight new

Alan Moss on Rigor Mortis, Castle Rock.   *Ron Kenyon*   244

climbs. Three of the best routes employed a substantial amount of aid; D.D.T. (6), Big Curver (7) and Rat Race (a large number!).

Adrian Liddell's free ascents of both D.D.T. and Big Curver in 1966 were notable accomplishments which have often been quoted as the spark that initiated the self-generated clean-up campaign of the late sixties. In truth, most Borrowdale pioneers spent much time trying to avoid pitons and the free-climbing ethic had never been in question. As Paul Nunn explained:-

'If some went too far away from the free climbing ethic, they were criticised; if a new climb used too much aid, it was soon done with less. The invention of new ideological positions can affect such things, but in the 60s that did not happen.' (*Mountain 44*, August 1975)

Nevertheless, it seems fair to say that although pegs continued to be used quite freely for a number of years to come, the emphasis on avoiding or eliminating aid gradually gathered momentum. It was not until the late seventies, however, that the valley could completely claim to be rid of 'The Borrowdale Piton Image.'

The South — "Whiter Than White"

'It was Austin's ideology that had profound effects on the later history of Lakeland climbing; so dogmatic were his ethics that their effect on the total British climbing scene is still gathering weight. As spiritual head of the Yorkshire purist movement, which is like saying *whiter than white*, he came to Langdale, and Pavey Ark in particular, with a virgin set of Yorkshire gritstone ethics.' (from 'Lakeland Community' by Pete Livesey in *Mountain 39*, October, 1974)

At best this statement is an exaggeration, at worst it is completely refutable, (see 'The Other Side of the Historical Coin' by Paul Nunn in *Mountain 44*, August 1975) but like all good stories it contains a grain of truth, and helps illustrate how the differences in attitude towards pegs and aid between the North and South of the Lake District originally came about during the mid-sixties.

Allan Austin, like Jim Birkett and Arthur Dolphin before him, is generally regarded as the foremost Lakeland pioneer of his day. In common with his two predecessors he concentrated his efforts on Langdale and throughout the sixties he totally dominated developments in that area. (It is an unusual fact that from 1940 to 1970 one in two of all recorded climbs in the Langdale area was pioneered by these three men.)

There is little doubt that Austin's attitudes and approach to climbing had a strong influence on his companions, and the fact that only two of the twenty-five climbs he established in Langdale during the sixties employed a peg for aid (one each on Astra and Rainmaker) stands in stark contrast to the developments in Borrowdale during the same period.

In 1963 Austin in the company of Eric Metcalf and Dave Miller made two fine additions to Gimmer Crag with Poacher and Gimmer String. The former is a surprisingly bold and exposed lead, and the latter was so named because all the pitches had been previously climbed by separate parties and it only remained to string it all together. Also that year Austin and Jack Soper regained some Lakeland pride by making the third ascent of Dovedale Groove and adding a new direct finish of comparable difficulty to the lower pitches. ('Dovedale Groove' by A. Austin. F.R.C.C. *Journal* 1964)

During the next 3 years only eleven new climbs were recorded in Langdale and Austin was on the first ascent of all of them. The best of these were Bowfell Buttress Eliminate, (Bowfell), Man of Straw and Chimney Variant (White Ghyll) and Gandalf's Groove & Razor Crack (Neckband). Austin returned to Neckband Crag in 1968 to add Gillette, thus completing a trilogy of superb short routes.

Elsewhere, Austin and Jack Soper opened up new crags with Cam Spout Buttress in Eskdale and Paper Tiger on Green Crag, Buttermere. Also in Buttermere the same pair along with Ian Roper added the fine and difficult Carnival to Eagle Crag.

In 1967, Austin's Langdale guidebook finally appeared, the first in a long overdue New Series of F.R.C.C. guides. The colour-coded plastic covers and the introduction of the H.V.S. and Extreme gradings were innovations. (Paul Ross had first used the Extreme grade in his pirate guide to Borrowdale in 1965 and the idea had been incorporated by Austin and Miller in the second of the F.R.C.C. *New Climbs* booklets in 1966.) In a review of the Langdale guide (*Mountain 4*, July 1969) Chris Bonington wrote; 'In Langdale, Allan Austin displays his contempt for artificial climbing by dismissing Trilogy in three sentences. He altogether ignores Paul Ross's spectacular, though artificial, line over the big overhangs on White Ghyll.' Reviewers of Austin's next Langdale guide in 1973 would have far harsher comments to make!

The West — 'All To Ourselves'

One of the more notable events of the mid-sixties was the renaissance of Pillar Rock by local West Cumbrians. In 1963, the new partnership of Geoff Cram and Bill Young ascended the impressive crack of Scylla and initiated an intense period of activity on the Rock which was to continue until 1972. More than thirty new routes were produced, almost exclusively at the hands of just five climbers — Cram, Young, Schipper, Eilbeck and Lounds. Many of these climbs were long and difficult and required a good deal of cleaning but here the use of pegs was generally kept to a minimum. The remoteness of Pillar had been an important factor in its total neglect for almost two decades prior to 1959, and its relative inaccessibility from the popular centres of Keswick and Ambleside in the sixties meant that the local climbers virtually had the place all to themselves.

In 1964, Cram and Young took time off from Pillar to make a visit to Castle Rock in Thirlmere to climb The Ghost. It was the hardest route in the area, and maintained a fierce reputation for many years to come.

Geoff Cram was the principal leader in the assault on Pillar Rock for several years and took most of the obvious prizes on the North and West Faces. Charybdis, Sheol, Puppet, Gondor and Ximenes, together with Electron and Necromancer on the Shamrock, provided him with an excellent string of trophies. The striking and awkward crack of Sheol, Puppet, Gondor and the exposed, bulging arête of Gondor presented challenges comparable with the hardest routes in the Lakes. Young, Eilbeck and Schipper also produced good routes during 1966 and 1967, particularly on the Shamrock.

In 1968, Bill Lounds appeared on the scene and in the company of Chris Eilbeck established six routes in as many weeks, the best of which were Eros, Thanatos and Vishnu. Another local team of Martin, Wilson and Cowan climbed The Black Widow, with four pegs for aid that were quickly eliminated by Lounds the following year to produce a very hard route. Lounds went on to eliminate aid from a good many Lakeland routes during the 60s and early 70s.

The long neglected Gable Crag had a visit from Cram and Young in 1966 resulting in the superb wall climb of The Tomb. Here again, though to a lesser extent, they began a revival of interest in the crag that was to extend into the early seventies. Interceptor in 1967 by Pat Fearnehough and The Slant the following year by the strong team of Burbage, Griffin, Fearnehough and Oliver provided the best routes.

The East — 'White Elephants'

Developments in the Eastern Fells during the mid-sixties were far less significant than elsewhere in the Lakes. Many small crags around Ullswater and in the Thirlmere area were discovered and climbed, principally by Neil Allinson and Jack Soper, but few have ever gained any popularity.

On Dove Crag, Mordor was started in 1965, by yet another top Welsh activist, Martin Boysen. It was not continued through the overhangs until 1968 (by Cram and Jones). Although the climb was very hard and serious, the rock was loose and dirty, and it did not compare with its illustrious neighbours.

Rainsborrow Crag received a great deal of time and attention in 1966 and 1967 by Roper, Allinson, Soper and others but here again it turned out to be something of a white elephant. The best route taking a fierce crack in the central Prow was left for Joe Brown, making a rare visit in 1969. The Groan used a point of aid that was soon dispensed with by Bill Lounds.

The Marauders

Not all the pioneers of the sixties were content to funnel their efforts into a particular valley or area. Some moved freely around the crags of the Lakes,

Geoff Cram and Bill Young on the first ascent of The Tomb, Gable Crag.   248
A.G.Cram Collection

poaching well chosen lines from under the noses of the local devotees. Most successful of these 'marauders' were Chris Bonington and Les Brown. Significantly, both these men soon broadened their climbing ambitions to beyond the confines of the Lake District — although this seems to be something of an understatement in the case of Chris Bonington!

In 1964 Bonington established two important and very contrasting routes on Raven Crag in Thirlmere. The central cave area of this crag, consisting of a complex array of overhangs, was to be the preserve of a future generation of climbers, but the only apparent weakness at that time was a huge bottomless groove in its left wall. Bonington and Martin Boysen — a climber rapidly attracting attention in North Wales and destined to become one of Britain's finest cragsmen — managed this improbable-looking line with three points of aid. The Medlar, named after the medlar tree which still sprouts from its foot , proved to be an outstanding climb and probably the fiercest undertaking in the Lakes at that time. Bonington returned the following month with Mike Thompson to add the delicate and elegant Totalitarian.

The following year, on the opposite side of the valley, Bonington with Ross, Henderson and Moseley added The Last Laugh to Castle Rock. Aid was used to climb the very steep groove on its second pitch, but the climb's reputation grew on the basis of its bold and serious first pitch. Also in 1965, Bonington and Thompson set off on an intended girdle traverse of the East Buttress of Scafell but realised too late that they had underestimated its difficulty and seriousness: 'it was a blind alley and I'd had it, the only thing I could have done was to jump off.' After an epic, Bonington managed to get to the top of the crag. (see *Lakeland Rock*, Chapter 4, The Holy Ghost.) The Holy Ghost has good climbing and was certainly a very hard and serious route for its time, but perhaps its main importance lay in providing the key to the outstanding problem of the girdle traverse.

In the mid-sixties Les Brown continued to pick off classic routes around the Lakes. In 1964 he added the highly technical Psycho to High Crag, Buttermere to provide the hardest route in the area. The following year after ascending the magnificent Praying Mantis (previously described) he turned his attention to Dow Crag once more and the big unclimbed groove in the centre of 'A' Buttress. The Balrog proved to be impressive and very strenuous, requiring three points of aid, and completed for Brown a brilliant trio of routes on this buttress.

In 1966, Brown solved one of the 'last great problems' of the period, the wildly overhanging crack in the wall to the left of Central Buttress on Scafell Crag. Operating in typical secrecy, Brown is reputed to have told inquisitive competitors that he was exploring a fictitious Far East Buzzard Crag. The initial crack was finally overcome after several attempts with two pegs and a nut for aid. The resulting climb Nazgul takes a direct line up the face and provided Scafell with yet another superb route.

Chris Bonington and Martin Boysen on the first ascent of The Medlar,   250
Raven Crag, Thirlmere.   *Bonington Collection*

Brown's other route that year, The Hun on Pillar Rock, added another fine, airy route to the crag's growing repertoire and signalled the end of his inspired explorations of Lakeland crags in the sixties.

1968-1970 Transition Period

It can be argued that climbing standards in the Lake District virtually stood still for most of the sixties. In the late fifties, several routes such as Post Mortem (1956), Phoenix (1957) and Eliminot (1957) had already broached the E2 barrier, and many of the outstanding classics of 1960 — Side Walk, Extol, Astra & Ichabod — were solidly of this grade. (Admittedly, each of the above-mentioned climbs employed a point of aid, which was subsequently eliminated, but they all possessed the aura of this new standard of climbing). During the sixties many formidable lines were ascended, opening up sections of cliff previously considered unclimbable, but purely in terms of the top level of climbing standards achieved it may be regarded as a period of consolidation of the E2 grade. It was not until the final years of the decade that new climbs began to emerge which showed signs of another rise in standards.

It is perhaps interesting at this point to compare progress with other areas. The advancement of climbing standards in Scotland roughly paralleled the Lakes, with routes like Club Crack (1956), Shibboleth (1958) and Carnivore (1958) representing the first E2's, but the next step forward did not occur there until the mid to late seventies.

Wales, however, was significantly ahead of both areas. As early as 1952, routes like Bloody Slab were breaking into the E2 grade and throughout the fifites the development of Cloggy saw the production of a whole string of new climbs which were firmly of this grade — Slanting Slab, Woubits, Taurus, The Mostest, etc. The ascents of November (1957) and Woubits Left Hand (1959), despite using considerable aid, already hinted at the next rise in standards. The almost traditional rivalry between N. Wales and the Lakes for producing the hardest climbs of the day has prevailed throughout much of Britain's climbing history. In the early fifties the death of Arthur Dolphin and the advent of Brown and Whillans on the cliffs of Snowdonia were crucial factors in swinging the pendulum strongly in favour of Wales. Many of the leading Lakeland pioneers of the sixties made regular visits to N. Wales but like everyone else at that time, their principal ambitions lay in repeating the earlier routes of the Rock and Ice. An equalisation in climbing standards of the hardest routes in Wales and the Lakes was not to be convincingly achieved again until the mid-seventies.

1968 and 1969 saw the dawn of a transition period in Lake District climbing which was to bring new faces, approaches and standards during the early seventies.

In 1968, Allan Austin climbed Gillette on Neckband Crag and the following year Bill Lounds added a hard direct finish. This latter effort together with

Lounds's free ascents of Black Widow and The Groan that year represented climbing at the upper limit of the E2 grade.

Many of the hardest routes pioneered during this period, however, employed direct aid and the level of difficulty achieved is now far harder to assess.

On Scafell, for instance, some notable completely free ascents were still being made: Minotaur by Syd Clark, Gold Rush by Geoff Cram and Bill Young, Gilt Edge Eliminate by Colin Read and most important of all, the long-standing problem of a complete girdle traverse of the East Buttress, by the freshly emerging team of John Adams and Colin Read. This marathon girdle provided serious and sustained climbing for 1,200 feet and took some 19½ hours over a two day period to complete. (See 'Lord of the Rings' by C. Read, in *Carlisle Mountaineering Club Journal* 1971) Lord of the Rings was a magnificent accomplishment, providing one of the best expeditions to be had on Lakeland rock. It was to be six years before it received a second ascent.

At the time, other routes were being ascended by the same pioneers using substantial amounts of aid, e.g. Chimera by Cram and Young and Dyad by Ken Jackson and Read. Unlike many of the partially-aided routes of the mid-sixties in Borrowdale and elsewhere, however, those of the late sixties tackled futuristic lines which were to become the E3 and E4 climbs of the seventies. Further signs of rising standards were also evident in the number of hard routes being accomplished in a single day. On Scafell during 1969, Lounds managed Nazgul, Ichabod, Holy Ghost and Leverage whilst Richard McHardy and Paul Braithwaite paid a rare visit from N. Wales to record an even better day. They climbed Leverage, Ichabod, Hell's Groove and another before soloing Mickledore Grooves, Trinity, Chartreuse and Overhanging Wall — all on sight. The same weekend, this team successfully ascended one of the districts 'last great problems'; the vicious overhanging crack on Tophet Wall, Great Gable. McHardy's lead of The Viking (1969) gave the Lakes its first route of an unequivocal E3 grading.

Elsewhere in the Lakes, Colin Read and John Adams made significant contributions. They gave Dow Crag's 'A' Buttress yet another impressive climb, Silence, and their route Great End Pillar opened up a new crag in Borrowdale. More controversial were their ascents of Peccadillo on Deer Bield Crag and Athanor on Goat Crag. Both these very fine lines utilized a number of pegs for aid — four and six respectively — to give routes which were to become hard free climbs by the mid-seventies. This trend of employing a limited number of aid points to tackle some of the more improbable-looking lines that remained in the area was adopted by a number of leading figures and continued into the early seventies. It was, I believe, symptomatic of the transition taking place. Most of the good lines of an E2 standard had been climbed over the previous decade. Standards were beginning to rise again and a new breed of climber was emerging with the will to take on more improbable-looking lines. The level of technical ability needed to free climb these lines of potential E3 and

E4 difficulty was still just beyond their grasp.

Thus, the sixties came to an end in a state of transition which held out great hopes for the future. The following decade more than lived up to expectations as a new regime of pioneers with better equipment, more refined techniques, professional methods and a whole new outlook began an intense period of development of the Lakeland crags. It was to be an era in which climbing standards rose dramatically, controversies flared regularly, and ethical debate intensified as many diverse factions competed for the best lines of the day.

THEN

NOW

FILMING THE NEEDLE — WHIT 1929

A SHORT HISTORY
OF LAKELAND CLIMBING
PART IV (1970 - 1985)

Ron Kenyon & Al Murray

The 1970's created more changes in the Lakeland climbing scene and attitudes than any other decade. At the beginning of the decade the Lakeland climbing scene was rather stagnant and awaiting the impact of a new generation of rock athletes such as Livesey, Matheson and the Carlisle lads.

The breakthrough in climbing standards led climbers into new areas of rocks once thought impossible to climb free, with routes such as Footless Crow, Shere Khan, Take it to the Limit and Das Kapital. Leading on to the 1980's this has brought about a general increase in climbing standards with more climbing the hardest routes. Climbers who stamped their marks on the decade were Jeff Lamb, Pete Whillance, Pete Botterill, Dave Armstrong and Steve Clegg from Carlisle; Colin Downer and the Keswick lads, Colin Read and John Adams; Ed Cleasby, Rick Graham, Rob Matheson and Andy Hyslop from the South Lakes, Martin and Bob Berzins and Ron Fawcett from Yorkshire, Bob Hutchinson and John Earl from Northumberland and Ed Grindley. However, one climber who really made his mark, was Pete Livesey. With a serious attitude to training he made a series of new modern routes on the 'outcrops' of Yorkshire and Derbyshire, such as Bulldog Wall, Jenny Wren, Mulatto Wall and Central Wall, Kilnsey. His route Footless Crow represented a quantum leap in difficulty in Lakeland climbing. It was the same in Wales with his ascent of Right Wall on Dinas Cromlech. This had a profound effect on the decade although it perhaps took two years for other climbers in the Lakes to gain the same level of ability. When they did a flood of new routes occurred. It wasn't exceptional summers that transformed East Buttress, it was the new generation of rock athletes.

The increase in standards was due to a number of factors. There was a change of attitude from the 'traditional' to a 'professional' approach with better training, and pre-cleaning (and inspection) of routes. This has now led to ethical arguments through the world on the way climbs are made. The traditional approach of starting at the bottom of the climb is now being attacked by different international ideals and the basis of the change occurred in the 1970's. As to the future we must wait and see or act accordingly.

Climbing walls were designed to be used as training machines to improve strength, agility and technical ability. Climbers were able to practise during the winter months and also wet weather. A lot of climbers seem to prefer them to the crags. The recently opened walls at Carlisle and Ambleside provide excellent wet weather alternatives. Most older climbers must be bewildered and

Chris Dale on Barefoot, Heron Crag, Langstrath   *Ron Kenyon* possibly horrified by these walls, but with the present levels of climbing difficulty the practice walls are an important part of the climbing scene.

The equipment moguls have devised various new ways of protecting climbs. In 1970 the development of nuts was in its infancy: the MOAC had been introduced just a few years earlier, and the baby MOAC was available together with an assortment of oddities. At the end of the seventies we had rocks and Friends — not to mention chalk. E gradings were introduced to make sense of the overburdened extreme grade — initially with gradings E1 to E5.

I am sure that any climber who stopped climbing in 1960 and started again in 1970 would have seen much less change in climbing attitudes over that period than someone who had stopped in 1970 and started again in 1980. Climbing is a changing sport.

1970

This was a relatively quiet year. The major routes of the year were in Langdale where Allan Austin climbed the excellent Brackenclock on Pavey, and Jack Soper was unearthing Oak How to produce Crossword and Gurt Gardin Stuff. Rob Matheson climbed Paladin in White Ghyll, initially with some aid, which he subsequently eliminated to produce a superb route. It heralded the start of a series of modern routes by this climber. At the time some were thought unethical, with the use of pre-placed pegs. Now they are accepted as excellent routes.

In Borrowdale Bill Robinson and Colin Read climbed Zoar and with Johnny Adams climbed Turbulence, on Hind Crag. Ray McHaffie was finding (is still finding and will forever find) routes throughout the valley with Autobahn and Green Cormorant.

On Gable Crag The Jabberwock and Trundle Ridge (Rod Valentine/Wilkinson) and Potheen and Bandersnatch (Dave Miller/Wilkinson) were climbed as well as The Serpent (Read/Robinson); good additions to this not too frequented crag.

On Buckbarrow L.A. Goldsmith and D.A. Banks climbed Lothlorien during a spell of development leading to the publication of a pirate interim guide in 1974. The crag's real potential was not appreciated until the 1980's when a sustained period of activity yielded many good routes of all grades.

1971

In Langdale Ragman's Trumpet (Pavey) was climbed by Valentine/Austin whilst in White Ghyll they completed Haste Knot Direct. White Ghyll Eliminate was climbed by Al Evans, and Pete Livesey climbed the slab right of Laugh Not to give Longhair — a serious lead. Back on Pavey Livesey climbed Sally Free and Easy. On Deer Bield Matheson, G.Fleming and J.Poole climbed the Graduate with a pre-placed peg and long sling and received the wrath of the FRCC who omitted the route from the 1973 guide. This route had been climbed by Les Brown and Ken Jackson in the 1960's and not recorded. It was climbed free in 1979 by Jeff Lamb.

On Dow Matheson showed the way with Holocaust, an audacious line with 2 aid points which he climbed free in 1975. On Esk Buttress he climbed Amoeba, a worthy companion to Red Edge. Lower down the valley on Heron the West Cumbrian team of Trevor Martin, Brian Smith and Joe Wilson climbed the Last Exit. On Scafell Bonington climbed two 'big' routes — Central Buttress Girdle with Mike Thompson and The White Wizard with Nick Estcourt. Much aid was used on the White Wizard but it was subsequently climbed free in 1976 by Martin Berzins/Gordon Higginson. The more direct pitch 3 was climbed in 1977 by Pete Botterill/John Taylor.

Just left of Narrow Stand Hugh Banner climbed the oft forgotten little gem of Last Stand. Tony Barley and Pete Long forced a line up East Buttress with Doomwatch — two points of aid were used on the first pitch which still awaits a free ascent.

Above Honister Pass on the side of Fleetwith Pike a new crag had been spied. Soper, Ian Roper, Colin Taylor, Neil Allinson, Mike Burbage and Geoff Oliver climbed between them four routes and a girdle traverse but the crag with its northerly aspect and slow drying has never gained any popularity. Along the ridge on Gable Crag Geoff Cram and Bill Young climbed Spirit Level, a girdle of the Engineer's Slab wall. On the right-hand side of Eagle Crag, Buttermere G. Tough climbed Vision of Julie (with Pete Fleming) and Fiesta (with D. Cook).

On Dove Crag Read/Adams completed a long-awaited girdle traverse, using some aid, but nevertheless a major achievement. On Raven Crag in Thirlmere Matheson/Poole/Fleming climbed the very steep Blitz using a fair amount of aid. This was climbed free in 1977 by Gomersall/Livesey and renamed Blitzkrieg. In Borrowdale Pete Downie climbed Parlophone (Shepherds) with some aid (now free) and in December MacHaffie climbed the fine Kaleidoscope (Gowder).

1972

In Langdale Matheson climbed the fine line of Cruel Sister (Pavey) but again received the wrath of the FRCC after having pre-placed a peg and sling. This route received scant mention in the 1973 guide but was climbed free by Lamb/Botterill in 1975 and included in the 1980 guide to give one of the best routes on the crag and one of the most popular E3's in the Lakes. Livesey came in on the act with Fine Time (Raven) with a pre-placed peg and a very long sling. This followed the line of the aid route Kaisergebirge Wall. It was climbed free by Botterill/Lamb in 1979. John Hartley climbed Mithrandir, the obvious groove of Gandalf's Groove on Neckband, and Ed Grindley started a campaign on Pavey with Risus. Bill Birkett went to Upper Spout Crag and climbed Dindale (with Mike Myers and one point of aid) and Spiny Norman (with

R.Gill and more aid) climbed free by Berzins. Recent routes by Whillance/Armstrong may attract more climbers here. In October Grindley/Roper climbed the pod-shaped groove on Pavey to produce Fallen Angel, an impressive route which used some aid but was climbed free in 1974 by Lamb/Botterill.

Beside the road to Coniston Birkett/Myers broke the extreme barrier at Raven Crag, Yewdale and climbed Albatross and Raven Girdle. On Dow Crag the Mathesons were active, climbing two excellent routes with Catacomb and Tarkus, and Austin/Grindley, Miller and Barley linked together 'B' Buttress Variations.

On Esk Buttress Young/Burbage and John Workman climbed West Point. On East Buttress Read/Adams climbed the impressive Incubus, with 3 points of aid — it was climbed free in 1982 by Berzins/Sowden. In the Buttermere area Read/Adams were active with the pleasant Grey Wall (Grey Crag), linked together Catalyst (Buckstone How) and climbed the difficult Deimos (Eagle Crag). This very active team also climbed Phobos on Dove Crag and opened up the left side of Greatend Crag in Borrowdale with Nagasaki Grooves — they employed 5 points of aid on the route which was climbed free, solo with a backrope in 1974 by Livesey.

On the remoter Pillar Rock Bill Young and Barney Barnes climbed the varied and interesting Megaton, Bill Lounds and Chris Eilbeck climbed the well-situated Soliton and Dennis Hodgson and John Workman found and climbed The Magic Rainbow.

1973

Rob Matheson and his father continued the opening up of Dow with the now popular Pink Panther and the short but awkward Hesperus. In Langdale Grindley was suffering Brain Damage on Pavey, Keith Myhill was receiving a Mindprobe on Bowfell and Pete Long found Pearls before Swine on Deer Bield. On Esk Buttress Young and Ian Singleton scored a Grand Slam, with one point of aid, which was subsequently climbed free by Lamb/Adams in 1974.

On Eagle Crag Buttermere the Northumbrian teams were active with Birkness Eliminate (John Earl, Banner and I.W.Cranston) and Warlock (Bob Hutchinson and R.Mitchinson). In the quiet dale of Newlands Read/Adams climbed the excellent little Bolshoi Corner. In Borrowdale little happened. MacHaffie climbed the short Black Icicle (Shepherds) and The Rack (Reecastle). Livesey and John Sheard climbed the very direct Raindrop on Black Crag, giving a true superdirect. On Raven Crag Thirlmere, Myhill and Ken Jones climbed the excellent Empire with 2 points of aid, subsequently climbed free by Lamb.

1974

Although there were only 3 routes done in Borrowdale these three gained the spotlight of the Lakes this year and represented a quantum leap in difficulty. Livesey was the main performer initially with the ascent in April of Footless Crow on Goat Crag, with Robin Whitham. This was by far the hardest route in the Lakes, being a long, strenuous and serious lead (no Friends then). It immediately became the milestone of Lakeland hard climbing and initially received a number of attempts but not many successes. Since then it has been cleaned up and received more ascents. Though there are now harder climbs in the Lakes it still has a great aura about it. Livesey/Sheard climbed the excellent and now very popular companion route of Bitter Oasis. On Upper Falcon, Livesey climbed the wall left of Route 1, solo with a back rope, to produce Dry Grasp. What a position it must have been in the middle of that wall! To complete the day he soloed, with a back rope, the first free ascent of Nagasaki Grooves.

In Langdale, Livesey and Al Manson climbed Eastern Hammer (Gimmer) which replaced the old aid routes of If, which had been climbed by Paul Ross in 1960. On Dow, Matheson and John Martindale climbed the pleasant Murray's Super Direct. It was also claimed as Lynx, a much more ingenious name! The wrath of the climbing world was directed at Valentine and Tut Braithwaite for their controversial ascent of The Cumbrian on Esk Buttress — 'one of the Lakes last great problems' — when they used 3 points of aid to force this much sought-after line in time for the new guide. It was climbed free in 1977 by Martin and Bob Berzins. Lamb/Botterill climbed the sustained and interesting Zeus left of Phoenix on East Buttress Scafell, originally starting up Morning Wall. The much harder first pitch was climbed in 1982 by Sowden/Berzins.

Earl/Hutchinson were active again on the less-frequented crags with The Hanging Chimney Direct and Pierrot on Eagle Crag, Buttermere and the excellent Heorot on Scrubby. On Buckstone How a new name appeared, Pete Whillance, who with Hughie Loughran climbed the loose Brutus. An attempted second ascent by Lamb ended when loose holds broke and he fell and broke his leg. On Pillar, Read/Robinson climbed the contrived Klingsor.

Just outside the Lakes, the Eden Valley and Chapel Head Scar were receiving much attention. Being out of the fells they have better weather and have developed into useful outcrops for locals and as wet weather alternatives to the Lakes — unfortunately not quite the same as Tremadoc.

1975

In Borrowdale there was interest in the Watendlath valley on Caffell Side with ascents of Blondin (Steve Clegg/Lamb), Slack Alice (Lamb/Botterill) and Juicy Lucy (Whillance/Mike Hetherington), and over the hillside there was the grand cleaning and opening up of Greatend Crag by the Keswick team of Colin Downer, Dave Hellier, Ian Conway and Dave Nicol. Equipped with an assortment of tools they unearthed this crag to produce Earthstrip, Greatend Groove and Greatend Corner. Botterill then started an intensive campaign on

Eagle Crag starting with The Cleff Direct (with Roger Clegg). Whillance/Clegg climbed the excellent Where Eagles Dare and Clegg/Botterill climbed Autopsy and Verdict. On Falcon, Pete Gomersall and Nigel Bulmer climbed the improbable Usurper and Nicol, Conway and Bob Wilson climbed the tricky Extrapolation. On Shepherds Birkett/MacHaffie climbed the vicious Savage Messiah (with some aid) — this was climbed free shortly afterwards by Berzins/Clegg — also Mike Lynch/Cleasby climbed the fine steep Jaws. On High Crag in Buttermere Cleasby/Birkett climbed the superb arête of Philistine.

Over on Dow Crag, Livesey and Jill Lawrence showed the way for the future with the two companion routes of Rough and Tumble, whilst Matheson/Martindale climbed the steep and strenuous Abraxas (with one point of aid). It was climbed free by Berzins in 1976. On Scafell, Adams and C.MacQuarrie climbed Overhanging Grooves Direct.

1976

In 1976 the action hotted up. Attention was directed at Dove Crag with Berzins/Cleasby teaming up for the serious Problem Child. Botterill/Whillance started on Explosion of Interest on the right of the crag. Cliff Brown and Birkett climbed Redex on the rather obscure Raven Crag, Threshthwaite Cove. This crag did not become popular until the 1980's, when realisation of its quality sparked off a wave of development.

On the better known Raven Crag in Thirlmere, Botterill/Clegg climbed the superb, hard Gates of Delirium and Creation — two routes which attracted much attention leading to the renewed development of this fine crag.

In Borrowdale MacHaffie was digging out the right-hand crag on Gowder to produce a number of routes, but only The Rib is worth any attention. Of more interest were activities on Goat Crag with the ascent by Botterill and Dave Rawcliffe of Tumbleweed Connection and by Clegg/Botterill of the stupendous Voyage. On Black Crag, Matheson/Cleasby cemented the Grand Alliance and higher up the valley on Long Band Crag Botterill climbed the Masochist. On High Crag in Buttermere Livesey/Sheard climbed the problematic Lost Colonies.

In Langdale Cleasby climbed the elegant Equus on Gimmer and on Pavey Whillance/Botterill/Clegg climbed the sustained Eclipse with one rest later freed by Berzins. Shortly afterwards the Berzins broke out of Eclipse on a girdle of the upper section of the East Wall, Startrek, whilst Cleasby/Matheson climbed the steep Mother Courage. On Gimmer Livesey and team climbed the eliminate Breaking Point.

On Scafell a period of sustained action was starting. Botterill/Clegg climbed the sustained Shadowfax, up the wall left of Botterill's Slab — he should have called it Botterill's Wall. John Eastham and Cleasby then climbed the often looked-at wall right of the Flake on Central Buttress to give the stupendous and surprisingly not too difficult Saxon. On East Buttress Livesey/Lawrence made a characteristically bold ascent of the central overhanging section of the crag with Lost Horizons. This was flawed by pre-placed protection and a point of aid, but nevertheless an excellent route which was climbed free by Bob Berzins and Mike Browell in 1982.

1977

In 1977 there was action everywhere — the fuse had been lit!

The action continued on Scafell with the Berzins brothers/Chris Sowden climbing the exceedingly steep Ringwraith, up the wall left of Nazgul. The Berzins also climbed Foxshooter up the wall left of the C.B. Flake. On the weekend of 28/29 May, Cleasby/Matheson climbed two excellent routes, the magnificent Shere Khan and the exceedingly elegant arête Edge of Eriador. Lower down the valley on Esk Buttress the Berzins climbed Humdrum.

On Dow Crag some new climbers came in on the act to produce a series of good routes. Initially Andy Hyslop and Ian Greenwood climbed Misty Mountain Hop on B Buttress and then Hyslop and Rick Graham climbed the companion Four Sticks. The same climbers also climbed Samba Pa Ti, to give a hard continuation of Isengard and the companion Brocklebank variation. Cleasby and Gordon Tinning climbed the athletic Issel Roof above the wall taken by Giant Corner. Just to the right, Hyslop/Graham climbed Born Free, an ascending traverse across Tarkus, Leopards Crawl and Pink Panther.

In the Eastern Crags there was a lot of action on the guide's three main crags. In Thirlmere on Castle Rock Gomersall and Bonny Masson climbed a variation finish to Barbican, Matheson Avenue, and then the steep crackline of Ted Cheasby. Across the valley on Raven Crag Clegg/Botterill opened up the year with Close to the Edge, an interesting climb starting up The Medlar and finishing up the groove between that climb and Gates of Delirium. On the same day the Berzins climbed The First Circle — an arduous crossing of the crag linking some very exciting pitches. Shortly afterwards Livesey/Gomersall stole the show with the exceedingly difficult Peels of Laughter and Blitzkrieg — a free version of the very steep Blitz. Over on Dove Crag Martin Berzins and Chris Hamper whittled down the aid on North Buttress to give an almost free and very airy route on the right side of the crag, to show what was possible there. Left of Extol Whillance/Armstrong climbed the good and steep Aurora. On the secluded Thrang Crag in Martindale Earl/Hutchinson climbed three routes — Jude the Obscure, The Wilderness and Locusts — to open up this little crag.

In the Langdale area the action started at Deer Bield when Armstrong/Whillance climbed Gymslip, a serious and technical route up the wall left of The Crack. Shortly afterwards this team returned and attacked the face right of The Buttress to produce the intricate Desperado. Later in the year Cleasby/Matheson caused controversy with their prior top-roping of Imagination — a bold and serious lead up the arête right of The Chimney. On

the very accessible Raven Crag Grahame Summers/Cleasby climbed the spectacular R'n'S Special with a wire for aid whilst higher up on Gimmer Crag the Berzins climbed the difficult mini-girdle of Enormous Room. On Pavey Pete Sansom and Bill Lounds squeezed in Kudos and the Berzins climbed another mini-girdle, Solstice. Fawcett/Gibb and Ian Edwards climbed the impressive Big Brother, just left of Cruel Sister; Mortimer/Allen climbed the oft looked at Rib, left of Rake End Chimney and that ever active pair of Whillance/Armstrong climbed Obscured by Clouds. Lower down on White Ghyll, Cleasby/Matheson climbed the sustained Warrior and Lounds/Sansom climbed the contrived Waste Not, Want Not. Over in Borrowdale the final routes were claimed before the new guide. Botterill and Doreen Hopkins climbed Black Sheep at Shepherds — definitely undergraded in the guide at HVS. On Black Crag Bill Freeland was active — with MacHaffie he climbed the excellent Jubilee Grooves and with Lamb and Syd Clark completed the contrived girdle High Plains Drifter. Livesey/Gomersall nearly free climbed the old aid route, Wack, renaming it Scrutineer — Lamb did free climb it later and renamed it Wack. Gomersall led the excellent and now popular Prana and with two other 'stars', Livesey and Fawcett, climbed Tristar.

Downer, Nicol and Co were still active on Greatend Crag producing the now classic Banzai Pipeline together with Punk Rock and New Wave, as well as the pleasant Point Blank on Goat Crag. These and other similarly excavated routes showed what could be produced with thorough gardening from abseil ropes etc. The route of Goat however was Alone in Space climbed by Tony Stephenson, Chris Sice and Ray Parker, a now very popular and good route up the centre of the crag. It was to have been named Flying Scotsman after a Scot who had fallen down the crag at that time but Alone in Space seemed more subtle. On Eagle Crag Lamb/Freeland continued developments with the impressive Inquest Direct.

On Great Gable the Carlisle teams were out in force. Whillance/Armstrong climbed the impressive Supernatural up the wall left of Tophet Wall; the fine Sarcophagus left of The Tomb on Gable Crag and then The Cayman, near Crocodile Crack on The Napes. Lamb/Botterill and John Taylor climbed the impressive overhanging crack above Tophet Wall to produce Sacrificial Crack and then Botterill/Lamb climbed the technical Golden Calf.

1978

This was certainly the middle of a golden era of development. On East Buttress, Scafell, Botterill/Lamb continued the flow of excellent routes with Talisman up the walls left of Trinity; the eliminate of Caradhras; the beautiful Equinox up the corner and faint crack left of Lost Horizon; the sustained Lucius and the deceptively difficult S.O.S. The Berzins, always close at hand, climbed Cullinan. On Esk Buttress Hyslop/Graham climbed the serious direct continuation of Trespasser Groove to give Strontium Dog.

In the Eastern Crags two fillers appeared on Castle Rock: with White Dwarf by Birkett and Ken Forsythe, a direct variant between Rigor Mortis and The Ghost, and Ecstasy by Cleasby/Wright/Matheson. Across the valley Cleasby/Matheson opened up with the technical Polytruk but Livesey/Gomersall replied with the super impressive Das Kapital.

On Dove Crag Lamb/Botterill/Taylor climbed the wall left of Dovedale Groove to produce Ommadawn. Hutchinson/Earl were scouring the lesser-frequented crags and found some interesting routes with Darth Vader on Scrubby, Heat Wave on Hutaple and the very good Bloodhound in Swindale.

In Langdale Whillance/Armstrong were again active on Deer Bield and produced the short but difficult Stiletto, The New Girdle and the super serious Take it to the Limit — a Whillance special — a route that gave second ascentionist Ron Fawcett some worrying moments.

On the excellent little Neckband Crag the Berzins climbed Cut Throat and Birkett/Forsythe climbed Flying Blind. Fawcett/Gibb climbed the very thin Heartsong on Pavey then free climbed the old Paul Ross aid route of The Horror in White Ghyll (since collapsed).

The production of the Borrowdale guide in the year sparked off a period of development in the valley. On Falcon Crag filmgoers Graham/Birkett squeezed in Close Encounters and Star Wars, then Botterill/Lamb linked together the fine Kidnapped. Hyslop led Wuthering Heights and Forsythe/Birkett climbed the steep Cyclotron.

In the quiet Watendlath valley action started initially on Caffel Side Crag with Everard and Apricot Lil, by Whillance/Armstrong and Martin Berzins. Across the valley Lamb showed the potential of Reecastle with his ascents of Guillotine, White Noise and Thumbscrew and Dougie Mullen, 'fresh' from the Carlisle M.C. dinner, climbed the now rather misnamed but good Widowmaker. These routes started the development of one of the 'hard' crags of the valley. On Black Crag Botterill/Parker climbed Silent Sun.

On the central area of Greatend Crag Livesey/Gomersall climbed the very difficult Hiroshima and Whillance/Armstrong replied with Trouble Shooter. A number of routes were climbed on Hind Crag and the Upper Right Wall of Gillercombe but have not become popular. On Goat Crag Ron Kenyon and Alan Hewison climbed Solid Air, then Colin Downer climbed Fear of Flying (with some aid, later free) and the excellent High Flyer. Bill Wayman climbed the oft 'inspected' line of the abseil on the right of the crag to produce Heretic.

1979

The flow of good routes continued this year. On Scafell, Lamb and the Berzins brothers found more excellent routes. Mythical Kings, a direct based on Ichabod finishes up the tower on the left; Roaring Silence (what a super name!) gives airy climbing right of Ichabod and Forbidden Colours attacks the wall further right. Lamb/Botterill climbed the deceptively difficult corner of

　Page 98: Al Phizacklea on Heartsong (E4), Pavey Ark.　　　*Phizacklea Collection*
Page 99: Pete Botterill on the second ascent of Close to Critical (E4), Dow Crag.
　　　　　　　　　　　　　　　　　　　　　　　　　　　　Phizacklea Collection

Burning Bridges and just to the right Berzins/Lamb climbed Subaudition. Botterill/Lamb climbed the intimidating slab of Chartreuse direct and finished up the very difficult headwall to produce Midnight Express. Down the valley on Esk Buttress Birkett/Hyslop climbed the very bold Fallout.

In Thirlmere Lamb/Botterill climbed The Ultimate Eliminate on Castle Rock and with the Berzins they climbed the difficult Relay on Raven Crag. On Gable Crag Lamb/Botterill squeezed in The Angel of Mercy.

In Langdale Lamb/Cleasby made the first completely free ascent of Trilogy, the deceptively steep corner on Raven Crag.

On Gimmer Crag Mortimer/Cleasby and team climbed the immaculate and popular Spring Bank.

Interest was then directed towards the Bowfell area. Kenyon and Rick Bennett went to investigate the central corner/groove just left of The Sword of Damocles, first seen by Kenyon in 1975. Thinking that such an obvious line must have been tried before, he thought it must be very hard but was surprised to find it a relatively easy E2, Mindbender. On Flat Crag Cleasby/Greenwood climbed the direct Fastburn then the Berzins climbed Slowburn and the exceedingly steep Ataxia. On Neckband Fawcett/Gibb climbed the thin Wilkinson's Sword and on Pavey they climbed the eliminate Supernova. Also on Pavey Lamb/Botterill climbed the impressive and sustained Coma. In White Ghyll Gary Gibson and D. Beetlestone climbed the serious Dead Loss Angelus up the Slabs left of the chimney.

Development still continued in Borrowdale. On Reecastle Lamb/Parker opened up with Ricochet, McHaffie followed with Bold Warrior and Whillance/Armstrong, the following day, climbed The Executioner. Lancashire climbers Knighton/Cronshaw found some excellent routes on the long forgotten Walla Crag with Blazing Apostles, Muscular Delinquent and Total Mass Retain (different names to the more traditional White Buttress and Snowstorm). On Shepherds Crag Whillance/Armstrong created interest in the overhung base right of Vesper with their Dire Straits. Lamb/Botterill turned attentions to the Shepherd's Chimney area and free climbed the airy Inclination. The Berzins replied with a free ascent of the dynamic Exclamation. On Bowder Crag Whillance/Armstrong changed things with their ascent of Wheels of Fire. Shortly afterwards Fawcett's free ascent of Hell's Wall stamped the crag on the lists of all aspiring hard men. On Castle Crag Birkett/MacHaffie climbed the big wall left of Libido to give Corridors of Power and on Goat Crag the ever active Berzins/Lamb team climbed the interesting eliminate of The Thieving Magpie.

An interesting guide appeared to Winter Climbs in the Lake District. Although not fully comprehensive this helped to distract the winter attentions from Great End and Helvellyn to a wealth of excellent ice climbs elsewhere in the Lakes such as on the Screes in Wasdale, Inaccessible Gully and Raven Crag Gully. This, with the general increase in ice climbing standards caused by better equipment and the 'coffee table' book of Cold Climbs, has led to new winter routes in the modern idiom during the 1980's. Traditional summer routes received winter ascents such as Jones's Route direct from Lord's Rake and Botterill's Slab on Scafell, Engineers Slab on Gable Crag and Bowfell Buttress — not to mention a complete winter ascent of East Buttress by Tony Brindle and Adrian Moore in the winter of 1986. And so the decade ended very much on a high note, with an emerging newer generation looking for any unclimbed rock, big or small.

1980

The new decade began with the rediscovery of Hodge Close quarry at High Tilberthwaite. Whillance and friends initiated development and by Easter were joined by the Cleasby/Matheson team. The result was a number of fine atmospheric routes mainly in the upper grades. Over on Dove Crag's North Buttress Graham/Birkett forced two impressive lines with Broken Arrow and Fear and Fascination. Botterill/Whillance found a number of short hard pitches on Deer Bield and Gouther Crag Swindale and during the latter half of the year began to tap the potential of Raven Crag, Threshthwaite Cove.

1981

That potential was realised the following year and most of Raven's major lines were snapped up by Botterill/Whillance in the company of Lamb/Armstrong, producing some superb routes like Top Gear and High Performance.

The unlikely Iron Crag, Thirlmere came under scrutiny during the year and a number of good quality climbs were found on the cleaned walls up and left of the main crag. The same team was also active up on Eagle Langstrath where they produced a fine trio of hard crack climbs; Dead on Arrival, Flying Circus and the intimidating Coroners Crack. On Reecastle Watendlath they breached the wall left of White Noise to produce the magnificent Penal Servitude, and in the west of the district pushed forward standards on the recently redeveloped and popular Buckbarrow in Wasdale with their ascent of the aptly-named Wild West Show.

Back in Borrowdale Rick Graham climbed a first pitch to Mirage on Goat Crag to produce an excellent route. Visiting American Mark Wilford bouldered up two hard pitches, Day of the Jackals on Goat and Rough Boys on Shepherds Crag, and on Bowderstone Botterill/Lamb transformed the old aid route Bulger into a brutal free route of the same name as well as adding Heaven's Gate to its right.

1982

There was renewed activity on Scafell with the Berzins brothers removing the remaining aid points on Lost Horizons and Incubus and Botterill/Lamb climbing the awesome Almighty left of Hells Groove.

On Dow Crag, Coniston, Cleasby/Matheson climbed the handsome groove behind Woodhouse's Pinnacle to produce Close to Critical and over on Dove Crag Graham/Birkett renewed their acquaintance with the North Buttress by climbing the withering Fast and Furious.

On the Bowderstone Crags the impending wall right of Lucifer was climbed by Jerry Moffat to give the as yet unrepeated De Quincy.

1983

By comparison this was a quiet year. It did however see the free ascent of the fine hanging pod left of Eclipse on Pavey Ark by Chris Hamper. This had previously been climbed back in 1981 with some rests taken on runners but had never really been accepted. Also of note was the first route to breach the futuristic crag right of Iron Crag Thirlmere's main buttress. This was the Committal Chamber and was the work of Graham/Downer. Up on Scafell during the course of guide book research Martin Berzins found the excellent Zeya.

1984

New route activity started early with Downer/Bacon hard at work during the winter months unearthing the hillside north of Grange Bridge in Borrowdale to reveal Grange Crags, much to the chagrin of the owner of the surrounding land. The end result was fifty worthwhile routes of all grades. They took their wire brushes and spades to Bleak How in Langstrath where a similar operation produced ten quality routes. Dave Hellier had earlier pointed to the potential of this long-neglected crag with his ascent of the excellent Bleak How Buttress at the end of 83.

Two very technical routes appeared during the year. One was Centerfold on Raven Langdale by Birkett and the other was Daylight Robbery on Reecastle Watendlath by Chris Sowden, stolen from under the local's noses. To round the year off Whillance/Armstong climbed the impressive thin crack between Vikings and Supernatural on Tophet Wall, Great Gable to produce Incantations.

1985

This year will be remembered most for the wettest summer for many years, and in consequence attention was focused on the low-lying crags, with many outcrop-style routes and variations appearing. Gate Crag in Eskdale saw a number of fine additions and the Eastern Fells came under the scrutiny of Bob Smith and John Earl, producing some good routes including their impressive Stern Test on Upper Thrang. In Langdale Birkett and friends developed the remote Crinkle Gill producing a number of hard routes. As in 1984 Borrowdale came in for much attention with the imminent production of a new guidebook. Dave Armstrong developed the steep Lower Knitting Howe and many minor

Phil Rigby on Maggie's Farm (E3), Pavey Ark.   *Pete Botterill*   274

gems appeared through the valley.

Summary

Rock climbing has evolved and is still evolving. Equipment designed to protect the climbers such as PA's, double nylon ropes, bolts, skyhooks, chocks and Friends now allow them to venture onto rock faces once thought too dangerous. Climbing walls and fitness programmes have been designed to increase strength and technique (and compensate for English weather!). Climbing competitions are held in various countries — thankfully this is not generally done in Britain. Imagine the crags relegated to vertical sports fields with top ropes flowing down them and closed for the day for a competition sponsored by a cigarette company!

All this was unheard of or indeed unimagined when Napes Needle was first climbed. The top climbers of each generation have broken down the frontiers of difficulty. As to the future it is difficult to imagine the climbing scene in ten years' time never mind another hundred years. Hopefully there will still be that special mystique which draws climbers onto the crags of Lakeland.

ROCK CLIMBER
1986 STYLE

Action on the Climbing Wall at Ambleside.   *Ron Kenyon*   276

THE NORTH-EAST SPUR
OF THE DROITES

Geoff Oliver

On the balcony of the Argentière Refuge, I lay dozing in the late afternoon sun, luxuriating in total inactivity. Around me was draped a cosmopolitan crowd; a mixture of walkers, already satisfied after their glacier walk to the hut, and serious alpinists unwinding in preparation for tomorrow's ascents. A conversation close by broke through my drowsiness and I opened my eyes. A lone Scots hardman was being questioned by the leader of the three Germans, very Teutonic in Afrika Corps peaked caps and sun-glasses, as to the feasibility of the Droites North Face in its present state. They were all smiles when he gave his view that it would go, but I could not share their enthusiasm. I had noticed on the way up the glacier that the ice apron which clings to the lower part of the face in good years had succumbed to the abnormally warm nights and collapsed, leaving only a narrow strip at the Western end to give access to the face, and this looked ready to follow at any moment.

I too was bound for the Droites; not the 'Face Nord' but the North-East Spur, or Tournier Route as the French call it. This had been a long-cherished ambition since 1964, when it was still up for grabs as a first British ascent. I had been eager to try it as the last climb of the season but my partner was equally keen on the Route Major of the Brenva. We decided it with the toss of a coin and I thoroughly enjoyed a fabulous September day on the Brenva face with the mountain virtually to ourselves.

In the intervening years the guidebook description had changed considerably. The 1957 version stated 'An impressive route, one of the finest and hardest in the Alps... the continuity of severe rock and ice pitches make this one of the toughest in the Alps — 19 hours from the hut.'

The new guide toned it down to 'an established classic' though still 'of outstanding quality in a magnificent position'. The time had also dropped to 11-15 hours. This really cut the climb down to size on paper but I couldn't help wondering if the mountain had been informed. The team had been changed too; my original companion, now spending his leisure time 'messing about in boats', was replaced by son Dave, in his fourth Alpine season, with several good ascents behind him and a few of the retreats from desperate situations that are the making of a mountaineer. His air of amiable imperturbability was always an asset on the hill, but along with this came an air of casual disregard at the planning stage of an ascent. This time around, he had arrived at the hut shirtless, simply because it had been too hot to wear one in the valley. He accepted the omission stoically.

As the shadow of the Courtes crept up the moraine towards us, the various groups filtered indoors; the Continentals to await the serving of dinner, the

The N.E. Spur of the North Face of the Droites. *G. Oliver*

British to prepare their own, and soon the room buzzed with animated conversations in half a dozen languages. By 9 o'clock we were off to bed with a motley crew whose common denominator was a desire to rise at 2 a.m. The dormitory was typically hot and stuffy, resounding with garlic-laden snores from some of our fellow alpinists, so sleep came slowly. My mind wrestled with the doubts that precede a big route; more so on this occasion because of an incident shortly before the holidays.

I am superstitious about climbing during the last couple of weeks before the Alps in case of injury, but this year a particularly sunny evening had lured me out to Castle Rock with sixteen days to go. I thought I had successfully passed through the danger zone as I reached the stance at the top of Thirlmere Eliminate but the gods had decided otherwise. I belayed to the tree and gazed contentedly across the wooded valley, feeling relaxed — *too* relaxed. As my thirteen-stone second removed a jammed stopper at the crux his foot slipped, and without warning he took to the air. The world was suddenly inverted as I pivoted on my waist belay and was flipped upside down to hang from the tree, my only contact with the rope being through my bare right hand. In a numb, detached way I was aware of rope zipping through the tightly-clenched fist as my companion glided smoothly down to the last belay ledge like a rather heavy pantomime fairy. With the emergency over, I opened my hand to survey the damage; much of the skin from the inside of three fingers and the palm had been torn off and dragged into a crinkled heap near the thumb and the whole thing stung abominably. When Spencer Tracy did a similar trick in 'The Mountain', blood gushed dramatically from his hand, but all that I could conjure up was a slight ooze of clear fluid. The hospital casualty doctor gave an emphatic 'No' to any climbing for at least two months, but climbers are optimistic creatures and after 3 weeks I found that, with a leather glove, the hand worked quite well, and I was now into my fourth route (and third glove) of the holiday.

I subsided into fitful dozing until, around 1 o'clock, a call of nature took me out onto the balcony. Around me, crampons and axes clinked as climbers stumbled down the moraine by torchlight. Feeble pinpricks of light against the black bulk of Les Courtes showed that some teams had left before midnight. Our German friends must have been among them for their lights were already well up the 65° ice apron of the Droites. Thus inspired I crept back to bed and instant deep sleep, oblivious to the moves and more significantly the shrill crescendo of electronic watch alarms at 2 a.m. We surfaced at 3 a.m., force fed ourselves (appropriately, with pâté) in readiness for a long day, then lurched into the darkness with that numbness of mind and body special to an alpine start.

For a major ascent of 1100 metres we were late in leaving the hut; it could prove costly if an afternoon storm should catch us high on the spur, but with a prediction of two days 'beau temps' from the Météo one can become complacent. Anyway, a bivouac on the summit or descent was all part of the masterplan so there was no real sense of urgency.

The glacier and the bergschrund at dawn went without a hitch, then on up a chimney couloir, moving together. The weather was a little too warm, giving melt-water problems as the rising sun scanned the bottom of the spur. Cagoules were the order of the day but Dave's turned out to be still hanging in the hut. Never mind — the lighter your equipment, the faster you travel. The ice-cold water running into my sleeves and down to the nether regions was certainly conducive to speed and we quickly broke free of the constricting chimneys. The couloir became open and snow-filled, narrowing again below the junction with the spur at brèche 3407 metres, reached at 8.30 a.m.

A light-hearted jaunt up to this point, the glacier and hut within spitting distance, on cresting the spur the climb began to show its teeth as the North Face made its chill presence felt and the first hard rock barred our path. Perhaps hard is not strictly the right word for it; with chalk bag, rock boots, shorts and warm rock it would have been a 'doddle' but with the ice-choked cracks, verglassed holds and the numb response of plastic boots, the dièdre gave us a fight. Easier chimneys and ledges unwound afterwards back to the sunshine and a huge smooth step which brought us to a dead stop. On our right was a 'traverse of the gods' line, fitting the guide-book suggestion that we should move that way. There was even a big detached flake to fit the description. Two horizontal pitches on loosely-stacked dominoes led away from the spur and into the dark regions of the North Face; a tilted wilderness of ice, rock ribs and shallow couloirs; typical mixed climbing. For those unfamiliar with this sort of terrain, 'mixed' is not readily definable, let's just say that there is not enough ice to be pure ice-climbing, but too much to be treated as rock; difficult to make the decision to move together or belay, in crampons or without; no one move of great difficulty, but add them together and you have a long drawn out encounter with the mountain, sapping the strength and concentration as the day wears on, which it always does.

On this part of the ascent, we could look across at the famous North Face route, stripped of its glamour at this angle. The pristine white slopes facing the glacier were now revealed in their true colour; a basic grey, streaked with avalanche runnels and pock-marked with stonefall. Way up to our right I spotted movement; the Germans 'topping out' on the skyline. I could hardly believe my eyes. With the time at 2 p.m. I mentally took my hat off to them. Some 14 hours for a rope of three was impressive. All very well for them, but we now had this big lonely mountain to ourselves and to add to the 'wilderness experience' the clouds began to close in. This in itself was not serious; the peaks often build up a little cloud in the late afternoon; but it did hinder our route-finding. The aim of the game was to rejoin the spur above the main difficulties, where it would become a simple gendarmed ridge. But how? A teasing couloir to our left, revealing just enough to lure us on, looked like the answer. To add further encouragement there were signs of recent traffic heading that way. A momentary gap in the cloud showed the couloir joining the ridge at a conspicuous notch, 500ft. above.

Upward hopefully, with the ice gradually steepening, but the crampon trail leading reassuringly upward; and where others had gone, surely we could follow? Then came the retreat sling, complete with karabiner, at the psychoplogical point where the couloir became too steep to hold ice. I don't like to see karabiners on retreat slings; it suggests a touch of panic in its erstwhile owner. It was certainly working on me; especially as the weather gods, who had obviously not studied the météo forecast, chose this moment to start a steady snowfall. The beetling walls ahead plus the falling snow around us started that old 'hunted' feeling gnawing at my gut. As the strategist of the team I felt responsible for the situation. If we could not gain the ridge, a bivouac in the storm would follow, with the issue still unresolved, and then what tomorrow? A long-drawn-out descent? UGH!

Getting a grip of my thoughts I tried to think objectively. It was still only 3 o'clock and the ridge was no more than 200 ft. away. One good lead would crack it. I composed myself and by the time Dave arrived, looking his imperturbable self, I was able to indicate his next lead up a downright nasty pitch in an offhand, casual manner.

He removed his crampons and eased his way up the compact gully wall, moving diagonally leftwards towards the base of a broad chimney. The holds were small, slicked in places with ice, and the rock yielded no protection. As the rope ran out to half length, without a runner to interrupt its graceful arc, he came to a bulge broken by a thin crack which looked crucial. My mind began playing the morbid game of 'What happens if he falls off now?', and the part of me that doesn't always enjoy Alpinism became positively unhappy. Then came the reassuring clunk of a stopper entering a tailor-made crack, a quick step-up on a sling (what the hell! — this is the Alps) and it was all over bar the shouting. The wide chimney, designed for Gaston Rebuffat legs, gave some trouble but led to a big, secure ledge. The last 50ft. to the ridge crest was OK but for a one-footed quick change into crampons as we suddenly returned to the realms of ice.

Thus released from our captivity, we dodged around gendarmes as the snow fell and the hunted feeling chased us along the clouded ridge faster than weary legs wanted to go. Then within minutes the snow stopped, the clouds parted and an early evening sun beamed benignly on the magnificent cirque of the Argentière glacier. Such is the human mind that not only did I stop worrying about our situation, but there was even a slight pleasure factor creeping into the game. Another diversion led us over the North Face again, now on easy but icy slopes, with one of the biggest voids in the range to aid concentration on the job. Back to the ridge for the last time and at 7.30 p.m. we chose a bivouac site among sheltering rocks just short of the summit and settled down to await the biting cold at 4000 metres. But it did not come; the temperature stayed above freezing point all night and a continual clatter of stonefall in the Lagarde

Climbing up to the Brêche on the N.E. Spur of the Droites.   *G. Oliver*   282

Couloir kept us on edge. We filled in a couple of hours trying to light our highly inflammable butane stove with a variety of boy scout tricks, cursing our lost lighter, but we were destined to have a dry bivvy. The rest of the night was spent alternately dozing and readjusting body positions to achieve comfort on our comfortless ledge.

The new day eventually dawned and we packed for a quick getaway while a lump under my long-suffering buttocks emerged as the missing lighter. The views towards Mont Blanc as we crested the summit were stupendous but utterly wasted on tired eyes. All our interest concentrated on the descent line, straight down the south ridge. This was to take up a goodly part of the day, first down a long snow arete, then by acres of broken rock and finally down a couloir which deposited us on the glacier at the worst possible time of day. Wending our way under creaking seracs and over the maws of hungry crevasses while the sun steadily grilled us left an indelible impression. At least we were through it with nothing but a snow plod to the Couvercle; then on down, through marmot country and the green line route on the Mer de Glace. One final obstacle remained: Les Echelles! — the iron ladders which take you in 200 leg-weary feet of ascent from the comparative peace of the glacier to the culture-shock of the Montenvers with its crowds, picture postcards and squalling kids.

There are those who complain that Chamonix is played out; overcrowded routes with queues at every stance. They could try breaking away from the first Midi Téléphérique of the day routine and go for ascents like the N.E. Spur of the Droites. It's much closer to true mountaineering, not merely following a line of pegs, and no pitch harder than IV, *if* you can find the right line.

ROCK CLIMBING IN NORTHERN ITALY

Al Churcher

Bormio, Christmas 1982 — just finished skiing for the day and entering the bookshop opposite the hotel for some postcards when something in the window catches my eye. Sandwiched between Italian translations of Harold Robbins, Alpine Floras, and How to Ski Like Franz Klammer in Three Days — a large glossy bookjacket with a climber in extremis below the legend *Cento Nuovi Mattini — Scalate breve e libere* . Even if I can't understand a word, at less than £10 this Italian cousin of *Hard Rock* is obviously a bargain, so clutching it to my chest I hobble back to my hotel.

There is certainly something unique about Italy — the food, the wine, the warmth and friendliness of the people, the many varied landscapes, the sense of history. Add a book of a hundred climbs on granite, limestone, conglomerate, quartzite, etc, in situations as diverse as the sea cliffs near Rome and the high valleys of Mello and Orco, and it's no wonder that Jill and I returned home with our next summer trip already planned, and I started work on the language.

So much for the start of my love affair with Italy and her climbing — all very nice, very romantic — but what's it offer you? So far I've only climbed in the North, (school holidays don't really fit in with trips to the even hotter, even sunnier South) but there's enough here to keep most people happy for the average lifetime. Very roughly speaking there are two main zones of interest to the crag-rat rather than the alpinist. The first of these lies to the North of Milano towards the Swiss border, and consists of the Lake Como area and the Valtellina/Mello region. Lake Como is surrounded by a sea of limestone and the cliffs developed so far vary from ones close to the lake (reached in 15 minutes from the road), to others high in the surrounding hills which often necessitate the use of rifugios. I've not climbed here yet, but many of the routes are said to be very good, although some of the older classics have their share of loose rock. I'll find out for myself in the summer.

The Mello valley is one of the most beautiful places I've visited — in August it becomes a little busy with tourists but once away from the main camping area you soon leave these behind, and the climbs are rarely crowded. There are good short and easily accessible routes — the classic being Nuovi Dimensione, Italy's first Grade 7 — but two of the most worthwhile climbs are probably Kundalini (HVS/E1), and Luna Nascente (E2). Each of these gives over a thousand feet of memorable climbing, and as one follows the other they could be combined to provide quite a day. Mello itself is still remarkably underdeveloped by British or American standards, but over the last two years bolts have begun to appear which should lead to the opening up of many of the untouched slabs and walls. The valley itself is full of boulders, and if that's your scene there's now a guide exclusively to the bouldering of Mello. But just outside the village of San

Martino (bars, new routes book, shops etc.) is the daddy of them all; Sasso di Remenno is over 50 metres high, and the new guide to this monster and its satellites has over a hundred more routes — all with E grades! Protection on the older routes is often by the rather suspect bolts of the 'drill a hole and knock in a peg variety', although the latest efforts (including several grade 9s) are equipped with modern 'spit' bolts.

Go down through Val Masino, (big walls and long alpine rock routes, but not easy to find information) and in the main Valtellina is the village of Sirta. Two minutes from the village square is the crag of the same name. Hot and steep, it has excellent two pitch routes and is usually in condition even when Mello is lost in the clouds — do a route, then drop down for an ice cream. If you're going up the Valtellina towards Bormio there are two small roadside crags that are well worth a day's climbing; Grosio and Migiondo. In the '81 guide book *Strutture di Valtellina* these have only a small number of routes, but they have since seen a lot of development by local climbers — particularly Giordano Senini and Adriano Greco who are rapidly filling in every gap with new lines — many of which are graded 8 and 9, and mostly with good 'spit' protection. The three successive roofs that make up Migiondo's 'Super Direct' (8—/E3 6a) are particularly memorable — even if I did have to be coached up it by Adriano!

The cliffs of the second major zone are those of Piemonte and Aosta, forming an arc running from west to north of Torino. Starting in the north with Aosta; the most well developed crags are those of Corma di Machaby. The 1,000ft main face of compact rosy-yellow gneiss is clearly visible from the motorway leading south from the city of Aosta. Most routes here are long classics of the 70's, often with the addition of later variants. Two of the best are the combination Banano e Galeon (VI—/5a), and Diedro (E1 5b). Both of these go right to the top (from where one has the choice of an easy walk off, or an abseil descent), although some other routes only go as far as one or other of the various giardinos (bushy ledges) which partly cross the face. Near the foot of the approach path is a steep quarried wall covered in fingery, one-pitch 5b/c's; plus a couple of 6a's and VSs. On the left of the main crag is the aptly named Gruviera — clue, think of cheese — a deceptively extensive area as much of it is shrouded by trees. The most obvious buttress contains the superb Topo Pazzo (VS) and the equally enjoyable Spigolo (E2 5c), as well as several other 2 pitch climbs. Behind the trees are two good HVSs, plus some modern horrors as this section of rock has seen the most recent developments, including Transea (IX — 6b?) by Torino hotshot Marco Pedrini. This year there have unfortunately been some access problems here, apparently due to climbers damaging the vines below the rocks.

The granite of the Valle dell'Orco forms one of the most important climbing centres in Italy — and in my opinion Europe. Less beautiful than Mello perhaps, but offering a far wider variety of climbing experience, ranging from the 'big wall' artificial routes of Caporal, through long varied free climbs on E1

Sergent and Caporal, to short desperate cracks or slabs on easily accessible roadside crags. Several European stars, including Italy's Manola, Bernardi and Pedrini, and France's Patrick Edlinger, have had a hand in Orco's recent developments; but it's interesting to see that it was a Briton, Mike Kosterlitz, who was part of the original group who unlocked the valley's potential. I don't propose to give further details here, as these can be found in my recent article in *Mountain 103*. The pictures in this — particularly Gogna's of Diedro Nanchez, one of the top ten routes I've done anywhere — should be enough to whet your appetite.

Running roughly westwards from Torino to the French border is the Val di Susa. This contains an enormous amount of rock — both limestone and granite. Of the former, the Orrido di Foresto is a gorge containing many steep routes of around 4 pitches — some of which start from near ancient dwellings built into the cliff. Above this is the forcing ground of Striature Nere; a black streaked wall containing enough bolt-protected 8's and 9's to keep any ambitious, tight-clad aspirant happy for a few days. So far, apart from a short day on an excellent granite 'Millstone' (part of Borgone), I've only viewed these and the other Susa crags from a distance, though I intend to remedy this as soon as possible. Being low lying and mostly south-facing, they tend to be rather hot during my August visits. The locals say they are at their best in Spring and Autumn, but can often be in excellent condition in midwinter when the ground is covered by snow — I wish you could say that for Scafell or Stanage!

In the upper Susa valley lie the ski resorts of 'The Milky Way'; Sestriere, Sauze d'Oulx etc. Just beyond nearby Bardonecchia is the Valle Stretta with its Parete dei Militi.

This enjoyed a brief period of fame/notoriety last Spring as the venue for the first organized European climbing competition — a commercialised multi-day jamboree that was given prime-time television coverage in both France and Italy. By a quirk of politics or geography the valley actually lies in France, although the only road leads in from Italy, and access from France means an Alpine ascent. Nevertheless, the Italian border guards carefully inspect all passports — whereas the French are conspicuous by their absence! The limestone crags are enormous, but the modern routes are all 2/4 pitch affairs in the Yosemite style; ending in fixed abseil points where the quality of the rock becomes dubious. Renato and I had an unfortunate experience here last summer; we'd had just roped up for our first route when a single falling stone struck his wrist. Despite our initial fears, an X-ray proved it to be merely badly bruised, not broken; but it meant no action for Renato for at least a week, and so the end of my Italian climbing for that year. The stone had apparently been dislodged by a party on the classic (i.e. grotty) alpine-style ridge which follows the right arête of the crag. We were well to the left of this, but the stone must have ricocheted across the wall. The high, unspoilt valley offers beautiful camping, somewhat reminiscent of Tuolumne with its high mountain air and pine trees. This would make it an excellent stopping off point for anyone travelling over the Susa Valley from France into Italy (or vice-versa). Personally I wouldn't make a special journey for the climbing — to me it bears too much resemblance to an oversized Pen-trwyn!

Outside the two zones described above there are other areas, many of which are frequented only by local climbers. To British climbers, the limestone of Finale (near Finale Ligure to the west of Genoa) is probably the best-known Italian centre, and Pete Gomersall has described this in his article in *High*. However, in reading this the average climber would probably not realise the wealth of lower and middle-grade climbing to be found there. In fact Finale has a very high concentration of good VS and HVS climbing.

The Dolomites seem to have been out of fashion for some time, although translating a selected guide from the Italian has reawakened my own interest in this region. I have included a comprehensive glossary in this, and although it is primarily intended to aid the understanding of the original Italian topos used in the guide, I deliberately extended the vocabulary to make it of use when reading original Italian guidebooks — whether to the Dolomites or elsewhere. In and around the Dolomites are several centres which are becoming known for the development of shorter, free climbs. Perhaps the most important of these is that of Arco (not to be confused with Orco), which lies close to the head of Lake Garda.

Well that's it — a brief run-down on a fraction of the rock to be found in Northern Italy. Fuller details of Machaby, Orco and Mello can be found in my various articles in *High*, *Mountain* and *Climber and Rambler*, and each of these contains a detailed bibliography. *Cento Nuovi Mattini* is now being imported by Cordee, and Gogna has also published a more recent compilation; entitled *Rock Story* (Melograno Edizioni), this is not available in this country as far as I am aware. Of course there are a couple of Crag Xs that I've not let on about — but I've got to keep something to myself to dream about during the long wet hours of winter......

13 MILES FROM THE EQUATOR

Ray Cassidy

A couple of years ago I managed to get involved in the International Mountaineering Jet Set. A mate called Dave persuaded me that Peru would be a good idea for the summer of '82. It was; but it didn't go down as an epoch making trip. The 'training route' on the S.W. Face of Alpamayo took two goes, and we had no grub left for a try at anything else in the few days we had left. I suppose we did learn one or two things; that high(ish) mountains are knackering, and that dead Frenchmen last at least two years on snowy slopes. My appetite was whetted, but it came sort of unwhetted when I tried to explain all the minus pounds to my bank manager. Banking traumas come and go.

About a couple of weeks later, at a leching-the-nubiles session in the Gloucester in Penrith, Steve Howe said to me. 'Fancy coming to Kenya next summer?', to which I replied. 'No thanks mate, I've just had severe bank trauma!'. Needless to say after a further couple of pints and a few eyefuls of under age beauty, it was all arranged. Nairobi in late July and via Moscow for a larf!!

Well, Moscow, Simferopol, Cairo, came and went, to leave us two innocents abroad trying to coax the Nairobi phone service into connecting us with Rod and Bar Bennet, our friendly local contacts for floorspace and shelter. And what a fantastic pair of people they turned out to be. Nothing was too much trouble! If you turn up in Nairobi with a few jars of Marmite it seems you can turn any of the expatriate community into the most hospitable people on earth.

After a couple of days shopping in Nairobi we left the care of Rod and Bar and headed off up country on the good old Mombassa country bus, which doesn't appear to go within 200 miles of Mombassa. Naro Moru Country lodge was an oasis of ex-colonial charm (does that sound right?). The following morning we got our first view of Mt. Kenya, a great upturned saucer with what looks like a little burst nipple on top. It was pretty neat, so out came the cameras for loads of piccys. It took us most of the day to get transport, porters and loads sorted out. We started to get a bit horrified by the cost especially as the Russians in Moscow had charged us £113 each for excess baggage on the way out. Luckily a fairly tough-looking female surgeon from New York and a Swiss lad called Peter came to our rescue, and split the price of the jeep. At about 3 o'clock in the afternoon the jeep, with about 10 people including porters hitching a ride home, pulled away and eventually deposited Steve and myself, the surgeon, and the Swiss lad plus porters at the Met Clearing. A couple of days later we had humped all our gear from Mackinders Camp, where all the touroids hang out, to American base near the bottom of Midget Peak. This is a really smart camping spot; it is off the main tourist tracks and gives an excellent view of the south face, whereon lie the classic ice routes of the equator.

First came the serious business of acclimatising in the oedema hot-spot of the world. Off we went for the ramble trek up Pt Lenana. It was a superb frosty dawn as we set off up the bouldery slope, strewn with the other-worldly shapes of the giant groundsels looming in the grey half light. To stay away from the crowds we scrabbled out way up the west side of the Lewis glacier and eventually found ourselves on a kind of crevassed ridge leading across to Lenana. The weather was superb where we were, but the plains all around us were rapidly covering themselves in a layer of clouds. We went bombing down the normal rubbly track to our tents where we were suddenly hit by monster headaches. When I could move again I got several brews going and gradually the knotted brains came unwound.

Steve had always fancied doing the Ice Window, and I, being a born coward and cheat, also fancied it when I realised I could sneak a look at the Diamond Headwall. A night in the five star bivvy below the Darwin Glacier was followed by a flog up the same slope that one of the army boys had descended head first after not quite reaching the fixed ropes on the south Face route. All the porters we had spoken to had been amused by his lack of fingers (one of the Everest boys I think), and the size of the bloody hole in his head.

The Ice Window starts in the next bay right of the Diamond, and takes a ramp line leftwards on to the buttress overlooking the Diamond Couloir. Steve set off up and found a nice shiny new peg after a few feet. When I followed I managed to lose one of my brand new, trendy goretex overmitts while I was nicking the army surplus peg. A couple of pitches took us into the hidden gully that parallels the Diamond and we moved together for a couple of hundred feet until we came to a steeper pitch. Out came the rusty front point techniques from last winter and up we skittered. Eventually we emerged from the confines of the gully onto the shoulder at the start of the traverse into the window. From here I got an all too clear view of the Diamond headwall and it looked steep and clean as cut glass.

Our route for the day traversed airily across the right wall of the couloir for about 300 feet, to the gaping cavity under the overhanging lip of the Diamond Glacier. Two thirds of the overhang were sealed in by a fringe of giant icicles, with the result that once you popped your head into the hole you were in a 16,500 foot luxury pad. It was a superb cave so we stopped and had a brew, all the while wondering if the glacier would choose that particular moment to nudge a few hundred tons of ice over the edge.

After the brew we set off on the next level of entertainment. This usually involves you in knocking a hole in the icicle fringe so that you can leap dynamically out above the Diamond headwall and sneak round the corner to climb easy-angled stuff. A couple of lads from Nairobi had already saved us the bother of hacking holes, so Steve only had to lower himself out, do a couple of steep moves to the left, and hey presto we were on the Diamond Glacier itself. It's a long pitch from where we had our brew to the first bit of belayable rock, and I suddenly found myself frantically undoing belays so that I could move across and pick up all the scattered debris from my rucksack before the rope ran out. In the end I had to crawl about twenty feet along the icy cave, stuffing food and clothes into my sack, before Steve managed to get belayed. The view through the actual 'Ice Window' is truly superb; straight down the Diamond Headwall and couloir to our tent, a tiny brown dot amongst the now tiny groundsel.

From there it was a steady four pitches up the glacier to The Gate of the Mists and a couple of hundred scrambly feet to the top of Nelion, slightly the lower of the twin summits.

We had a superb doss in the little coffin on the top, including waving at a light aircraft that buzzed the top several times, and an excellent lamb curry which we only had to heat up. It's a bit confined in the bivvy hut, but there's room for four people to stretch out on the foam mattresses, and you could cram a few more in, in a crisis. Entertainment consists of trying to read all the Spanish graffiti scrawled on the polystyrene tiles that the hut is still partially lined with.

Next morning we poked our heads out just before dawn to see a rich orange glow along the cloudy horizon. Soon a lurid orange ball seemed to rise out of the cloud itself. Looking over our shoulders, the shadow of Mt. Kenya seemed to beam down out of the night sky. We ran the few yards to the summit and watched as this torch beam of darkness settled on the cloud tops far away to the west. All around us the rocks had a rich orange glow. We sat for ages, just soaking in our first real equatorial sunrise. We seemed totally isolated above the clouds that obscured the lowlands around us. The air was still and pleasantly cold. There was no threat that morning, just a calm beauty that seemed to say, 'Don't rush off lads!'. So we didn't.

About nine or ten o'clock we finally had a brew and set off down the abseils and snowy scrambles that led back to the Lewis Glacier, and the scrambly ground that brought us home to American camp.

A couple of days later we did the Diamond via the Headwall and got to the top of Batian. It was another great day out on some very steep ice, that was in perfect condition for us. Other days were spent on Midget Peak, and the Window Ridge of Pt. Peter. This was a superb slabby corner which goes at about 5b, two-thirds of the way up, and is definitely worth doing.

ALL OUT

W.Heaton Cooper

At nine o'clock on this June night it was still light enough by Loch Coir' a' Ghrunnda to draw the purple-black spur of Sgurr Alasdair against the sky as it swept down to the sandy shore of the lochain, the rough gabbro foreground and the Siamese-twin shaped island of Soay that led the eye over an immense space to Rhum and Canna on the horizon.

There is something about the Cuillin that is different, even beyond the fact of its magnificent position, rising in the south a sheer 3000 feet out of the sea, encircling the hollow that holds Coruisk, and even beyond the great expanse of water with the family of islands standing around. Possibly half-remembering the ancient sagas from my Norwegian childhood and being alone with the wind moaning among the midnight rocks, I felt that anything might happen here.

Around three o'clock a gentle glow began to spread from the east across the thin high canopy of cloud, revealing immense space and a sense of expectancy. Rhum and Canna, purple amongst the pale gold, seemed to emphasize the continuity of the earth beyond the horizon. The slowly increasing light intensified the turning of our sphere and oneself with it.

The painter now needs to do several things simultaneously. First and most important is the need to be entirely free, like a child, to lose himself in wonder and delight. At the same time he needs to make a cool appraisal of the priorities of design and of the tone values, and to organize the sequences of colour, especially if using a transparent medium. All the way to the conclusion it is of vital importance to retain the vision, wonder and delight that made him first want to paint it.

On that morning upon the Cuillin ridge time no longer existed. After several hours, which might as well have been minutes, the painting had enough vitality and emphasis for me to use it, together with the previous evening's drawing, to carry out at leisure in my studio a larger oil painting: the drawing — a record of form and structure — to give information, and the colour sketch — the subconscious emotional content — to produce a fairly subjective result.

In choosing a route on a crag the process is, in some ways, rather similar. The intense appreciation of the whole mountain and the crag as part of it; the compelling urge to climb it; the cool assessment of an interesting line to take, of the problems on the way and, possibly, of variations, as far as one can judge from below. Then the total commitment to the whole route and, from the first few feet, to every move, every sign of a hold and to every one of the hundreds of decisions to be made, as in a painting. Time has no more meaning, especially if one is climbing solo. Then the exhilaration of achievement, the sudden change of eye focus from close detail of rock to the relief and delight of unlimited space and far horizons.

Sgurr Alasdair and the Cuillin Ridge.
p. 132 New West.

Abraham Collection
p. 133 Stanley Watson on Sepulchre.

One element seems to be common to both activities, that of total commitment. I find this is true, also, of the whole art of living if one is to 'go far enough for fun'. Without vision, life would be a very dull affair, and the 'person' could perish, especially among the many and powerful de-humanizing forces of our time. Without real assessment of oneself and what needs to be done while still retaining the vision, the whole journey might not add up to very much.

One thing that seems to be common to all humans is the desire for wholeness — to be all-of-a-piece oneself and often to be part of a greater whole.

The only truly satisfying kind of wholeness, I find, comes with the whole total commitment to co-operating with the Creator in his design for his universe, especially for our own planet and for everyone who lives on it. Then everything, even the adrenaline, begins to flow.

> 'Thou art clothed with honour and majesty,
> Who coveredst thyself with light as with a garment,
> Who stretchedst out the heavens like a curtain,
> Who layeth the beams of his chambers in the waters,
> Who maketh the clouds his chariot,
> Who walketh upon the wings of the wind.'
> Psalm 104.

THE ABRAHAM COLLECTION OF MOUNTAINEERING PHOTOGRAPHS

June Parker

The photographs in this collection are a fascinating record of the early days of rock-climbing, from about 1890 to 1934. As we are now looking back on the one hundred years that have passed since the first ascent of the Napes Needle, it is an appropriate time to say a few words about this collection and the two 'Keswick Brothers'; George and Ashley Abraham, who were responsible for the photographs in it.

The collection was presented to the Club by Ashley Abraham's second son Geoffrey on his retirement in 1967, at which time the family business closed down. It was a sad day for many when the shop at the corner of Lake Road closed after 101 years of producing thousands of photographs of the Lake District and other areas. The Club was and is very grateful for this valuable gift and hopes to continue to make copies of the photographs available to future generations. The photographs presented to the Club are mainly of rock climbing and mountaineering; most of the purely scenic ones, of which there were many thousands, are now in private hands.

Both George and Ashley Abraham were closely associated with the Club over many years. George, the elder brother, was an honorary member from 1907 until his death at the age of 93. Ashley, four years younger, was the Club's first president and was a member until he died aged 75. Except for a brief period when George went to Manchester to study art, the Abrahams lived in Keswick all their lives. They were drawn towards the mountains as young boys, and after scrambling on local crags such as Castle Head they were soon borrowing a clothes line to use as a climbing rope. Fortunately when they ventured to Pillar with this they met more experienced climbers who lent them a climbing rope. Soon they were competent and experienced climbers themselves, and it was not long before they had a new climb to their credit: Sandbed Gill in St. John's Vale, climbed when George was 19 and Ashley 14.

They began to take photographs about this time too, both of them working in the family business started by their father G.P.Abraham. The combination of their passion for rock climbing and their skill in photography was a fortunate one, and they soon launched themselves into the task of trying to record the thrills and pleasures of climbing and the attractions of the mountain scenery. Their success was outstanding, as thousands who gazed at the display in the Lake Road shop will testify. Their spectacular action photographs were an inspiration to a whole generation of climbers. Many of the photographs still stand as comparable with the best being taken today, and all of them have the added value and interest of being part of the historical record. A classic example of this is the photograph of Jones's Route from Deep Ghyll, one of the first to

George and Ashley Abraham with A.S. Thomson on the 'Stormy Petrel', Ogwen.
Abraham Collection

show a new route being made. It is interesting too to see the details of the clothes worn for climbing; the tweed jackets, cloth caps, nailed boots and long trousers tucked into socks, and a little later the first 'rubbers' or cheap Woolworth's plimsolls as worn by Stanley Watson on the layback on Sepulchre. Rope technique (or sometimes almost complete lack of it) is another feature, although there are a number of photographs, probably taken towards the end of the period, especially to demonstrate safe climbing methods.

Taking photographs then was not the simple matter that it can be today. The camera they used was an Underwood whole-plate camera which was basically a large wooden box with a leather concertina bellows at one end and aperture which would take different lenses at the other. The whole kit with tripod and a dozen unexposed glass plates weighed over twenty pounds. They used plates with a very slow emulsion which therefore required lengthy exposures, often of several seconds. Rusty Westmorland could recall being asked to hold a pose for 40 seconds. All this meant a great deal of patience and co-operation from climbers who were often asked to balance on small holds for a long time while maintaining a dynamic pose. Not the easiest thing to do. It was the use of this slow emulsion however which resulted in such good quality negatives, capable of considerable enlargement without loss of detail, and in prints which showed the nature and texture of the rock so well.

The Abrahams have been criticised for 'working over' their photographs. After many months of sorting and studying the negatives during the preparation of the catalogue, I do not think this is a valid criticism. Certainly in some cases masking tape or paint has been applied to the negative in order to make the edge of a rock or the outline of a climber stand out against the sky. As they preferred to take photographs in diffused lighting to avoid the contrasty effect of direct sunlight, and as this would often mean a dull grey lighting, then this technique seems to me perfectly justifiable. In one case, a more dramatic photograph has been achieved by painting out a rock buttress which filled the gap between two pinnacles. This is the picture of the 'Crazy Pinnacle' on Crib Goch and it was absolutely necessary to do this to show the true nature of the situation. In yet other cases, people have been painted out of the foreground, presumably to emphasise the peace and tranquility of the landscape. This must have been a personal whim as most photographers today seem to prefer a figure in the foreground. Not many people will realise that there was someone sitting in the boat in Plate 9 in *Camera on the Crags*.

It is true that there is a photograph taken in a quarry but with an Alpine title. As far as I know there is only one such, and I think it was probably a joke, arising from the sight of a photograph of the Needle in Chamonix bearing the title 'Aiguille de la Nuque'!

In 1896 something happened which had an immense impact on the lives of the two brothers. O.G.Jones, who was in the course of writing his book *Rock Climbing in the English Lake District,* called at the Lake Road shop and invited

301   On Crazy Pinnacle, Crib Goch, with an emphasised gap.   *Abraham Collection*

George and Ashley to climb with him. Jones knew the power of a good photograph because he himself had first been attracted to climbing by Dixon's photograph of the Needle which he saw in a London shop. When Jones's book came out in 1897 it was illustrated with 30 Abraham photographs.

The brothers were already very good climbers, but the partnership with Jones led to a whole spate of excellent new climbs such as Walker's Gully on Pillar, led by Jones in icy conditions, after removing his boots. Jones not only introduced them to the mainstream of the sport which had been going on at Wasdale Head for a decade or more, but also to climbing in Snowdonia which they visited for the first time at Easter 1897. Sadly, the partnership with Jones came to an early end when Jones lost his life on the Dent Blanche in 1899. After this, George and Ashley combined to write *Rock Climbing in North Wales*, using Jones's notes as a base and taking many photographs to provide the illustrations. It was published in the same format as the Lake District book and became equally popular. Later Ashley made his last venture into mountaineering writing with his *Rock Climbing in Skye*, which forms the third volume in a classic trilogy now very scarce and much sought after. George went on to write many more books, two of which were as influential as the photographs. These were the *Complete Mountaineer* in 1907 and *British Mountain Climbs* in 1909. The former was a massive book of nearly 500 pages, packed with information on the history of the sport, advice on equipment and detailed descriptions of climbing in the British Isles and abroad. It is a chatty and very readable book with 75 photographs. Until 1920, when two important mountaineering books were published, (Geoffrey Winthrop Young's *Mountain Craft* and Harold Raeburn's *Mountaineering Art*), it was the only book which gave such information. *British Mountain Climbs* was the forerunner of modern pocket guidebooks, but encompassed the whole of the British Isles. It was used by climbers for decades, even going into a 6th edition in 1948, although by this time it was somewhat out of date.

After Jones's death George developed even more strongly as a lead climber. He was a natural, described by Geoffrey Winthrop Young as being 'graceful to watch and one of the earliest to climb by balance rather than grip'. Ashley was the ideal second man, being patient, heavy and cheerful. He also took almost all the photographs, so that it is George who is seen most often poised on the rocks. (Ashley can be seen in plates 4, 5 and 6 in *Camera on the Crags*.) The two climbed together for many years, making several new ascents not only in the Lakes but also in Snowdonia and Scotland. Their favourite was the New West on Pillar, which they first climbed in 1901 and which was the scene of their last climb together in 1936.

There are over 700 glass negatives in the collection and these are in the care of the Abbot Hall Art Gallery and Museum in Kendal. They are bulky, heavy and fragile. They survived a fire in the Lake Road shop but many suffered damage by heat, smoke and water. To sort them out, identify them and arrange them was a formidable task. Thanks to Alan Hankinson, one hundred of them were published in his *Camera on the Crags* in 1975. A few years later, various working parties of Club members got together and spent many hours on the task of identifying and sorting the others. It was not until 1983 that there was an opportunity to finish the job, when the present writer left full-time work and was able to work on the collection for one or two days every week. The biggest job was to get all the negatives arranged in some kind of logical order, so that all photographs of the same area were together. This makes the catalogue easier to use and also facilitates examination and searching of the negatives. At the same time as the sorting was going on all the negatives were cleaned on the plain glass side with methylated spirit which removed a lot of soot and other stains. A catalogue was finally prepared and several copies made. The photographs used in *Camera on the Crags* were kept in the same order as in the book, so that the book can be used as a reference for these. All the others were then arranged by place; the Lake District, Snowdonia, Skye and the Alps. There are a few not identified but these were noted descriptively in an addendum.

The catalogue is not illustrated but the inclusion of references to published photographs in the Abrahams' books has proved very helpful to users. Work is in hand to produce either positive transparencies or contact sets from new negatives of all the photographs so that the collection can be used without too much handling of the irreplaceable glass negatives.

It is good that the photographs that were taken with such care and effort are still being used to illustrate books and for display in both private and public places. Long may it continue!

Main publications illustrated by Abraham photographs

1887 *Rock-climbing in the English Lake District*
      by O.G.Jones. Longman.
1906 *Rock-climbing in North Wales*
      by G.D.Abraham and A.P.Abraham.
      Keswick: G.P.Abraham.
1907 *The Complete Mountaineer*
      by G.D.Abraham. Methuen.
1908 *Rock-climbing in Skye*
      by A.P.Abraham. Longhman.
1909 *British Mountain Climbs*
      by G.D.Abraham. Mills & Boon.
1910 *Mountain Adventures at Home and Abroad*
      by G.D.Abraham. Methuen.
1911 *Swiss Mountain Climbs*
      by G.D.Abraham. Mills & Boon.

1912 *Beautiful Lakeland*
      by A.P.Abraham. Keswick: G.P.Abraham.
1913 *Some Portraits of the Lake Poets and Their Homes*
      by A.P.Abraham. Keswick: G.P.Abraham.
1913 *Motor Ways in Lakeland*
      by G.D.Abraham. Methuen.
1919 *On Alpine Heights and British Crags*
      by G.D.Abraham. Methuen.
1923 *First Steps to Climbing*
      by G.D.Abraham. Mills & Boon.
1933 *Modern Mountaineering*
      by G.D.Abraham. Methuen.
1975 *Camera on the Crags: a portfolio of early rock climbing photographs by the Abraham Brothers*
      by Alan Hankinson. Heinemann.

Victorian Climbers below the Requin.   *Abraham Collection* 306

THE WASDALE CLIMBING BOOK

Muriel Files

George Sansom, writing in the 1974 *Journal** about climbing at Wasdale before the First World War, mentions the 'climbers' book' which was kept at the Inn** for recording descriptions of new climbs; he adds 'I wonder what has happened to that'. An editorial footnote suggests that 'Muriel Files has traced the whereabouts of this book and attempts are being made to secure it for the Library'. Unfortunately my efforts were unsuccessful. The last I heard of it, about five years ago, was a rumour that it had been sold. If anyone can supply up-to-date information it will be gratefully received; the book itself of course would be even more welcome.

In the meantime, the few established facts may be of interest. The Minutes record that on 15th April 1922 H.P.Cain, the Librarian, informed the committee that he intended to have a copy made of the original climbing book in the Wastwater Hotel. His intention was unanimously approved with the result that there is now a typed copy in the Club's Archives, although it lacks the photographs and diagrams which illustrated the original.

On making enquiries in the dale in 1975, I was told that J.Ritson Whiting (Proprietor of the Hotel 1907-1951 and an Original Member of the Club) had taken the climbing book with him when he retired from the Hotel to Lingmell House (formerly the vicarage) and that, after his death in 1956, it remained there in charge of Miss Edith Long, his sister-in-law who had been his partner at the Hotel after Mrs Whiting's death. Miss Long had known many of our members and I hoped that she would regard favourably the Club's desire to acquire, in order to preserve it, this important piece of climbing history. However, by 1976 when I wrote to her, she had left Wasdale and was living with a nephew near Sheffield. In answer to my letter to Miss Long he wrote that she was failing in health and could no longer remember what had happened to the book, but that the next time he visited Wasdale he would make enquiries. He did not write again and the next I heard was the rumour that the book had been sold.

I recently wrote to Alan Hankinson who, in *The First Tigers*, mentioned the Hotel visitors' book several times. He confirmed that his references were indeed to the visitors' book and that he did not know, until he received my letter, that a separate climbing book existed. I think he probably saw the visitors' book 1873—1900 which the management showed me in 1980, saying that it was the only early one they had.

Not many references to the Wasdale Climbing Book have been found in mountaineering literature. O.G. Jones related in *Rock Climbing in the English Lake District* that, on arriving at Wasdale Head on foot from Drigg after a night travelling by train from London in April 1891, he enquired at once for the

---

* 'Goodbye To All That', *FRCCJ. 64, 1974.*
** According to George Seatree (*FRCCJ, 5, 1911, p206)* its name was changed from Huntsman's Inn to Wastwater Hotel when it was extended in the late 1880's; but climbers continued to refer to it as the Inn. It officially reverted to Inn recently.

An Abraham classic — Head of Wastwater.   *Abraham Collection*

Climbing Book to ascertain the latest developments. He found that the *Pall Mall Budget* article of 5 June 1890 on the ascent of the Needle had been inserted, and read how it might be vanquished. This he proceeded to do the same afternoon, not without difficulty. George Abraham writes in *The Complete Mountaineer*, page 131: 'No organized records of the Cumberland climbs had been kept until the year 1880; about that time the Climber's Book was presented to the Wastwater Hotel and eventually put under lock and key in order to retain its pages for entries of first and second ascents, or matters of special interest to the climber in contradistinction to the ordinary tourist'. He was ten years out; the book was presented in 1890.

Recently the Wasdale Climbing Book has again become news. When writing about early scramblers on Scafell in the 1985 *Journal*, I suggested that there was probably much still to be gleaned from contemporary press accounts. In pursuit of early references to rock climbing in the Lake District, Jean Cram investigated the resources of Leeds Reference Library and found a number of relevant entries in the catalogue, mostly of items already in our Library. However, one entry greatly interested me: the Climbing Book from Wasdale which Leeds had acquired as part of a bequest by G.T.Lowe, an eminent Yorkshire Rambler and author of 'Climbs in Lakeland,' a chapter in Edmund Bogg's *A Thousand Miles....along the Roman Wall....Lakeland and Ribblesdale*. Jean examined the Climbing Book and described it as starting with C.N.Williamson's 'Climbs of the Lake District' (published in *All the Year Round*) stuck in; then followed a foreword by John Robinson indicating that the book was to be for the use of climbers; then climbing items 1863-1890 copied from the visitors' books; then, from 1890 to 1898 it was a continuous climbing record with diagrams and cuttings pasted in.

This description fits our typed copy of the Wasdale Climbing Book. The differences are that our copy continues until 1919. The Leeds book ends in 1898 (14 October) and is hand-written whereas ours is typed. Puzzling features are that the Leeds book is in various hand-writings and is illustrated by photographs and diagrams, giving the impression that it is an original work. It is possible that the original was copied by different people; the diagrams could have been traced; and the photographs could have been different ones of the same subject; and, as the Leeds book was contemporary with the original, other copies of the printed matter could have been obtained. However the fact remains that a comparison is impossible, the original Wasdale Book, 1890-1919 not having been located. In the Fell and Rock typed copy the press cuttings have been typed and there are indications in the typescript of where the diagrams and photographs were placed.

The last entry in the Fell & Rock copy is: Pillar Rock & West Buttress (sic.) Route 1. 9.8.19 and is signed H.M.Kelly. C.F.Holland. The route is now known as Sodom. The companion Route 2 (Gomorrah) pioneered by Kelly and Holland the same day, is not entered, presumably because there was no more room in the Climbing Book. An explanation of the nomenclature will be found in H.M.Kelly's article 'Memorabilia' in the 1979 *Journal.*

Many climbs recorded between 1890 and 1898 are first ascents of classics such as the North on Pillar (a culmination of many attempts by W.P.Haskett Smith); Eagle's Nest Direct (oddly, the lead is not allocated to Solly but might have been by any other member of the party); Moss Ghyll (many later ascents are recorded — it was clearly a popular route); O.G.Jones's many first ascents including the Pinnacle Direct from Lord's Rake. Many other well-known names are to be found: John Robinson (many entries); Archer Thomson; Norman Collie; Hastings; Charles Pilkington; the Hopkinson brothers. Haskett Smith's first ascent of the Needle was made four years before the Climbing Book was started and might be found in the visitors' book, 1873-1900 which is still at Wasdale Head. Many of the routes, now well known, were not then named and were identified by names long out of use such as the Pinnacle Ridge for Needle Ridge.

O.G.Jones's descriptions of his climbs are brief, but Botterill's account of his ascent of his eponymous slab on 3rd June 1903 is very detailed; a note follows it, referring to its daring leader; a second note advises that the route should be left alone.

In the next few years, the names of Herford, Sansom, Laycock and Jeffcoat (two of whom were to lose their lives in the first World War) dominate the entries; Harry Lyon, George Abraham and H. (Rusty) Westmorland also appear. After 1911, the year he joined the Club, Herford's name frequently occurs until 14th April 1914 when the ascent of Central Buttress is recorded. This marks the end of an era. There is a gap of five years and the next entry is for 11th June 1919: Tophet Bastion, H.M.Kelly, Mrs Kelly and party. A new era had begun. Kelly, Crawford, Holland and Gibson are now the most frequently recurring names (Gibson being the only one who appeared before 1914) sometimes accompanied by Pritchard, Odell, Bower and (once) Dorothy Pilley.

Mystery now surrounds the Wasdale Climbing Book. It is hoped that someone among our readers will be able to answer Sansom's question as to its present whereabouts; and that the further problem provided by Jean Cram's discovery at Leeds may also be solved. The mystery is indeed compounded because it must now be disclosed that, in fact, Jean found *two* manuscript copies at Leeds, both included in the G.T.Lowe bequest. The one I have described is referred to by the Leeds Reference Librarian as 'the original'; the second as 'the copy'. He informed me that in 'the copy' the entries are only prior to about April 1893 and that it lacks some of 'the sketches', photographs and cuttings. The solution of the mystery of the climbing book would be a welcome by-product of the interest aroused by the Centenary of Climbing.

Wasdale Climbing Books in the FRCC Archives
1. *Wasdale Hotel Climbing Book, 1863-1919.* Typed copy.
2. *Wastwater Hotel Climbing Book, 1920-1939.* For recording first and second ascents.
3. *The Fell and Rock Wasdale Climbing Book, 1907-39.* All the 'centres' (Borrowdale, Buttermere, Coniston and Wasdale) had books for recording climbs, now in the Archives.

Photo by   *G. P. Abraham & Sons, Keswick.*   *(Copyright)*

THE ASCENT OF THE FLAKE CRACK.

SCAFELL CENTRAL BUTTRESS

G.S.Sansom

Reprinted from the FRCC Journal, No. 8, 1914

Some two years ago, Herford and I, in an inquisitive spirit, climbed up a grassy scoop leading out of Moss Ghyll on to the Central Buttress. We did not seriously believe that we should find a new climb on this rock face, for it appears to be singularly unbroken and almost vertical for over two hundred feet. It was, however, an unknown region, and as such appealed to us.

The scoop was not very difficult and we were soon looking around a corner at the top along a narrow grassy ledge which apparently extended right across the face to Botterill's Slab. The rocks fell away very steeply below and a sheer smooth wall rose up to a great height above: its regularity was interrupted at one point, it is true, by an enormous rock flake which tapered out to nothing 70 feet higher. For some obscure reason this ledge suggested vague possibilities, which we did not fully appreciate at the time. The Great Flake looked quite hopeless as a means of ascent and we dismissed the idea at once and concentrated our attention on the Moss Ghyll side of the buttress, which was broken up by right-angled corners running upwards from west to east at a uniform angle of 65°. The nearest of these corners stopped us in less than 30 feet, but we determined to try the next. It appeared difficult of access from this ledge: accordingly a descent to the Ghyll, and an awkward traverse from the top of the next pitch was effected. I climbed up this groove with some difficulty until the slab on the left almost gave out and upward progress seemed scarcely feasible; the groove immediately on my right continued upwards for a considerable distance, but the traverse into it appeared too difficult and I returned to Herford. We thereupon decided to give up the attempt and climb Pisgah Buttress instead. We did so, with searching eyes on the rock face which had so successfully repulsed us, and I for one returned to Wastdale with the opinion that Central Buttress would not go.

That day's work was not, however, wasted, for it led indirectly to the discovery of the Girdle Traverse, inasmuch as it apparently demonstrated the possibility of reaching Botterill's Slab from Moss Ghyll and thus over-coming the most serious obstacle to the expedition. Some three months later Herford made the second ascent of Botterill's Slab, and a few days afterwards the Girdle Traverse was completed. My belief, that the ledge on the Central Buttress actually joined the Slab, was founded on insufficient data, and the credit for the discovery of a feasible connection between the two is due to H.B.Gibson.

Consideration of other climbs, which led up apparently impossible but actually feasible rocks, impressed on us the necessity of not judging by appearances, but of trying all places, however impossible or impracticable they looked. The proverb "Better is the sight of the eyes than the wandering of the desire" is inimical to those desirous of finding new routes on a much-explored rock-face. We accordingly assured one another that, as we had not actually attempted the ascent of the "Great Flake," there was still a chance of finding a feasible route up the Central Buttress.

It was not until June, 1913, that we had an opportunity of putting this theory into practice on the Central Buttress. It is however one thing to talk lightheartedly of trying to climb a narrow 40 foot crack, of which the top overhangs the bottom some 12 feet, and quite another thing to stand at its foot prepared to do so. The crack proper started some 30 feet above our grass ledge (the Oval) and obviously could be reached without great difficulty. I ascended about 25 feet and found myself below a large bulge in the side of the flake; I could have got over this bulge, but the sight of the crack above was too much for me, and Herford took my place and climbed to the foot of the crack. He also decided that to attempt to force it, without knowledge as to what lay above, would be unjustifiable.

I was abroad all that summer, but Herford and Jeffcoat spent a profitable afternoon in exploration from above. From the top of Keswick Brothers Climb—below the variation finish—they traversed out on to the face of the Central Buttress, first downwards some 30 feet, and then horizontally to the right for about the same distance to a large flat rock, "The Cannon," which is a conspicuous feature in the profile view of the face. From this point they descended a narrow shattered ridge for 40 feet to a good belay on an exposed platform known as Jeffcoat's Ledge, and a further descent of 12 feet gave access to a shelf of rock some 3 feet wide proximally, narrowing gradually down to 18 inches and supporting various large rock flakes in a state of doubtful equilibrium. Distally the ledge was concealed by a rather larger detached flake some 10 feet high and barely 3 inches wide at the top. Herford traversed out on the ledge, climbed on to this detached mass, walked along it and climbed down the opposite side. He now realized that he was on the top of the Great Flake, which formed the left retaining wall of the crack we had tried to climb from below. The flake narrowed down to a knife-edge, so thin and fretted that it was actually perforated in some places. Crawling carefully along it to the end, Herford descended the overhanging crack, whilst Jeffcoat paid out rope from the belay. Unfortunately the rope jammed during the descent and Herford had very great difficulty in getting down. He considered, however, that the crack was just climbable, and wrote me to that effect. Thus ended what is probably one of the most remarkable and bold explorations ever carried out in the district, and it is to be greatly regretted that Jeffcoat, who had lent such valuable assistance, was unable to join us in the actual ascent of the climb.

On April 19th of this year Herford, Gibson, Holland and myself repaired to Scafell for the attempt. Herford and Gibson ascended Keswick Brothers Climb and traversed out on to the Central Buttress, whilst Holland and I climbed direct from Rake's Progress to "The Oval." Gibson lowered me a rope down the crack and after removing my boots I attempted the ascent. As far as the bulge, above-mentioned, the climbing was comparatively simple, but from this point to a large jammed stone 20 feet higher it was extremely difficult, as the crack is practically holdless and just too wide to permit a secure arm wedge. Two fairly good footholds permit of a position of comparative comfort just below the jammed stone and I noted, as Herford had suggested, that it was possible to thread a rope there. The stone itself afforded quite a good hand-hold, but the crack above overhung to such a shocking extent that the ascent of the remaining 12 feet proved excessively difficult. My arms gave out long before the top was reached and a very considerable amount of pulling from Gibson was required before I joined him. Herford then tried the ascent on a rope and just succeeded in getting up without assistance. We thereupon decided to attempt the ascent in the orthodox manner, and preparatory thereto descended by Broad Stand and rejoined Holland on the Oval.

Our plan of attack was to climb up the crack and thread a loop behind the jammed stone, and I undertook to do this if Herford would lead the upper part, which he was quite prepared to do. My first procedure was to soak two feet of the end of a rope in wet moss, to render it stiff and facilitate the threading. I then attempted the ascent, but six feet below the jammed stone found my position too precarious to be pleasant and called to Herford for a shoulder. He came up without the least hesitation and standing on the bulge at the foot of the crack, steadied my feet on small holds until I attained a safer position and was able to climb up to the chockstone. The stiff rope threaded very easily, and making a double loop I ran my own rope through it for the descent, which was, under those conditions, quite safe.

After a brief rest Herford tied on to the threaded rope and speedily reached the level of the chockstone. He made a splendid effort to climb the upper part, but his strength gave out and he returned for a rest. A second equally fine effort was also unsuccessful, and he climbed down to the Oval. I then made one attempt, but soon abandoned it, and we unanimously agreed to postpone the ascent till the morrow, leaving the threaded rope *in situ* . As Holland had already spent *seven* hours on the Oval we decided to waste no more time, and accordingly descended via the traverse into Moss Ghyll.

The next day we climbed to The Oval direct from the Progress and one member ascended to the chockstone to renew the loop, which showed signs of wear from the previous day's use. We decided that combined tactics would be necessary, and accordingly ran a second rope through the loop. Herford tied on one rope and I on the other, whilst Gibson and Holland manipulated the respective ropes. I followed Herford closely up the crack and hung on to the loop whilst he used my shoulders as foot-holds. Directly he vacated them I climbed three feet higher and hung by my hands from the top of the chockstone, whilst he again employed me as foot-holds, which are most sorely needed at this point, for the crack is practically holdless and overhangs about 20°. A minute or two of severe struggling and he reached the top—to the great joy of all members of the party.

Photo by   G. S. Sansom.

CREST OF THE GREAT FLAKE.

Herford thoughtfully hung a short loop over the tip of the flake to assist us in the ascent, but even then we required much help from above, and it was with a sense of great relief that we found ourselves on the crest of the flake. Murray, who had been observing us from the recess with some interest, was delighted with an invitation to join the party, so we lowered him a rope down the crack and induced him to remove the threaded loop on the way up.

We were well satisfied with the day's work, but not with the climb, inasmuch as it left 150 feet of the Central Buttress still unclimbed. Two days later, therefore, we set out, greatly regretting Gibson's absence from the party, to explore the upper part of the face.

Fifty feet above the top of the Great Flake on the Central Buttress is an irregular V shaped grass ledge, from the western end of which springs a wide chimney, which is the lower section of a conspicuous Bayonet-Shaped Crack, running up to the very top of the crags. The upper section of this crack was, we knew, easy; the lower portion looked very unpleasant, but we hoped to avoid it by climbing the steep face on the left. With Holland and Slater belaying us, we climbed down steep rocks to the V shaped ledge 100 feet below, and from there were able to look down a remarkably smooth and almost vertical wall to the top of the Great Flake, 50 feet lower. The wall was broken at one point by a right-angled arête, which, in spite of the fact that it overhung slightly, possessed sufficiently good holds to permit of a comfortable descent of 25 feet. From its foot a wonderfully exposed traverse across the almost vertical face on the left enabled us to pass behind a large detached pinnacle and climb slightly downwards to the shattered ridge against the foot of which the Great Flake abuts.

Much elated at this discovery we climbed back to Holland and Slater, and the three of us at once descended the easy rocks to the "Cannon." Belayed from this point I led across the traverse and up to the V ledge. Herford then took the lead, Holland going second. Now the way by which we had descended necessitated an extremely difficult hand traverse, on bad holds, in an exposed situation, and we therefore cast about for a better route. Herford first tried the Bayonet-Shaped Crack, but it looked repulsively difficult and he abandoned it in favour of a most exhilarating traverse across its foot, on to the vertical wall beyond, and upwards across the latter for 30 feet to a steep slab, which he followed, for another 25 feet, to a good belay at the top of the lower section of the crack. We soon joined him here and climbed easily up the left wall of the upper portion of the Bayonet-Shaped Crack to the top of the Crags.

The Central Buttress climb as a whole is extremely interesting and the situations absolutely unique. As regards difficulty: The direct ascent to the Oval from Rake's Progress is decidedly difficult and entails an 80 foot run out. The Flake Crack is unfortunately excessively severe and requires very careful management to render its ascent safe. The traverses and ascents on the upper wall are extraordinarily exposed, but not unduly severe, and the climbing is exceedingly enjoyable. The climb is certainly the longest in the district.

MORE OF C.B.

Bill Birkett

When the editor asked me to do a piece for our *Journal*, celebrating 100 years since the first ascent of Napes Needle, I felt a certain buzz of excitement. I wondered how I could fit a piece in when there would inevitably be so much written about our Lakeland rocks — but he replied over the telephone that there was plenty of foreign material, could I actually do something about Lakeland rock climbing.

Well, actually, I thought I could, because, as everyone knows, I don't know anything about foreign stuff. I mean I haven't been up Everest or even walked in the Pyrenees (walking at altitude makes me frightfully dizzy). Then I thought what can I do — A hundred years of rock climbing? I took me a whole book to do it last time! No, it's got to be something a little bit different. Personal experiences; how Bobby Files guided a pathetic 13 year old up Napes Needle or me and Rick on the North Buttress or actually getting up Centrefold after even thinking it's not too good an idea. But then that's all too near the bone.

So then I thought perhaps I'll try to capture the spirit of the thing, the excitement of the movement, the feel of the rock, the wonder of the hills. So then again it had to be a day of real experience in the Lakeland Fells. More of the same in fact — but then that's what I like. Because if nothing else I am a rock climber and Lakeland is where I am and I'm gullibly honest in these simplicities.

So here we go with an article on Central Buttress, that's on Scafell you know and some people walk past but Bill and I couldn't. (Essay from *Classic Rock Climbs of Great Britain* to be published by Oxford Illustrated Press in summer 1986)

Central Buttress

Because 'CB' is so famous, clichéd, and popular, I for many years avoided it like the plague. When people said 'You mean you haven't done CB?' I would smile and inform them that this was one I was saving for my old age. I meant it.

A rather remarkable man, Bill Peascod, changed this situation for me with his infectious enthusiasm for life in general and climbing in particular. Bill thought CB to be the single most distinguished Lakeland route he had climbed and described it as having a unique blend of size, steepness, character, quality of climbing, difficulty and atmosphere that made it incomparable*. This was recommendation enough and on one rather damp and greasy day we set off to climb it.

Scafell is a mighty lump of rock, the pride and focal point of Lakeland rock climbing, and the rock for climbing stretches in a long semi-circle from the Shamrock up to Deep Ghyll Buttress and then, growing in stature, arcing round through the Pinnacle, Pisgah Buttress, Scafell Crag and finally, on the Eskdale side of Mickledore, the East Buttress. All steep and impressive ground and all, on the Wasdale side of Mickledore, dominated by the highest and steepest face of rock; the daunting Scafell Crag. Here a 250ft. clean, vertical wall intimidates both age and mind, seemingly exhibiting no weakness, no compromise, in its domination. Yet, on interested inspection, beneath a faint wisp of a horizontal crack, a magnificent leaning groove, only initially hidden by the sheer size of the wall, plucks at the heart of the climber. This is the Great Flake and provides the

* *Journey After Dawn* by Bill Peascod

key to a great climb — Central Buttress.

The boys were playing on the rocks around Moss Ghyll when they spotted the Great Flake;

'The rock fell away very steeply below and a sheer smooth wall rose up to a great height above; its regularity was interrupted at one point, it is true, by an enormous rock flake which tapered out to nothing 70 feet higher.... The Great Flake looked quite hopeless as a means of ascent and we dismissed the idea at once....' wrote G.S.Sansom in his article 'Scafell Central Buttress'*.

The following year they returned but were turned back at the flake, and shortly after this Sansom went to Brazil for the summer. Herford's letter which reached him there spelt out the inevitable;

'We then made an exploration of the CB. We found that it will go without serious difficulty except the top 20 ft. of the flake crack.'

They finally put it in the bag in 1914. Even allowing for the fact that Herford stood on Sansom's shoulders, whilst Sansom had lashed himself to the jammed chockstone near the top of the flake crack (in fact I'm far from convinced that this would make it easier) and that they worked on the route, it was a very bold and brilliant effort. It still is!

C.F.Holland wrote, in his *Climbs on the Scafell Group* (FRCC Guide, 1926);

'**The Central Buttress**: The most arduous ascent in the Lake District; unexemplified exposure; combined tactics and rope engineering essential at one point; not less than three climbers. Rubbers.

'The ascent of this buttress, the final problem presented by the great facade of Scafell, was made for the first time in April, 1914. It has as yet been repeated on two occasions only, and the difficulties met with are so great that the expedition ranks among the world's hardest, and is possible only under practically perfect conditions.'

All was quiet at Hollow Stones as Bill and I approached, and the clouds rolled menacingly up and down the crags. The atmosphere was dark and forbidding, the rocks were damp and greasy and it was the kind of day when one fully expected to see Herford's ghost walk unobtrusively past. A huge wet streak ran down the wall from beneath the chockstone of the Great Flake and I realised that the climb for my old age was in fact going to be a sizeable and difficult undertaking.

I set off, feet slipping and sliding, and found the so-called easier pitches up to the Oval absolutely desperate. Secretly I hoped Bill would want out and present me with some reasoned case for so doing. But I didn't, then, fully appreciate the tenacity or depth of character of the man, as I do now.

He climbed those wet, greasy slabs with grace and style, proving he was still the master of precarious balance climbing. There was not the faintest hint of wanting out. Then it was up to me and I knew we were going up, greasy rock or no.

The Great Flake from the Oval is very steep and, not so obvious from the

* *Climbing at Wasdale Before the First World War* by G.S. Sansom

ground, rather overhanging. It feels as though it's going to be demanding even before you start, and, as proved by the multitude of falls and failures seen at this point, it is. Under the prevailing conditions it was going to be an entertaining proposition.

Fortunately the wet streak stopped at the chock and the crux above looked dry. So up to the chock I went, all the time feeling worried and insecure. The protection is little better than in 1914. Pretty soon I was clipping the cluster of old tat round the chock and, with faint heart, wrapping my own long sling round it, too.

I attempted it at least three times, with skidding feet and pumping arms, each time retreating to the poor rest below the chock. Conflicting advice ran through my troubled mind;

'Jim (Birkett) jammed it, in nails. Bloody hell in nails. Dolphin laybacked it.' Gazing down to the Oval and Bill, patiently belaying, was an alarming feeling. I got the impression of being on a big crag, in a way out position, and the grade of HVS at that time seemed entirely meaningless. I've climbed countless routes that have been graded much harder and yet rarely experienced such a powerfully gripping fear.

Shouting down to Bill I got the first word in. 'It's all in the mind, I'm going to layback the bastard next go so watch the ropes.'

Bill chuckled on the ledge, 'Dolphin fell off lay-backing in nails'. But I'd got a grip and was definitely going to go for it.

'Watch us' and I went. Once I had made that mental commitment it wasn't so bad and it actually felt as if there was a good hold after a few scary moves.

I shouted down — 'There's a hidden jug', as you do, and proceeded to grab the top, a wafer-thin edge, the ultimate handhold.

I was interested, now, to see just how Bill, then 62 years of age and reascending the route after some 38 years, was going to cope. After various contretemps with my threaded sling and clipped in situ gear, necessitating his going up and down three times, he still powered up the edge like a cork exploding from a champagne bottle — an exceptional performance.

The mist lifted, the sun shone through and we laughed and hallowed, as only climbers can. Bill subsequently wrote in his autobiography, *Journey After Dawn*;

'It was the kind of moment that will live in a climber's memory as long as life.' It's a sentiment that I'm sure, Herford and Sansom felt; a feeling of trying and winning and the joy of sharing something unique.

The climb by no means ends at this point and the traverse across the upper wall, high above the Great Flake, gives delicate climbing with breath-taking exposure. We took the original finish, a traverse across into the final groove of Moss Ghyll Grooves, as this seemed a fitting and logical end to a satisfying route. For my part, if someone ever asked me to recall one of my finest days out on the mountains, I would tell of the day I climbed the immortal Central Buttress with young Bill Peascod.

CLIMBING IN THE MIDDLE AGES

Tony Greenbank

Hangover was first climbed in 1939, the year two farmers met on Hardknott and pondered if war had been declared. Finally agreeing it probably had they parted, one of them commenting: 'Aye, aye, well — Bonny day for it.'

In October 1985 Hangover lost its wardrobe-sized block way up the long pitch (95ft 4c) when it was inadvertently torn clean out from its socket by Golden Rule landlord John Lockley.

John wasn't to know. The Constable *Selected Climbs* guide suggests you use the block. And thousands had — including, on that same ascent, myself (who runnered it too). But the comment of the climber it shaved as he stood watching 150ft below ranked for its super-cool with that of the Eskdale shepherd: 'That'll make it harder.'

A po-faced demeanour, which is somewhat different from a panic-stricken one, can be a mark of someone who has digested the adage: Look well to all things, hold fast to that which is good. The only thing being — how exactly do we find what is the real McCoy? And not just in handling loose rock on climbs, but in Life itself.

It is something the majority of our Club will know. As will members of the SMC, CC, Yorkshire Ramblers, Pinnacle Club and the Alpha, Rock and Ice and Abraham Club too.

For in climbing, unlike many other pastimes where danger is the key, age need not stop the activist for literally ages. There are many 50-year-olds climbing in the VS and even E-grades today. Attend any Club annual dinner, Buxton gathering or Kendal film festival and you will find climbers not segregated by age but integrated all together, and frequently with those of the more advanced years making more row than the fledging rock jocks of the day.

This is what above all else I mean by holding fast: that is, climbing (God willing) — I repeat, God willing — to the end.

By Middle Ages I don't mean when the Battle of Evesham, the Golden Horde and the death of Roger Bacon were all happening. I refer instead to those pivotal years when dentures can fall out from a mouth dry with apprehension, and the arms are no longer long enough as you strive to read the guidebook by pushing it further and further away.

Climbing in the Middle Ages, providing you've hung on in there to reach them through earlier formative years, perhaps when the Tarbuck Knot was the vogue, can be a breeze today. Friends, sticky boots, chalk and the rest — oh, wow! And should things not go quite your way then a British Rail disabled card will give you cheaper travel. But, joking apart, it's experience that really adds the power to your tennis elbow.

Once climbing Moss Ghyll with Peter Moffat I was gobsmacked (just temporarily) as a Clint Eastwood lookalike cruised adjacent Slab & Groove. Then, as now, there was only one 'Ron'. In the 1950s it was immaculate Ron Miller. He made it look so great I shouted up to tell him so (and an embarrassed Pete told me to hush). It wasn't until my Middle Ages I managed to follow Ron's example. And that evening I phoned its creator from the pub to say 'Slab and Groove — out there!' Robert James Birkett let me down lightly. 'Actually,' he said, 'Len (Muscroft) and I thought it was only severe.'

Bobby Files put me in my place during my early days in the Club. We climbed Troutdale Pinnacle and I went a bit over the top at the top, 'Hey wowing' it or whatever you said in those days of Suez and the Windsor knot. 'Ah, yes,' said Bobby, spectacles fogging in the rain, 'And now we go down.'

'OK,' I said, running rope out still on the scramble up to the descent path. Bobby reminds me of the Yorkshireman who clean-bowled Bradman, namely Bill Bowes, and climbing with such a respectable figure — man, it was good to be alive.

'Ah, no,' said Bobby, now some distance behind. 'I mean down.'

And so he did. Back down every one of the 375ft we had climbed of this classic, its wonderful top pitch now highlighting the Club's Borrowdale guide.

Then again I learned to hold fast to good values the day my world collapsed on Brown Tongue. Gunn Clark, who was soon to make the first British ascent of the Walker Spur, was psyched up to climb CB. Together with Pete Moffat, he and I were toiling upwards when I suddenly remembered something. 'Oh, hell! Oh, no!' I think I said.

'Oh, hell!' I repeated. 'I said I'd bring the guidebook. Well, I forgot it.'

For moments we made a tragic tableau silhouetted high above the valley in the sun's westering rays.

Giving us both a kindly gap-toothed grin, Peter told us not to worry.

'I think we'll see where CB goes.'

The same thing could not be said of the Brackenclose roller-board. On this fiendish piece of equipment anything could happen.

To ride the roller-board you balanced gingerly on a short thick plank that rested on a wooden roller the size of a Tesco toilet roll (unused). Then, timed by a wristwatch, you see-sawed for as long as you could maintain your equilibrium and contact with the polished wood beneath the soles of your stockinged feet.

Aces like Ron Miller, Arthur Brooks, Joe Griffin and Albert Ashworth not only kept in balance, but flicked the board around the room like a skateboard, performing a variety of tricks along the way.

They made it look all so deceptively simple.

On my first attempt, however, first one end of the board went down as I applied my weight, and the other end went up. Then the end that had gone up fell rapidly down again only to snap back up then once more down — and so on with increasing speed — like the staccato rat-at-tat of a machine gun. At the same time these movements grew more violent until — and looking as if a thousand volts of electricity were passing through my body — eventually they fired me through the air like a space shuttle while plank and roller went hurtling in the opposite direction.

It was a costly trip totalling (as the Americans say): ½ bucket of coal (overturned); 1 dish of Phil Wormell's delicious Women's Institute-recipe lemon meringue pie; 8 mugs of steaming Ovaltine; 1 plate, at that precise moment being carried through the room by Sir Geoffrey Howe lookalike Lewis Smith, of wet liver; and the glass front to the bookcase beside the kitchen door through which my head became inextricably jammed.

All these happenings, please note, took place in the Fifties.

But to climb then in the Fifties and *still* to be on the rock and ice in these Fifties (even if a different kind of Fifties).... Hey, heavy number!

There's a lot of us about.

All still striving to hold on to that which is the genuine 18-carat. All going for the second chance. And all keeping the Middle ages, even with the occasional wobble, on course.

And when they finally cut this bloody plaster cast off my left leg I'll be back there still searching for something rather better than the last hold I used — hey, can YOU win them all?

THE MAN WHO BROKE THE NEEDLE

Graham Sutton

Reprinted from the FRCC Journal, Lakeland Number, 1936-37

It was no place to have teeth out — an October morning in Borrowdale and Ronnie dumping our three sacks into the Doc's old car, to go climbing on Gable.

But I'd no choice. An army marches on its belly, and I'd been marching on that rotten molar all yesterday; and the Doc swore he couldn't deaden it, it would really have to come out. So after breakfast, when we'd phoned a dentist, they made for Seathwaite and I caught the bus into town.

He was ready, with his accomplice — I mean his anaesthetist. I'd ordered gas; but when he'd violated the tooth a bit, the chap said: 'H'm trouble! I'd recommend an injection. Gas may not give me time enough....'

I said: 'I've got to climb today, and I can't climb full of dope. Gas goes off sooner, doesn't it?' But he dodged that, and countered me below the belt with a prophecy.

'If you come round before I'm through, it'll be no fun!'

I said I wasn't there for fun and I'd chance it. I caught them swapping a nasty look: as though they weren't sure whether to humour me, or tell me to mind my own business. The accomplice picked up a needle-gun, and began practising an approach-shot; he lacked the delicacy of the dentist, who had put his pliers in a shaving-jug and was pretending they weren't there. But I said: 'Gas or nothing!' and climbed on board.

So the accomplice laid aside the needle-gun, and started juggling with that sinister conglomeration of tubes that they pump gas in you with ('Death of Laocoon,' you know). And the dentist said 'Open please!' and rammed a gag in my mouth — a thing that tasted like a cold hotwaterbottle and felt like a dumbell. He said: 'I'd hate *you* to get violent! What's your weight?'

I said: 'Eighteen stone' — at least I said 'Hay-hee-ho,' because of the gag. But I knew he was only making talk; it didn't mater whether he could understand me or not. He went on: 'This gag's in case you bite! It wouldn't do to have you clench your teeth when I was giving you an injection. You might break the needle.....'

I said: 'Huch-hi-hoch-*hach*ha....' Then I spat out the gag, and started again. 'But I'm not *having* an injection.'

He said: 'No, no, I don't expect you are. But I can't operate with your mouth shut.' So he replaced the gag, and asked if it was comfortable: sarcastically, I suspect. And I said: 'Hoch!'

Then the snakecharmer weighed in with his gas-machine, and told me to inspire deeply. And I inspired, and hoped like billy-o they'd have the nous not to begin too soon; and they didn't; and that was that....

After all, it was not too bad. I lay recovering in an anteroom, and read the obituaries in last week's *Cumberland News*, and sucked the hole with my tongue. And the first minute I felt good enough, I tottered out into the Keswick market place and caught the Seatoller bus.

The Styhead track on a fine fresh October day would put anyone on his feet. When I arrived below the Napes the others weren't visible, but I heard their voices above. So I lay out on the Dress-Circle, and began probing that infernal hole again — it's queer, your tongue won't give a place like that any peace — and stared at the old Needle.

The Needle has been compared with lots of things; but what it most reminded *me* of, just then, was a great tusk of a molar. It seemed the very thing for today — appropriate, and a nice heartening job of work, and not too long if I tired. So before long, when the other two came down off Eagle's Nest, we crossed the gully and began to scramble up to our rock. The Doc led it, by the ridge; and I came second on the rope, and Ron brought up the rear.

You'll know the ridge-route, of course? In the old days, one used the central crack; and the crack's still the merriest way down, you just slide, like down banisters. But the ascent's not so popular. The footholds were always slim; and they've been worn so smooth, and you're so liable to jam your leg and have to leave your boot behind, or perhaps even your breeches, that a lot of modest men rather jib at it, and prefer to go upstairs by the ridge. From the main crack you edge out horizontally, on rather sketchy holds with a long drop beneath; but once you're there, you'd be surprised how much less difficult it is than it looked. The ridge is jagged and sharp, with a belaying pin the size of a cricket bat halfway up; and at the top, a regular armchair of an anchorage, where you can brace your feet across a gap and safeguard the next man. Then comes a scramble up some easy rock to the shoulder; and there, trouble begins.

You're on a broad step — lots of room for three of you; and your next job is to surmount a smooth little wall, on which the summit-block stands. It's like a mantelshelf — they call it The Mantelshelf — a long ledge, chin-high, and four inches deep. You can catch hold of it, and then press upon it, to put your knees where your hands are; and the whole problem would be simple enough, if only you had more room. Try climbing any ordinary mantelshelf and you'll find out what I mean. You want to lean well forward across the shelf, but the top wall won't let you. You must perform the trick erect, like a toy monkey; only the monkey's nailed on to the stick, and you're not. At home, you could catch hold of something like a picture-rail; but here there's nothing at all.

My turn came when the Doctor was perched on top, out of sight; and I just couldn't make it! Three times I pressed up on the shelf; but when I tried to squirm a good knee on to it, I conked out and slid back. Ron mocked at me, from the ledge: 'What's your weight, G.S.'

I said: 'The dentist asked me that. I'm hay-hee-ho, less a few ounces for the tooth....'

Ron's voice came up: 'You've spoilt your balance, having that tooth out; it's left you too light in front and too heavy behind!'

I said: 'Forceps to you —!' But in the end, by gosh, I got up. Half up, anyhow. I'd still the worst bit. I had to raise myself from my knees to my feet, without falling backwards.

It's not easy, any time; and today — thanks to that beastly dentist, probably — it defied me. So I did something very wrong: reached up and helped myself in secret to a nice pull on the rope. Most unorthodox. The wrongness is, that if you pull up on a rope the leader feels that it's taut, and doesn't haul in the slack. So, as you rise, you get a two-or-three-foot loop hanging down by you; and if you come unstuck just then, of course, you're going to drop so much, clear. And that's what happened to *me*. I was just upright when my toe slipped, my knuckles grazed the rock, a stinging pain made me let go the rope, and I swayed over backwards. I dropped two feet before the slack ran out; and my full hay-hee-ho came on the Doctor's rope with a bang.

I must explain now, how the Doctor was fixed. He was up out of sight of us, on the flat summit of the final pyramid, with the rope belayed round his shoulder. And by the way, people ask sometimes if it isn't rather worrying, on a rock-climb, to have nothing beneath you. Well, it's not, really; you don't think of it; and you couldn't do anything if you did. It's much more of a stinker to have nothing above. You see, the leader's job is to tie on to something firm above, in case the next man comes off: some flake, or spike. But on the Needle, you're on top of everything and there's nothing left to tie on to. The only safe thing you can do is to drape several loops of rope round the peak itself, beneath where you're sitting; you have to loop yourself below yourself, if you see what I mean — because there *is* no above. The Doctor'd done that all right. But when I fell, the jerk on my rope dragged him off his perch and he half dropped, half slithered down the face of the pyramid, until his own belay held.

The whole thing happened in a flash; but if you've followed me so far I think you'll see how it landed us. I'd been left dangling over Ron, a few feet above the ledge; the Doctor's fall released my rope, and I came tumbling on to Ron, who collapsed with me. But the Doctor's case was more serious. He must have come down a good fifteen feet before the belay stopped him. Then the rope snapped — it wasn't built for such a strain. They make 'em good for a hundred and something pounds, you know, dropping umpteen feet — probably in a vacuum; but the Doctor's gravity's a bit plus-ish. Still it broke his fall; the wonder was, it didn't bisect the beggar. It stopped him dead, a yard above the pair of us; and when it parted, down he slumped on to us.

But, by jove, we weren't finished yet! As we lay there, half dazed, and sorting ourselves out, we heard a kind of rumbling. And Ron let our a yell. And I looked up and saw that the huge pyramid which forms the Needle-tip was adrift!

It's a poised block, you know: not part of the main mass. I'd always heard you could vibrate the thing, if you rocked on it. And now, the mighty jerk our rope had given it must have started it off. Not towards us, luckily. The fissure slopes west, towards the Needle Gully; and the block was creeping that way. It slunk down, almost imperceptibly at first, but soon faster: with a queer, frightful, grinding noise. And then it passed beyond its centre of gravity; and the noise stopped; and the whole thing leaned very gently outward: and fell.

It hit the rock one single glancing blow, above the top of the crack. Then a long silence — minutes, it seemed like. And then a most almighty crash down below, as it struck the bed of the gully. We craned after it; we thought we'd see it go on walloping down into Wasdale. But it never budged. Just stuck embedded bottom up, in the loose scree of the gully. And a big mushroom-cloud of sunny dust spread on the still air. And Ron and I hung, gaping down at it, and heard our own hearts beating.

The Doctor was still laid out; his fall had winded him. By and by, when he sat up, he got the devil of a shock to see the needle-tip wasn't there; he thought he must be delirious — doctors are easily alarmed about themselves; dare say you've noticed that — but we assured him it was all correct, and he cheered up a bit. And when he'd satisfied himself that he'd not smashed any ribs, we got down as quick as we could.

We didn't say much; we were too scared; and if we'd overturned the Albert Memorial we couldn't have felt more guilty. You see, the Needle is a sort of national monument; men come back happily to do it again, year after year, from the far ends of the earth; and now....! So we just slid the crack and dropped into the gully bed, and ploughed across with our eyes turned away from the great foreign-body sticking there, and scrambled up to the Dress-Circle again; and there we sat and took stock.

The Needle looked pretty awful without its tip. It looked forlorn and stumpy and undignified. It looked *wrong*! We stared at it without speaking. And — you know how it is, when you've come through a nasty fright and the reaction sets in, it plays queer tricks on you. Ron began to laugh.

He said: 'O lord, G.S., you've been and gone and done it now! You'll go down in history! The hiking heavyweight! The man who left no stone unturned! The man who crashed the old Needle! My hat, whatever will the Fell and Rock Club say? Oh, G.S., you've surpassed yourself!'

I couldn't see anything to laugh about. I was too ashamed. I felt like that chap in the *Ancient Mariner* — 'For I had done a hellish thing' — you know the passage I mean? And there's another tag, in scripture somewhere; it came into my mind: 'Cursed is he that removeth his neighbour's landmark. Amen!'

I said: 'Oh, shut up! I've two more days' holiday; but I'm off home to-night, before this gets out.'

Ron rolled back, helplessly. 'Gets out! Hear that, Doctor? How long d'you think we'll keep it dark? Oh lord, I'm going to be sick!'

Then we heard nailed boots clicking on the rocks, and three fellows hove in view; they must have been on Abbey Buttress or Arrowhead, round the corner. And when the first man came in sight of where the Needle ought to be, he stopped dead. 'Great Scott! I say, George, look here — !'

Ron punched me. 'You're too late, G.S. — it's out!' And then he must needs jump up and point at me and say: 'He's broken the Needle!'

And the newcomers glared and shook their fists at me, and said: 'The big stiff! He ought to be handcuffed.'

And Ron's voice gurgling: 'It's out — !'

I hadn't heart enough to say anything. I sat there overwhelmed with shame, with my eyes shut; I felt feeble and limp. And the voices kept on at me: 'It's out....he's broken the Needle....ought to be handcuffed, the big stiff.... its *out!*'

At last I opened my eyes: and saw the accomplice groping on the floor, where I'd kicked all the bag of tricks; and beside me the dentist, holding up triumphantly a great pyramid of a tooth.

THE OLD MAN AT STOER

Ed Grindley

'Yes, definitely over there' said MacInnes, pointing to the left of a low mist-fringed hill. 'I was here on a reconnaissance a couple of weeks ago'. At Hamish's command our assorted and heavily-laden party began to move across the bog. We were here to make a film.

Within five minutes the party was scattered across the moor; camera men fell into old peat cuttings and tried vainly to thrust their cameras onto dry ground; sound men tripped over peat stacks and rammed their gun-mikes into highland cattle pats.... chaos.

Bathgate and myself had the ladder. We set off with it horizontal, one at either end, our heads through the rungs. The ladder was piled with boxes. One of us tripped. If you've ever been garotted and hit over the head with a metal trunk at the same time, you know how it felt. Practice should have made perfect, but in a bog like that it didn't. Finally we stretched the ladder across the next mire and walked across carrying the boxes. And the next mire.... and the next....

Some hours later we all reached the cliff-top from different directions.

'No bad thing that' observed Hamish, 'More chance of finding the right path if we spread out'.

After five minutes rest it dawned on everyone that the sea below was empty. All eyes turned to Hamish.

'Must be the other side of the hill. Difficult to tell in this mist', he mused. 'You lads start fetching the rest of the gear and I'll go and look'. With that he disappeared, empty-handed.

Three hours and five trips later it was done: trunks, aluminium boxes, tripods, food for a week, a marquee and twenty crates of McEwan's moved to the top of the cliff. Just at that moment Hamish re-appeared. 'Took some finding in the mist', he noted.

All that remained was to move the huge mound of gear up and over the hill. Reassured of our safety, Hamish went to investigate the path down to the foot of the Old Man.

Next day Hamish descended the line of ropes we'd put down the steep cliff path, poking the odd belay and tutting. Bathgate, Brown and myself made no comment; we'd just arrived down with the 30 foot ladder.

Between us and the Old Man was a narrow and deep sea channel, normally crossed by swimming. Hamish had other ideas — the ladder.

'Should be no problem; used the same technique on a crevasse in the Western Cwm. That was 35ft wide, this is only 30 ft.'

Hamish sat down to supervise the operation. Under his direction the ladder was raised to 45°, by Joe and Dave using side ropes, and myself pushing. Slowly we got the base of the ladder to the channel's edge.

'Let go' said Hamish.

A couple of hours later we succeeded in removing the ladder from the channel, along with several tons of sea-weed and two conger eels. The channel, it seemed, was 31ft wide. As a man experienced in the ways of MacInnes, Joe then produced an inflatable boat from his rucksack and rowed across. After that things went smoothly for a spell. Joe and Dave did a new route and Ian Nicolson and myself did the Original Route to check the belays for the girls' ascent the next day.

The start of the Original route traversed greasy twin cracks above the channel; why I don't know, because we walked around the back and avoided it. An easy pitch followed, up a crack to a ledge on the south rib 60 feet above the sea. The next pitch was the crux — an awkward crack, slanting up rightwards over a bulge. From the stance above, a rising traverse led rightwards; roofs above and roofs below; to a ledge. The ledge contained a bird: unmistakably a fulmar, I thought. This surprised me as my 'How the fulmar spreads' map didn't show them this far south. Suddenly the air was thick with puke; cracks and ledges dripped and I wondered if I'd misinterpreted the map's title. Fortunately I remembered the words of Hamish. 'Flick a sling at them till they run out of ammo'. After five minutes it seemed safe to proceed. Whoosh!

'You have to watch that' Hamish remarked later 'they sometimes keep a bit in reserve'.

Green-faced, I climbed the final chimney and pulled onto a ledge just below the top; there was a fulmar to each side. I tried quickly to remember what Hamish had said about his experiences in the Ypres salient; I believe the correct military term is enfilade fire.

The top and as the Americans are so fond of saying, high man, high.

Next day the misty weather cleared, Cynthia and Dot climbed the Original Route and Joe and Dave repeated their line for the cameras. Don't think the epic was over; far from it. Hamish had decided that Joe and Dave must Tyrolean from the summit to the mainland. A special steel-cored rope had been made and eventually this was hauled up and tensioned across the 300ft gap.

'OK Joe, across you come', shouted Hamish.

'No way mate. It's your idea, you can try it first'. Hamish went pale.

'Nothing to worry about Joe, I had the rope made specially, 20 ton breaking strain, steel core. It'd hold a tram'.

'After you mate'. Hamish went white and had to be helped down to the rope, a broken-looking man. The rope held, the acrobats were filmed and Cynthia and Dot abseiled off to film Cynthia's swim across the channel.

At last the Old Man was cleared and the circus departed. Months later the film went out. A plain enough tale. Four climbers arrive at the Old Man, swim and Tyrolean the channel and climb two routes, one new. With the help of a couple of handy walkers they stretch one climbing rope across the gap, and two Tyrolean over; the other two abseil.

The camera never lies? Well it doesn't tell the whole truth either!

THE MODERN ICARUS!
(A HANG-GLIDER'S GUIDE TO THE LAKE DISTRICT)

Ed Cleasby

Introduction

My first glimpse of a hang glider was the novel sight of a crude rogallo, wheeling like some pre-historic pterodactyl around the sky over Chamonix. This was late in the summer of 1974, and America's latest craze had found its inevitable way to Europe. The rudimentary structure looked decidedly unsafe, but it worked and provided a cheap and exhilarating way to take to the air. Having been very air-minded since a child it almost tempted me away from my new-found passion, climbing. To this day I retain a hazy, scratched instamatic slide of the occasion, little realising at the time that it was the embryo of what was to become my dominant activity a decade later.

During the seventies, this new sport developed, as new things do, at a tremendous pace, but firmly immersed in the climbing scene and with little desire or time for anything else, I maintained no more than a distant technical interest. Until, by chance one warm summer's afternoon in 1978, the long dormant desires were reawakened. From a belay, high on Falcon Crag, I watched as two 4th generation gliders, the latest 'hotships', soared by the cliffs above Borrowdale. No longer was it a flapping deltoid-shaped kite, but a sleek, taut aircraft that displayed a mastery of its environment. Within days I'd enrolled myself on a course. Winter intervened, but eventually, around Easter the next year, the snows had drained away and I enjoyed four glorious days, emerging the proud owner of an Elementary Pilot's Certificate, with a whole twelve minutes airtime.

With the onset of summer, climbing again exerted an irresistible pull, dampening my new-found enthusiasm, but it proved only temporary, for by November, money set aside for other purposes had been diverted into purchasing a flying machine. The 'Spirit' was dated, even at that time, but she was safe, had the stability of a Sopwith Pup, and would carry the dreams of this young Bleriot. Alas, she was destined to gather more dust than airtime as three more summers quickly passed and I couldn't bring myself to break the bond with climbing.

Early in July 1982, just as I was preparing for a Norwegian holiday, fate again intervened, when out of the blue I was introduced to a young Finnish pilot. Gliderless, and looking for one to borrow, he'd heard I might have one available. Certainly he could use it, but I sensed his initial joy turn to disappointment as the sails were unfurled to expose years of accumulated dust, smothering a piece of what was now hang-gliding history. Still, it was basically sound, and for the next couple of weeks I followed him around, becoming more captivated by it all, until eventually, noticing my keenness, he clipped me in and talked me off a few hills and from then on I was hooked.

This was now the age of the 5th generation glider, a fast, double-skinned, fully battened aerofoil that was a quantum leap in performance on anything that had gone before. Lengthy cross-country flights were becoming quite common, with the hundred mile barrier broken, but an article I read at the time really brought home to me its potential for exploring the Lakeland fells from a new perspective: not isolated from the environment by a cockpit, but part of it and using it to progress.

Well, that was my ever-so-gradual introduction and finally last year, after several seasons of dedication, the hard-earned skills began to pay off when I managed, not once but twice, to achieve a dream, the classic Lakeland trip; a north-south traverse. Along its length it takes in some of the area's highest and finest peaks, including Skiddaw and Helvellyn. The second half of this article inadequately attempts to describe the experience.

The Flight

During the night the cold front had moved quickly through, dampening the ground a little, but leaving in its wake a much clearer airflow. The wind was back in the west again, and with pressure rising, it had all the makings of an excellent flying day. But where to go to exploit the conditions? Although spoilt for choice, the obvious site was the ill-named Cockup, on Skiddaw's N.W. flank overlooking Bassenthwaite village. Lenient of wind direction it offered the most northerly launch point for the high level run to at least Windermere and who knows how far beyond.

By 1pm, six of us had assembled, and, risking heart failure, successfully negotiated the steep hillside with 80lbs of glider and associated equipment to the 600' launch plateau. With the wind dropping, rigging was a hurried affair and within fifteen minutes gliders were being tensioned bow-tight, harness and parachutes donned and final adjustments made to instruments and radios. However, the conditions were decidedly marginal, and the finishing checks were dragged out as six pilots waited to see who would break first and test the air.

First to weaken was Ian, his 'Demon' working hard to gain a few hundred feet over take off: no-one was too impressed and we declined to join him, so giving up the struggle he came back in to land and wait for an improvement. Nevertheless, the sky looked good, and as things can improve quickly we clipped in and watched for signs of passing thermals, timing the cycles. As the wind was light it was going to take more than pure ridge lift to stay up.

The wind slackened further but the air felt slightly warmer, so on a half-hunch I launched. It was weak, but the vario warbled slightly indicating I was going up. Slowly the 'S4' ascended till the lift died after a mere 200'.

Taking a chance I came in close, and almost at stall speed cruised along the rising fellside towards the small closed valley of Barkbethdale. The valley was short: at its head, steep scree funnels swept up towards Skiddaw's summit;

natural thermal courses but a hostile environment for a hang glider. As I entered the valley the air became rougher and I unconsciously eased back on the speed bar countering any turbulence: there was lift here somewhere. The glider was sinking fast, vario silent until a light tug on the bar stopped the slide and the vario needle slowly rose, the first gentle tones rising to a high trill as it reached 8up (800'/minute climb). Quickly I had enough height in hand, and banking over, began circling, mapping out the lift and trying to exploit it to the full. Like riding a wild horse I stayed with it, rising above sheep trails and summit-bound walkers until all the paths converged on Skiddaw's final cairn. Six hundred feet higher I'd lost it, and could relax, able to take in the sheer grandeur of the panorama spread out below. Ahead to the west lay the sharp rising spur of Ullock Pike, the sunless east flank in deep afternoon shadow, and streaming out towards it, looking very small, the rest of the gliders, eager to be on their way.

Just south of Ullock we were all together again, the three of us fortunate enough to have radios working together to exploit the good lift. Eventually Steve, Ian and I reach the murky chill of cloudbase and momentarily the ground disappears as stringy tendrils swirl about us, trying to suck us in. Circling together under the same cloud we steadily progress, drifting in tune with the sky and maintaining our height whilst, far below, Latrigg, Keswick and the snaking A66 slip silently past. Our first objective, Clough Head, lies three miles away across the St. John's sink hole. Sometimes it's a hard gap to cross, but this time it goes easily, and an hour after take-off five of us have made it. For the sixth pilot the day ends prematurely when he blunders into sink and is forced to land a mile short: nothing is worse than being on the ground whilst others drift by overhead.

The next four miles down to Helvellyn take a little nerve. Technically it's quite easy, but the landing areas along Thirlmere are very limited, even for a hang glider, unless the reservoir is low. Clough Head enjoys our attention for a while, the steep gullies carving up the hillside from St. John's Vale making an interesting place to explore. Sandbed Ghyll especially evokes memories for me of a winter ascent a few years earlier, and flying past the upper crag I'm amused to find I can't break the habit of searching for new lines.

Someone goes for it, and chicken-hearted, the rest of us are content to watch until with no problems his 'Magic' is no more than a dot in the sky above Helvellyn. Working independently I manage to build up almost 3000' over the valley and, with the confidence that height gives, turn south towards Thirlmere. Soaking in the view, the next ten minutes is pure nostalgia. Drifting past Castle Rock I can easily pick out the ant-like climbers — it looks a busy place today. Across the valley Raven Crag hides in the shade, just a lone couple visible, basking on the heathery summit. Did I really do routes on these cliffs? — from this unreal vantage point it seems a world away now. On down the length of Thirlmere, nothing disturbing its smooth, black surface. The level is high: no chance of landing there today.

Aware that I'm gradually losing height, I have to start thinking again and decide to crab towards Helvellyn's shallow upper slopes to see what they have to offer. Having completely forgotten to maintain radio contact, I'm suddenly surprised to see Steve and Ian come floating over just above me having followed a more direct route along the main ridge. Tacking back and forth we gradually move southwards towards Dollywagon Pike, using every minor bump and bowl in the terrain to gain the best lift from the quartering wind. Occasionally we fly within a few wingspans of the hillside. Sheep and fellwalkers pass close below, often oblivious of our presence, as with bowed heads they concentrate on the task in hand.

Crossing the gap towards Seat Sandal we blunder into a small but well formed thermal rising out of the broad ghyll below. At first weak, it strengthens with height till we're rocketing up in steep spirals and dropping over Grisedale Tarn. To Ian, a keen fellwalker and Munro bagger, it's an incredible experience, and on reaching over 4000' his gasps and whoops of amazement fill the headphones.

Time is now pressing, and regretting our late start we quickly head off towards Heron Pike. As we pass over the deep gash of Tongue Gill, level with the top of Fairfield, the sun is well past its zenith and with all lee sides now in shadow, thermal activity is decreasing. Grasmere basks beneath a sky almost devoid of cumulus, and our hopes of a final boost to clear the difficult ground around Ambleside fade.

Ever the optimist, Steve abandons the weak ridge lift produced by Heron Pike and heads out over the valley, whilst unconvinced by this last-gasp tactic, Ian and I are content to watch. Although visibly sinking out he makes no attempt to turn back, and when all hope seems gone he is rewarded by the best lift of the day. Suddenly the whole valley seems to be lifting as a deepening shadow of cool air noses slowly in from Easedale and triggers it off. Pulling speed we dive off into the rising air and as turn follows turn we achieve our best height gain of the day, topping out at 5000'.

From high over Snarker Pike the view is magnificent, with the whole of the Lake District spread out like a giant relief map, whilst in the distance, beyond the dark silhouette of Great Gable and the Scafells, is the gentle shimmer of the Irish Sea. Now more than ever I curse my clumsiness in pulling the air release off the keel mounted camera over Ullock Pike.

As Steve strangely heads south towards Lake Windermere, Ian and I continue out drift over Wansfell and Troutbeck, steadily losing height. Despite having enough altitude in hand to reach Staveley three miles ahead, we take a last chance on Troutbeck delivering up a final offering of the day. But the day is finished and after twenty futile minutes roaming back and forth on the ridge below Ill Bell, we give up and elect to land. At 5:30pm we touch down at Limefit Park. Shortly afterwards Steve lands at Staveley to a hero's welcome and tea and biscuits, but now for me the hard part begins: a twenty-five mile hitch into the night to retrieve the car — nothing is entirely for free.

CLIMBING IS MORE A DANCING THING
Angela Soper

On a glorious summer day in 1967 when Kipling Groove was the hardest route in Langdale, I fell off it at the end of the traverse. With only one move to make, my fingers, on which I was depending, simply uncurled and let go. Well I remember how the rope cut into my waist as I dangled from the peg, and how ashamed I felt at this unseemly débâcle.

On a miserable autumn day in 1984, when Kipling Groove had long been just another 5a pitch (though probably the most popular one in Langdale), I stood in balance in the middle of the traverse, took off one hand at a time and confessed the story to the girl who held my rope. Could it really be the same place?

Strange, how I used to believe that climbing was a matter of strength and courage. Was it because the other climbers were men, much stronger than me? Why did I depend so much on my fingers, unreliable at the best of times? Just because the old brown guidebook described a hand traverse, why didn't I think of feet? It took me far too long to realise that climbing is more a dancing thing, especially for a woman. *Technique* and courage. Then, the leader never fell. Now, if she doesn't fall occasionally (onto perfect protection) she isn't climbing at her highest standard. Then, four points of contact. Now, put your spare foot out in space and feel your balance improve. Push up, rock over, lock off.

In these days of indoor climbing walls, you don't need to make a new start after every winter, but can resume at the standard you feel 'trained up to'. I used to be apprehensive to the point of terror, especially when seconding. Once I thought my difficulties were due to lack of strength, but now it's clear that they were due more to lack of perception. Over and over again, I must have tackled things the wrong way. Now, guided by the technical grades, I approach a lead with only mild 'butterflies', expecting to see what to do and enjoy doing it.

Like Extol. I'll always remember the scorching day when we arrived at Dove Crag so early that we waited for the sun to go *off* it, then climbed that soaring pitch beautifully with new 50m ropes that were none too long. As I brought Stella up, the part of me that always stands aside from our antics seemed to say, 'What are they doing, these middle-aged women?'. And the active part replied, 'Rubbish. Let them stay young and daft until they're old and strange'. Still in a 'go for it' mood, we went onto Dovedale Grooves, and next day climbed Central Pillar and Red Edge to compile surely the best weekend's climbing I'll ever know.

Hard Rock has become a good source of routes for the girls and Sirplum in Chee Dale was on my list. Jenny, a student, had only been climbing six months but had already followed Sirplum, so naturally I offered her the lead. As we walked along the disused railway she told me that dancing and teaching dance were other leisure interests. Jenny danced up Sirplum without hesitation, taking in her elegant stride the steepness, the exposure, the polished rock. Afterwards

whispered happily, 'Guess what — that's the first E route I've ever led'. I could only think, surely the first of many.

'Butterflies' were in evidence before Vector, probably because of the early days when I was refused access on the grounds that I would only fall irretrievably into space; the rope could be of no assistance. Now, I'm eternally grateful to whoever said that and set me up for a sight lead, even if it was twenty years later. My partner Judy (of the clean-hands brigade) had led the route before and her friendly presence nearly amounted to cheating by me for, as soon as I made the first interesting step, she mentioned, 'I found that as hard as any move on the climb', and added similar helpful remarks as I continued. Vector was beautiful, marred only by chalk. It is done in the head like an intricate dance; think of the right sequence and the rest happens. Technique and balance, judgement and timing, grace and style are the things which matter. But why didn't I know that before?

THE WELL-OILED MACHINE — TWELVE MONTHS ON

Tony Burnell

COMPONENT PARTS	SPARE PARTS
MARTIN BERZINS	GORDON HIGGINSON
CHRIS SOWDEN	NICK HALLAM
MARK SPREADBOROUGH	GRAHAM DESROY
TONY BURNELL	

'The Well-Oiled Machine' was christened by Graham (Streaky) Desroy on the 30th of September 1984, which incidentally was almost at the end of a hyperactive year. The event that inspired this title was the team's enthusiastic assault on a mediocre discovery, Ravenscar South.

The team was first assembled in the closing days of 1983. Three quarters of the team, that is to say Martin, Chris and myself, were exploring above Arncliffe. After struggling through knee-deep snow we eventually came to what we thought was Yew Cougar Scar. We were not impressed; our eyes beheld an almost vertical stack of rubble. It was obvious that someone had climbed there before, however the crag's true worth had quickly been evaluated and no routes have been recorded there. We carried on up the valley and eventually struck gold (black gold some might say.) There, half immersed in the hillside like a black nugget, was the true Yew Cougar Scar. The crag is on average eighty feet high and bulging all the way to the top. Apart from a little damage sustained during the sixties and seventies from the whap and dangle brigade and, rumour has it, a rebuffed assault from members of the Y.M.C., we had a virgin crag. On that cold wet afternoon even the most obvious lines looked somewhat futuristic: time alone would tell.

The next mention of crag 'X' was at one of the early guidebook meetings. Chris and Martin spent the evening keeping straight faces and playing innocent as they listened intently to Frank Wilkinson extolling the virtues and obvious potential of a one hundred and fifty foot high, three hundred foot long, steep limestone crag called Yew Cougar Scar. Fortunately Chris and Martin were successful in playing down the significance of any of these comments and reluctantly accepted the responsibility for checking the crag.

Gordon, Chris, Martin and myself started checking routes at Attermire in February and notched up the first new route of the year. Albeit a somewhat insignificant route, nobody was prepared to solo Green Beam; eventually ropes and runners were brought into play and the first gap was plugged. Thoughts were refocused on Yew Cougar and on the 18th March, 1984 the Machine headed off into the Dales; conveyed on this particular occasion by Mark's twenty-four hour old Vauxhall Cavalier. Whilst travelling past Sleets Ghyll in close proximity to an old Honda (one week old to be precise) a screech of brakes

accompanied by the smell of burning rubber resulted in both Cavalier and Honda being instantly customised. Later that same day Yew Cougar yielded its initial routes, Power Play and Cavalier Crunch. Development continued at Yew Cougar throughout March and April, the only major problem being cleaning. Chris was given the task of procuring some angle iron stakes. We assumed a man so conversant with mechanical engineering would be best suited for this job. This following weekend we set off into the dales secure in the knowledge that Chris had succeeded and we would soon be able to abseil in safety. On parking at the crag, Chris proudly produced several lengths of Dexion slotted angle; we were not impressed and Chris could tell. An hour later we had managed to persuade three rather disfigured pieces of Dexion that they really should stay in the ground. Martin was the heaviest and as such volunteered his services as test pilot; all went well. The belay was really put to the test when Martin decided, for reasons best known to himself, that he would set off solo and put some runners in whilst Chris was still cleaning. The inevitable happened, retreat was impossible and after much bleating a rope was swung into position and Martin swung into space. We now knew the belay was capable of supporting two bodies at one time.

The team moved back to Attermire, picking off several new lines like Ultra Brite, Lemming Essence, Blind Panic, Chrome Yellow etc. etc. On one such visit half the team were ensconced on Whizz Popping and Escapologist, whilst Bruiser had lashed down Chris, elected himself as team gymnast and set to work on his own creation Red Terror. It was a sight to behold! Imagine if you can, flying through the air with all the aerodynamics of a brick, the thirteen stone sylph-like figure of Martin Berzins grasping for non-existent holds, undercut at that. It was also around this time that Mr Careful, alias Chris, forgot what a bowline was and how they were formed. The result of this minor oversight was the first, albeit unintentional, solo of Legal Limit, carefully removing the runners placed by Martin when he led it. I think the mere thought of it scared him more than his rather vocal ascent of Blind Panic a few weeks earlier.

For the next few weeks Trollers Gill was the scene of fervent and hushed activity, so hushed in fact that one half of the team forgot to tell the other half where it was going, hence routes like Angel Dust and Barguest were followed by Book Up and Sour Grapes.

After a short recess in Verdon I teamed up with Gordon and, taking our lives in our hands, we headed for the escarpment at Attermire. After cutting one rope in half, as a result of a landslip, which didn't curtail our activities for very long, we managed to check a number of routes and added No Hiding Place, probably the most stable route on the crag but still no real reason to walk all the way up the hill.

Loup Scar was another crag that, although known about, had been left for better days. However Ron Fawcett's ascent of Guadaloupe stirred the Machine into action. Five routes were salvaged, most of which were done in the evenings after work and a high speed race up the dales to beat the darkness. Climbing in the dark however does not lead to accurate grading and the second ascentionists, namely Martin and myself, were left to correct the grade from E1-5b to E3-6a; so much for the team's ability to grade routes.

September 1984 brought about the episode that earned the team its name. It was a wet day when Martin, Chris, Mark and myself, closely followed by Streaky in his Tonka Toy, went to check out a minor crag, Raverscar South, and of course do a little exploring on as yet unreported crags. As with all Yorkshire's unexplored rock, from a distance they show a lot of promise, however, the closer you get the smaller they become until finally you arrive at yet another esoteric gem. Within four minutes of arriving at the crag one ascent was under way from the bottom up and two other routes were being cleaned from the top down. To say the least, Streaky was impressed (so much so that he returned mid-week to pick off the last remaining line); needless to say it was not by the quality of the routes but by the ruthless efficiency with which they were being exploited.

Evening activity was centred on Kilnsey at this point in time, due partially to the weekend climbing ban and partially to the prying eyes watching our every move at weekends. On one particular evening Martin was engaged in the first free ascent of Ice Spurt Special. Under normal circumstances an event such as this would be preceded by an abseil inspection/clean; however, due to the imminent onset of darkness, Martin considered the route looked fairly clean and pretty straight-forward so a direct assault was employed.

It quickly became apparent that the route was not as clean or straightforward as it appeared. Blocks cascaded down from on high and the meek cowered under whatever shelter was to hand. It was about this time that a visiting southern climber had the misfortune to witness the ongoing pantomime and appeared totally unconvinced as rocks and curses rained down, in between which Martin was extolling the virtues of his adopted crag in terms of quality and potential. It was after the umpteenth airborne incident that Martin disclosed that this was in fact the first free ascent and not an aid route. The route did in fact concede somewhat later the same evening.

The Machine gathered momentum as the year drew rapidly to a close, culminating with the exploitation of Gordale's upper right wing, reputedly pre-empting Martin Atkinson by twenty-four hours, and, surprisingly, the left wing at Malham, with many thanks to Dave Cronshaw for pointing the way. Gordale's upper right wing yielded seven excellent routes while Malham rendered another *fifteen*. Possibly the most memorable (or, if you like, epic) was the ascent of Night Moves. Prior to setting out for Malham on the nineteenth of December, Dr. Berzins had just invested in his latest piece of mountaineering equipment, (probably as a charm to ward off the possibility of any snow in the forth-coming winter) a new-fangled head torch. I cleaned the route by abseil and due to the lack of runners decided to split the route on the half-way ledge, working on the principle that this would probably give the second a chance to grab the unfortuate leader should gravity take control. Things were not however going well. I had led the first pitch and returned to earth in order to allow Chris to continue his siege (oops sorry Chris): eventually the crag submitted and Chris succeeded in climbing the excellent Ship Of Fools. He was followed in double quick time by Martin and myself. I returned quickly to my position on the half way ledge and brought Martin up to the belay. Frantically we changed places and I got to grips with the top pitch. It was now twenty past four, the sun had set about half an hour previously and I was getting nowhere fast. In the gathering gloom I changed places with Martin and passed him the runners, one number three friend, one number two friend and a number three rock. Standing on the edge of the ledge looking up at forty foot of unknown rock he looked totally unconvinced; unconvinced the rock could be climbed, unconvinced the runners were good and unconvinced that he could see where to put the runners. It was now completely dark. The bleating coming down from above my head would have put many a woolly sentinel to shame. Spasmodic lurches, grunts and curses were the only evidence that the ascent was, if not going well, then at least going up. A tight rope around my waist summoned me upwards and an hour and a half after sunset we let the root of our problems, Chris, ascend the route. Needless to say the new head-torch was lurking in the car boot.

Another atmospheric addition to Malham's left wing was the title track The Well Oiled Machine. Fittingly, after leading one pitch each, Martin and myself were joined on the first ascent by Chris, Mark and of course Streaky Bacon.

P.S. The team has always assumed Graham's title to be a compliment for its efficient activity. It could of course be attributed to the time served by the team at the bar......

A SKI MOUNTAINEERING JUBILEE

A.Harry Griffin

While we are celebrating a century of rock climbing in the Lakes it may be appropriate to notice the golden jubilee of skiing in the area. In January 1986 the Lake District Ski Club modestly celebrated, with a dinner and a club journal — only the second in its history — its fifty years' existence. The inaugural meeting of the club, shortly after New Year's Day, 1936, was really the bringing together of a few small groups of Lake District ski mountaineers to share information about snow conditions and the best areas for the winter exploration of the fells. The occasional skier was seen on the fells in the early 1900's, and early last century the Glenridding miners are said to have descended from their mountain huts in winter time on 'barrel staves'. Presumably, though, this desperate-sounding expedient — did they have closing hours in those days? — was for convenience rather than sport.

As far as I am aware our Club played no official part in the formation of the Lake District Ski Club; 'our healthy relative' as one of our *Journals* put it. The early officers were largely Fell and Rock members; the formation and activities of the new club, especially in ski mountaineering, were reported upon at some length in several of our *Journals*, notably by Edmund Hodge; and our Club was favourably disposed towards the upstart. Some climbers might look down their noses at skiers but not — at least at that time — the Fell and Rock. Perhaps this was partly because our esteemed Leslie Somervell was the first president of the Lake District Ski Club, holding down the job for ten years, while Bentley Beetham, the first vice president, held unbroken office in that rank for 12 years. Rusty Westmorland succeeded Leslie Somervell as president of the ski club and other Fell and Rock members who served as president of the LDSC are Dick Cook, Eric Arnison, Bill Kendrick and the writer. Another Fell and Rock member, Jim Bannister, is the present vice president. John Appleyard was an early vice president, Edmund Hodge an early treasurer and would-be ski guide writer and Phyllis Wormell secretary for some years. Molly Fitzgibbon served in several offices, almost continuously, for nearly 30 years.

The mountaineering flavour these names give to the ski club — and other Fell and Rock members have also been active in the LDSC — is perfectly understandable since, in the early days, piste skiing had not reached Britain, let alone the Lakes, and skiing was largely ski mountaineering; going up and down mountains on skis. To most of the early members of the new club skiing was an enjoyable alternative to ice-axe work in the gullies and skis useful pieces of equipment for exploring the hills in winter. They fitted skis to their nailed boots, wore their ordinary mountain clothes, often carried axes for the steep, icy places and fastened on their skins — originally, sealskins — as soon as they reached the first snow. Even my own first skiing, about forty years ago, was in

the same mould — primitive skis without steel edges fastened on to nailed climbing boots, after first gouging out grooves in the heels to take the elementary bindings, for an ascent and descent of Harter Fell from Longsleddale. The ascent, using skins — naturally, in those days, acquired at the same time as the skis — was straightforward enough but the descent, since I had no idea how to turn, quite disastrous — a succession of falls, all the way down. In retrospect, though, there had at least been the delightful sliding along the easy bit at the top and the dramatic views across winter Lakeland. No doubt, on that distant day in the 1940s, a would-be ski mountaineer, with a very great deal to learn, emerged.

It used to be called ski touring in the early days and a few of us old stagers, more interested in mountains than in careering down the same bit of fellside, time after time — and, also, let it be admitted, no longer athletic enough for icy moguls — still prefer this sort of skiing and seek it out whenever there is general snow cover and we can summon up the necessary energy. For ski mountaineering certainly needs more continuous effort than ordinary piste skiing where as much time, or more, is spent in being whisked effortlessly up the slopes, not counting the time standing in the lift queues. Piste skiing is, or should be, neat and elegant and, in its higher flights, demands considerable technical skill, but these skiers don't need to know anything about mountains or even about the vastly-varied types of snow as the ski mountaineer does. To ski, away from the piste, the Lakeland fells, the Scottish hills, the Alps or any other mountains, competently and with enjoyment, it certainly helps considerably if you are a skilled technical skier, but an average skier with winter mountaineering experience will probably cope just as well. It is far more important, in the mountains, to be able to ski slowly, under complete control, while assessing the changing quality and suitability of the snow, as well as of the weather, than to be capable of fast, elegant descents. Many a mountaineer whose parallels or short swings leave much to be desired has skied the Haute Route.

Living within the Lake District national park and retired, now, for more than ten years, it is comparatively easy for me to seize ski mountaineering possibilities on the fells seen from my windows — or, more likely, others that might have better snow — whenever there is general snow cover or, at least, snow down to, say, 1,000 feet. The winter of 1984/1985 was one of the worst for skiing, any sort of skiing, in the Lake District for many years but, at one time, four months of weekend skiing — even if only shortish drifts high in the fells could be expected and the fells have been skied as early as November and as late as May — and, in 1979, in the middle of June, a few days before Midsummer's Day. But ski mountaineering, needing a fair blanket of snow on the fells, is not normally feasible for anything like as long as ordinary downhill skiing and the opportunities have to be quickly seized as they occur. There are obvious places such as the round of the Dodds, the Helvellyn range, the Skiddaw-Blencathra area, the Fairfield Horseshoe, the High Street fells, the Howgill fells and so on

347   Ski-mountaineering on Hellvellyn.   *R.J.Kenyon*

but sometimes it has been rewarding to get on the skirts of Bowfell around The Band or on the Easdale edges or, better still and potentially best of all, on to Esk Hause and the Scafells. The traverse of the Coniston heights can be good and, occasionally, quite unlikely-seeming places like Blea Rigg or Red Screes have proved enjoyable and even the steep slopes above Helvellyn's Red Tarn have been descended on skis. It was the unusual sight, at that time, of skiers descending from High Raise to Grasmere in long, elegant turns that first inspired me to try the game but I soon found that the slow ascent of any steepish fellside, using skins, working out the best line through different or craggy terrain, can be, as in a fell walk or climb, just as important, and sometimes as interesting, as the descent. Even to climb Caudale Moor from Kirkstone Pass on skis, descending by a different route, is infinitely preferable to an afternoon cavorting down the slopes near the inn, in company with shrieking sledgers and maniacal cagoule glissaders. And a quiet traverse along the Helvellyn ridge, ticking off the tops, is usually more enjoyable than a dozen or so runs down Savage's Drift on Raise — with the help of the tow — in much the same grooves that people have been using for at least 40 years now.

Skiing the tops one is usually either alone or with a chosen companion, seeking out the way in untracked snows; on the piste, you are generally with dozens, even scores, of others, either queuing for the lift or tow or trying to get out of one another's way on the descent. On the tops one can enjoy one's thoughts, the scenery or the intricacies of the route in silence, with, perhaps, the occasional monosyllabic grunt; on the piste you sometimes might just as well be in a fun-fair. I remember once skiing, with a friend, several of the Cairngorm four-thousanders on the most perfect day for powder snow, weather and sunshine I can ever remember enjoying in Britain, seeing nobody else and finishing off with the swoop down the Lurcher's Gully and the traverse across the floor of the corries. As we reclined in the heather on the Fiacaill Ridge after our long round we looked down at the scurrying ants on the White Lady and in Coire Cas, listening to the distant rattle of machinery and the cries of colliding skiers. One of us asked: 'What about a couple of quick runs?' and the other, wisely, replied: 'Too much of an anti-climax. Mustn't spoil a marvellous day. Let's go down for a pint'. And we did, leaving the noisy, crowded snows to the mob.

It should be made clear that I do not write of cross-country skiing with narrow Nordic skis and lightweight boots since I have never tried this. I suspect that this equipment is not the most suitable for the steep or icy places regularly encountered in mountain skiing. Ski mountaineers dress like winter mountaineers — not like the gaily-bedecked whizz-kids you see in the advertisements or the racers on television — and carry rucksacks and, when necessary, ice-axes. Nowadays, my tours are unambitious though still rewarding and memories of earlier, more challenging days, remain. Somehow, you never forget ski mountaineering days, whether in sunshine or in storm. The happy, crowded days of piste skiing in Lakeland, Scotland or the Alps have now all merged together in a hazy, mixed-up picture of sun and sprindrift, good turns and bad ones, superb swoops and ego-dashing falls, whereas I think I can recall, in some detail, all the dozens or scores of ski mountaineering days in their more natural environment, far from the crowds. A fortnight's successful alpine hut-to-hut tour, some wonderful mountain rounds in Scotland and, in Lakeland, a fine circuit of the sunlit Kentmere Horseshoe in superb powder snow, are remembered with particular pleasure.

It has to be confessed, though, that my most recent skiing, with a daughter living in Vancouver, has been on the beautifully-laundered pistes of Cypress Bowl and Mount Whistler in British Columbia and Mount Baker in Washington, USA, where skins — and even rucksacks — seemed unknown, where nobody walked or climbed more than ten yards, and where hired, fancy-looking downhill boots were used instead of my heavy ski mountaineering footgear. It was all so easy — by car on cleared mountain highways to the foot of the lifts and then up and down one run after another on superb, pisted snow, so flattering to one's style that I began to wonder, after all these years, whether perhaps even I could really ski. There were no queues or crowds — we avoided the weekends — the sun blazed down all day and, from the top of the lifts, we looked across at wave after wave of real mountains. At 75 years of age there is now the temptation to settle for this sort of thing — or might be if it was more readily available — but, back home, the sight from my windows of snow-covered High Street, Harter Fell, Red Screes or the Howgills is still alluring and, now and again, and, indeed, as often as possible, I have, forgetting all the effort involved, got out on the tops. The skiing on these untracked snows may not be so neat and elegant as on the pistes — 'rough-neck skiing' is how Rusty Westmorland described it in his 'It's Tough but It's Grand' in our 1948 *Journal* — although I can think of many splendid slopes in our fells that have provided perfect skiing. But, bagging winter summits in this way, you feel you have had a real mountaineering day.

Regrettably, to a would-be ski mountaineer, probably most members of the Lake District Ski Club are downhill fanatics — and some very good at it indeed. But we should commend the club for its energy and enterprise in hut building, tow construction, Scottish and Alpine meets, and, now, ski racing and congratulate them on fifty years of mountain activity and much good fellowship. Skiing, whether on smoothed or untracked snow, is a wonderful outdoor exercise and for myself, as for many members of the Fell and Rock, there is always the recurring problem in winter — whether to climb, walk or ski. Leslie Somervell started off a lot of things when, in the early 1900s, inspired by Nansen's Greenland adventures, he made himself a pair of skis which were still in use by younger members of his family 30 years later. He had the right idea about mountains and skiing, and perhaps in its next half-century more and more members of the club he helped to found — and other skiers as well — will be encouraged to leave the crowded pistes and seek quieter, but even more rewarding, adventures on the heights.

WAY OUT WEST

Tom Price

Though the Lake District has become an important part of the nation's heritage, the pride of the north of England and known throughout the civilised world, the industrial strip in the west — Coronation Street transplanted on to the Cumbrian coast — tends to be passed over and ignored like a poor relation. Traditionally as a community it looked west and north rather than east, but nevertheless it has always had its climbers and devotees of the hills.

When I came to live there after the war, not many people had cars, and so the Sunday bus of the Workington Ramblers was a useful facility for climbers, and offered the added attraction of a rendezvous in the evening at some tea-room or pub, and congenial company on the way home. We used to think that the acquisition of a car would bring about an increase in climbing, but I doubt if it did. When travelling was difficult we were much more inclined to come out for both Saturday and Sunday and stay at a hut, and it was surprising how well one could manage on public transport. The railway line from Workington to Penrith was open at that time. You could on Saturday mornings buy a return ticket to Penrith or Foxfield for two shillings (i.e., ten pence). It was a workman's ticket valid only on the 0630 train but with no restriction on the return journey. For a further half-crown you could take a bicycle along. Using the ticket made a day out into quite an expedition, especially in winter. The stealthy departure from home, the gruff greeting at the station, the sleepy ride to Keswick, and then the eight miles of pedalling to Seathwaite, gave an importance to the occasion which was quite absent when, later, we did the same journey by car. Eight o'clock would generally see us at Edmonson's, where we would treat ourselves to a second breakfast of bacon and eggs before going on to the Napes, or Great End, or even Pikes Crag or Scafell. We generally headed for the higher crags in those days, though the routes we did might be modest enough. On the return journey, waiting for the train, or, worse, hurrying to try and catch it, could make a tiring and chilly end to a long day, but our reward was to return home to an evening of warmth and ease, drugged with fresh air, and the memory of rocks competently scaled.

Climbers in those days were I think less well accepted by the general public then they are now. There was an undercurrent of feeling abroad that the sport had something perverse about it, as though scornful of ordinary human concerns. This may in part explain the incident that took place one evening on Keswick Station. The train drew in and we stood by the guard's van waiting to put our bicycles on board. Two porters were hurling parcels out on to the platform. I was with Jack Carswell, and those who know him will not be surprised that he turned to me and in a flat voice made the remark: 'Handle with care'. The porters gave not the slightest indication of having heard, except that

The Wasdale Head Inn from Great Gable. *Phizacklea Collection* one of them picked up a parcel, examined it elaborately, and said to his companion: 'Can't see owt that says "Handle with care", can you? 'No' said his mate, 'I can't'.

They went on unloading and when they had finished we stepped forward to put in the bikes. The guard was already unfurling his green flag. But one of the porters barred the way. His face showed no expression and his voice was mild and impartial. 'Can't put them on without a label' he said.

I was inclined to expostulate and eat the necessary humble pie, but Jack said 'Hold my bike' and disappeared at a full run into the booking hall. Within seconds he re-appeared with two scraps of a discarded cigarette packet. 'Pencil' he rapped. I hadn't one. Charging back into the booking hall he borrowed one from the clerk and scribbled Workington on the bits of paper. We stuck them on the saddles with spit and presented the bikes again. They were accepted and we caught the train. It was one of those fortunate outcomes where both parties feel they have won.

Occasionally we took the Foxfield option on our workmen's tickets. From Foxfield we would cycle up to Coniston, leave the bikes in the village and climb all day on Dow. This gave a long but inspiring day. On one such occasion, heading for the last train at the end of a summer's day on which we'd climbed several classic routes, Jack Carswell lost a pedal from his bicycle, and his only recourse was to keep on trying to kick the crank round until the other pedal came into position for downward pressure. His riding was erratic but we made progress. Unfortunately his corduroy plus-fours kept catching and tearing in the machinery and on arrival at the station looked more like a divided skirt. But we caught the last train.

One of our ways to climb on Gimmer was to go by bus to Borrowdale and walk over from Stonethwaite. Gimmer took on a new and more impressive appearance when one started climbing from the top. Setting off down A or B Route made an alarmingly abrupt transition from fell-walking to climbing.

Buttermere and Ennerdale, however, were our nearest climbing areas, and attainable by bicycle. Following Bill Peascod's development of the climbing there, Buttermere was probably our most frequented valley. The roadside cottage at the foot of Fleetwith Pike was then occupied by Miss Nelson, who would serve teas with home-made scones. Her front room became the rendezvous for many a cheerful gathering of damp and pungent climbers, their patched knees stained with moss and their fingernails black with dirt and lichen. Miss Nelson spoke with a high-pitched fluting daleswoman's voice, and gave a warm welcome to climbers. She kept hens and her life was an endless battle of wits against the foxes, which, nevertheless, she was fond of. She reared several fox cubs at different times, and they were free to depart into the fells when they felt the call to do so. Her charges for tea and scones revealed a disdain of trade.

Another meeting place was the Travellers' Rest inn in Workington, where, on Tuesday evenings, we got into the habit of foregathering. On Monday we would still be licking our wounds or coping with the shock of returning to work, but Tuesday was the evening for reliving the exploits of the weekend and for planning the next. It was a pleasant and informal arrangement and could well have gone on for years. But alas for mutability someone one evening made the remark: 'You know, we've become a sort of a club' and from that moment on the conversation moved away from climbing talk and centred tediously on the formation of a club. Though our climbing was modest enough we felt proud of our status as rock-climbers, and we envisaged a club wholly devoted to rock-climbing and not to be infiltrated by fell-walkers. We proposed a continuing membership qualification like that of the Groupe de Haute Montagne. Anyone failing to attain an annual quota of climbs — on a points system taking account of difficulty — automatically reliquished membership. We would call ourselves the West Cumberland Rock-climbing Club.

There was no debate as to who should be the first president. It was Bill Peascod. A treasurer was found without too much arm-twisting: George Rushworth. But the secretary, the man who was to do all the work, took several meetings to determine. A sustained effort to get S.B.Beck to do it failed in spite of a wealth of blandishment and flattery. In the end Ronnie Wilkinson, a reporter on the local paper, and a warm, companionable man who could recite the poem 'I have been faithful to thee, Cynara, in my fashion' in its entirety, allowed his good nature to get the better of him and consented to do it.

The founder members paid a first subscription. Headed writing paper was ordered. The club was set fair to make its contribution to climbing history, and it began with a grand inaugural dinner at the Fish in Buttermere, to which all the flower of Lakeland climbing was invited.

The dinner was an immense and unqualified success. The notion that social events go best late at night in the winter season is quite mistaken. Conviviality smiled upon by a summer sun has a special warmth and luxury. It was a lovely June weekend and we stood in a long line outside the inn, glasses in hand, for a group photograph. Speeches were made after dinner forecasting a distinguished future for the club. The President, in his, kept finding his way round to the same lines time after time, repeating them word for word, but this spoiled no-one's pleasure and he was warmly applauded. It was one of those occasions which show how gregarious a sport climbing is in spite of its claims to individualism. At the end we walked through the balmy and night-scented dark to Gatesgarth, where we slept in the barn.

The interesting thing is that that inaugural dinner proved to be the one and only function of the West Cumberland Rock-climbing Club. It was as though the dinner's great success consumed the club like a fire, blazing with such splendour as to leave nothing behind. Or almost nothing, for somewhere, I imagine, there may be a forgotten stack of headed writing paper, and in some bank or building society, perhaps, a small stagnant pool of club funds.

But of course climbing went on exactly as before, and though in quantity and severity it was of little account compared with what is done today, it filled our imagination just as much and called for the same concentration and commitment. On the day after the dinner, Bert Beck and I walked over to Pillar, climbing up the North West, down the West Wall, up the South West, and down the New West. Down-climbing was considerably in vogue among those of us who pursued the ideal of competent cragsmanship. At one stage we sought to climb down as many routes as we climbed up. In the days of comparatively little dependence on rope technique this led to a useful increase in mobility on the rocks and made retreat a more acceptable option. 'Going for it' was really against our climbing philosophy, and when as sometimes happened we took a chance and got away with it, I for one would be troubled in conscience by it and brood about it in the night with superstitious dread. I remember climbing one day on Pillar in bad weather. We were descending the west side of the Rock in the rain, and the West Face of Low Man, that unfriendly and slightly concave crag rising out of a steep gully, gleamed wetly through the murk, its top lost in mist. Strung out towards the top were five climbers, with Joe Williams from Whitehaven in the lead. They were on the West Wall Climb which has a difficult exit on the last pitch. Joe, within a few feet of easy ground, decided to come down. His calm and methodical retreat, with such a large party, in ever-worsening conditions, commanded our admiration, as did his decision not to 'go for it' on that last move.

Long ropes of climbers were more common in those days. It maximised the leader's contribution. Once I was at the end of such a 'caravane' in an ascent of Stack Ghyll, and had time, while the leader was fighting it out ahead, to brew tea half way up, using water from the back of the Ghyll. But most of my climbing was in a leading-through partnership with Jack Carswell which lasted several years. We were so used to each other's climbing that we seldom needed to communicate by word of mouth and we were embarrassed by people who shouted to each other on crags.

We climbed quite often in bad weather and since the current wisdom was against impermeable fabrics for climbing we got wet. I remember one occasion when Bert Beck and I, at the end of a dry spell, were just approaching the top of C Gully on the Screes when the weather broke. We finished in pouring rain, and, already so wet it did not matter, drove up Wasdale in Bert's open tourer with the hood off, knowing that the comforts of Brackenclose were to hand. The rain settled in in earnest, and with the satisfaction of C Gully snatched in the nick of time we were quite resigned to the prospect of spending the rest of the weekend in the simple enjoyment of being under a sound roof with a good fire. But on Sunday morning the only other occupant of the hut asked us if we could recommend a suitable solo rock-climb for the day. Our advice was to read a climbing book in front of the fire, but in spite of the fierce spattering of rain on the windows he seemed determined to go out. Conscience smote us. After all he had come all the way from London for this weekend. We offered to go with him, chose Upper West Wall Climb on Scafell, and put on plenty of clothes. It was I believe the wettest climb I had ever done, and it was hard work dragging all that sodden clothing upwards. When we got to the top we just had enough left in us to be able to raise a grin and turn to our friend with the question: 'What shall we do next, then?' But he had had enough too. When we stripped off our wet clothes in the hall at Brackenclose I found a small round spot, about the size of a ten pence piece, on the front of my innermost vest, that was still dry. It made me very careful in the use of such terms as 'wet through' and 'saturated'.

Another West Cumbrian I climbed with was Frank Monkhouse. Whereas Jack Carswell's approach to climbing was one of sober judgment, Frank went in more for audacity. One winter's day we went to Dow. The crag was well plastered with snow and ice but it was not freezing. We started up Woodhouse's Route on B buttress. There was a slanting icy chimney up which I struggled to a bay. Frank followed. The next pitch, a crack in a corner, was deeply buried under a vast festoon of icicles which hung down like a candelabrum: our way was barred. 'What about this slab up here?' I asked. 'That leads to Giant Grim on Eliminate B' said Frank. 'But', he added brightly, 'there is Abraham's on B! The only difficulty is moving round that corner on to a roof. After that it's straightforward.' A preliminary look at the hard move and I came back down and took off my boots. I returned to the corner, spent some time scratching the snow out of the holds, and swung up and round on to a new and inimical aspect of the crag. I was now on my own, out of sight of Frank, on the bottom edge of a steeply inclined roof that rose above me for thirty or forty feet. Round my waist, tied in a bowline, was my Kenyon three-quarter-weight manila line, not a rope one could put much faith in. Through the waist loop was stuck my long ice axe, ready to gore me in the event of a fall. I stood there in my socks, unable to believe my ill-fortune. My chief enemy became a creeping paralysis of the will. The line from Henry V: 'Would I were up to the neck in Thames, or anywhere but here' kept running through my head, hindering my efforts to face up to the task in hand. Meanwhile my toes and fingers were getting colder. I made one move by hooking the pick of my axe over a little hold. Gradually I goaded myself upward. Every new perch I reached, comfortless though it was, seemed preferable to moving on, so I fought inertia all the way. I was also wooed by spurious ways sideways off the slab. Every hold had to be cleared of snow, and I found nowhere to place a runner. My last move was a kind of mantelshelf. Supported on the heel of one hand I groped above my head with the other, and found the jug handle that represented the end of the ordeal. I remained motionless for some time before I finally made use of it and hauled myself into safety. Frank came up Giant Grim using the rope, and helped me on with my boots.

Nylon ropes were available but hemp and manila were still much in use. Vibrams had not fully taken over from nails. As late as 1953 I climbed Kern Knotts Crack in tricounis. There was a shoemaker at Grange in Borrowdale who made me a pair of boots nailed with Ortler clinkers, and after that I switched wholly to vibrams. It was not easy to get stiff-soled boots and a Whitehaven climber, I forget who, had a pair of clogs planed flat and fitted with Vibram soles. This gave a rigid sole plus a pointed toe and was a precursor of the modern rock-boot.

Nails came into their own in winter climbing, crampons being unheard of except for the Alps. Long bouts of step-cutting could turn a simple gully into a worthy expedition. I remember one such ascent when except at the top there was nothing but water-ice in Central Gully Great End and we had to cut steps all the way. On the main pitch a big ice-bulge produced an overhang. By standing on Jack Carswell's shoulder I was able to cut hand and foot holds and overcome the bulge. Ahead now lay a cataract of transparent ice, up which I kept cutting, desperate for a runner. I'd taken every inch of rope out by the time I reached a belay. For Jack there was no rope left for manoeuvre, and I wasn't for descending. Darkness was only an hour or so away. With the rope twanging taut between us we were at a stand-still. Providentially at this moment another party appeared from below. As they cast a jaundiced eye on the options Jack said, in a matter-of-fact way that precluded refusal: 'Just stand here a second and give me a shoulder' and the next moment he was on his way, and we reached the top at dusk. We often wondered how the other two got on.

And so, weekend after weekend, we made our small pilgrimages out of the west, returning homeward again with the evening sun in our eyes. In this way the Lake District retained its magical quality, and our concept of the picturesque remained unimpaired by too much familiarity. We went home to the ordinary world which began at about Frizington or Cleator Moor or the top of Fangs Brow, and in parts so resembled L.S.Lowry's Salford that he occasionally painted there. Where we picked up this clear awareness of where the mundane ended and the picturesque began I cannot think, but it was in our consciousness like a fundamental truth. They were good days in West Cumberland. One remembers fondly many names like Jack Carswell, Bill Peascod, Bert Beck, Ronnie Wilkinson, Stan Dirkin, the brothers Banner-Mendus, Brian Blake, Austin Barton, George Rushworth, the Monkhouses, Jim Joyce, and young fellows like Don Greenop and Eric Ivison; and one forgets many more. One looks back and wonders what it was all for, all that passionate interest and energy, and where it sprang from. Just as one wonders why one still keeps responding to the siren song, even when one is old enough to know better. Perhaps it has something to do with that warm golden light that floods Scafell Crag on about one summer evening in a hundred.

THE DAY I BROKE THE NEEDLE

Stan Thompson

In summer 1941, as a young climber active in the Lakes prior to going into the R.A.F., I saw a good deal of George Basterfield, particularly on Gable, where I often climbed with the few active climbers who were not yet doing war service. George expressed great concern about the stability of three large blocks perched on the arête of the Needle, just below the Shoulder. (These can be seen on older photographs.)

After some discussion and examination of the blocks, from which climbers frequently abseiled despite their instability, George decided that they should be 'removed'! Our help was enlisted, as we operated from Wasdale Head each weekend and could get to the crag at a time when no-one was around and perhaps push the blocks off without danger to other climbers, walkers etc. — apart from a few of Joe Naylor's sheep! We set off one morning at 5am and climbed up to the Shoulder by about 7am. It was the day that Germany and Russia declared war, so it is clear in my memory: a bright summer day with no-one around. Removing the blocks was easy. They were supported by a slender finger of rock, separated from the main rock of the arête. (It was around this finger that people threaded abseil ropes.) This flimsy support was easily knocked out, and the three blocks, each about 2-3' cube, were very delicately balanced. It only required one shove with my foot from above to send them off into space with dramatic effect! One landed in Needle Gully and is still there, one went across Gable Traverse, and the largest one bounded down the scree almost as far as the Styhead path — Mr. Naylor swore that he heard the crash of these descending stones in Wasdale Head! The Needle was altered in shape quite considerably and we were well aware that, in a sense, we had modified the FRCC emblem and all the badges etc. were now inaccurate. It was said that, for some time afterwards, if one went into Abraham's shop in Keswick to buy a postcard of the Needle, the assistant would get an eraser out of his pocket and carefully rub out the blocks before selling the postcard — the Abrahams were all for moving with the time despite being a bit ancient in their shop-front display.

Subsequently I got rather a strong note from the Club Secretary of the time — I think it was Mary Leighton — saying that I had exceeded my responsibilities (as a very new member) by altering the shape of the Club emblem without permission! However, it was accepted that the blocks were very unsafe and that we had been acting on the instructions of a most venerable and famous member in doing what George had suggested. I think we were forgiven? I hope so!! It was a memorable day for me (and for the world) and I always think of it when I climb the Needle and move up to the arête where the blocks used to be. I was one of those who really 'broke the Needle'!

SCOTLAND

The Fell and Rock members come in their droves
To walk on the hills and the ridges,
They come to 'Knock Off' a few more Munros,
They're never bitten by midges.

Their tales of achievement defy repetition,
Brave exploits on crampon and ski,
They tell of the views that defy definition
Everyone's seen them, but me.

They Love Scotland.

I trudge up the mountains muddy and tired,
By peat bog and slippery heather,
The mist shrouds the peaks but undaunted we stride,
And pray for a break in the weather.

The boots before me are boots that I know,
The wet rock's the same as before,
The rain that beats down has just turned to snow,
And we slither and slide and are sore.

'This one's a beauty, the view from the crown
Is the best that you ever did see,'
But when we arrive the fog has come down
And the top is no place to be.

I Hate Scotland.

And then in the evening over their malt
They'll tell you how good was the day;
The campsite is boggy, the midges all bite
And the pub is a long way away.

They plan for tomorrow, Oh No not again!
What fun it all is they agree....
    Except Me!

PAA.

Page 188: Winter ascent of Jones's Route Direct, Scafell. Grade VI ice.

Phizacklea Collection

Page 189: The first winter ascent of Mayday Direct, Scafell. Grade V ice.

Phizacklea Collection

THE YEAR WITH THE CLUB: 1985

Jim Sutcliffe

I suppose that, when the Editor decided to resurrect this resume of club activities, he chose the Chronicler because I should have a fairly close knowledge of the Meet Reports. At any rate, I have at least read them all.

So, this article will be a short account of other people's reports.

The New Year Meet brought change, yet returned to tradition in revisiting the Old Dungeon Ghyll Hotel. It was very much Harry Ironfield's idea and it must have been enjoyable, as it was decided to hold it again there this year.

In mid-January, Andrew Paul led a meet at Beetham Cottage which seems to have been mainly memorable for the excellent weather on the Saturday and the foul weather on the Sunday. Most people went home early, but Andrew was dragged out into Ruthwaite Cove where they found very good ice, thus justifying the long, wet walk.

I remember the Salving House Meet at the end of that month because of the amazing thaw which took place during Satuday night. As Ron Kenyon, the Meet Leader, said in his report: '....where had the snow gone? Looking down the valley the scene was of green grass and bracken.' That day, in South East Gully on Great End, both Peter Moffat and Malcolm Kate were hit on the head by falling ice. Malcolm needed five stitches!

47 members and guests attended the Meet in early February at Raw Head, led by Ray Moss. Although there was little snow, water ice in the ghylls provided 'impressive displays' for the walking parties.

The Salving House Meet in early March was led by only one of the two Leaders, Joan and Ruth Moffat. Ruth really showed maturity beyond her years when she exercised 'sound mountaineering judgement' in pouring rain on the Sunday. She packed up and left in the early afternoon.

The weather up at Black Rock Cottage does not sound to have been much better on the Saturday, but they had a good day on Sunday. Tim Pickles reports that temperatures were 'into the double figures — above zero!'

Syd Clark led the Ben Nevis Meet at the end of March and had fairly good conditions and some good routes were climbed.

The Ski Meet at Meribel was a great success. This was the first time such a meet had been held. It was largely Harry Ironfield's idea and was led by him and Brian Cosby. The weather was good and the only dark cloud was due to John Wild being hit by a 'piste-bomber' out of control, a misfortune I know only too well since I was hit by one at about he same time on the La Plagne system.

The Easter Meet was once again held at Brackenclose and met the fate of so many meets that year — poor weather. Ken and Pat Andrews, the Meet Leaders, claim that the sunburn on the faces of members returning from the Ski Meet went unnoticed due to the poor lighting conditions.

June Parker reported much better weather on the Saturday of the Birkness Meet in the middle of April. The day was excellent for both walking and climbing, with 'warm, sunny spells between snow showers.' But the Sunday followed the more usual pattern and the Fish became a strategic target for many.

The North Wales joint C.C. Meet at Ynys Ettws, led by Brian Swales, also did not fare very well with the weather. Some climbing was done on the Saturday and some of the ladies went out on what Brian describes as 'talking parties.' Thereafter the Padarn and the Moon feature prominently in his report.

One remarkable exception to the weather pattern was experienced by Margaret and John Wild at the Torridon Meet at the beginning of May. Munro fever seems to have taken hold but I am glad to report that some climbing was also done.

At the end of that month the weather returned to the 1985 norm for the joint Meet with the M.A.M. at Brackenclose. The problem seems to have been that fine weather would entice people out in the mornings only to let them down later. Several ascents of Tophet Wall were made in wet conditions and many people enjoyed some very soggy walks. At least Jill Evans and Norma Precious, who led the S. Cairngorms Meet at about the same time, started with 'storms and rushing torrents and ended with hot sunshine'.

George Lamb, leading his maintenance meet at Birkness early in June, made a remarkable contribution to medical science by his report on the local phenomenon of 'Jennings Fever.' The source of the infection seems to be The Fish!

Although the Coniston Meet, at the beginning of July, led by Frank Alcock and Ron Brotherton, fared much better for weather, at the end of the month Chris and Ron Lyon seemed to have been met by floods of almost biblical proportions.

The Beetham Cottage Meet early in August led by Roy Summerling was lucky in striking one decent day — the Saturday — and the majority of people enjoyed an excellent walk across most of the hills around High Street. Stan Roberts and Colin Shone found normal 1985 conditions at the end of August for the North Wales Camping Meet. The only dry places on the Sunday sound to have been either the underground slate mines or the girdle of Carreg Hyll Drem. The weather did pick up for the Monday and everyone was out climbing or walking.

After two damp meets in September at Raw Head, the early one led by Geoff Cram and the later one David Rhodes' Maintenance Meet, it was a change to read reports of good weather and good climbing from the Derbyshire Meet, led by Roy Precious and Roy Townsend, and the Northumberland Meet led by David Rhodes. The answer seems to be to avoid the mountains!

The London Section enjoyed favourable weather on the Saturday at their meet in October at Salving House led by Eric Finch, but the Sunday was back to normal.

363 Members at the Salving House Meet, January 1986. *Ron Kenyon*

Amazingly, the weather was excellent for the Dinner weekend. At the dinner, David Roberts gave his first formal address to the Club as President. In it he looked with optimism to the future of the club. Chris Bonington replied for the guests, as he had only recently been accorded honorary membership.

The last report to appear in the last Chronicle was for the Brackenclose Meet, led by Eric Ivison early in November when 'heavy rain and gale-force winds, starting in the early evening, resulted in postponement of the traditional bonfire to the Sunday Night.' I have received another report from Richard Morgan for the Birkness Meet early in December which seems to have suffered the same fate as so many of the earlier meets as far as the Saturday went, but the next day 'the clouds lifted to reveal a sharp and clear winter day'.

I hope that this indicated a change in the pattern for 1986.

365 Ullswater.   *Ron Kenyon*

NEW CLIMBS AND NOTES

Alan Murray & Phil Rigby

New route activity in the Lake District during 1985 has marched on despite one of the wettest summers for many years. The steady downpour didn't curtail all activity though, and a remarkable number of new routes have emerged from the gloom despite the so called "drying up" of Lakes rock.

Following the trend of recent years development has centred on the many outcrop-style crags that have been unearthed by budding gardeners. Many of these crags can now boast excellent one-pitch routes covering all grades.

In Borrowdale Colin Downer and Andy Hall developed Hanging Stone Crag, above Seathwaite, while guide book research by Dave Armstrong resulted in the discovery of the futuristic Lower Knitting How. At the other end of the valley C.Thwaites and R.Curley braved the unstable roof of Lamplighter on Lower Falcon, and the Jaws of Borrowdale exhumed acres of rock in his quest for yet another Borrowdale classic for the new guide.

Across in Langdale Bill Birkett wire-brushed the remote Crinkle Gill into the limelight to produce some worthwhile climbs. In Eskdale the popular Burnt Crag had some obvious gaps filled, and the scattered buttresses of Gate Crag saw eight new additions, mainly the work of D.Hall and D.Hinton.

Over in the Eastern Fells, Raven, Threshthwaite and Thrang Crags came under much scrutiny from Bob Smith and John Earl, producing some good routes, while at Raven, Thirlmere, Scottish raider Dougie Dinwoodie snatched some very obvious lines from under the local's noses.

The main sources of information have been the new routes books spread around the area. Our thanks go to their custodians for their continued co-operation, and to Dave Armstrong and Ron Kenyon for help with the Borrowdale section.

Most routes remain unchecked and the usual caution should be exercised.

BORROWDALE

LOWER FALCON CRAG (273205)

Breaking in Space. 40ft. E5.

Belays at the junction of Lamplighter and Illusion and climbs the overhang just left of the finish to Lamplighter Eliminate.

6b. Gain the short groove in the overhang from the right using large unstable holds and climb it exiting right to better holds. Two peg runners and fixed sling. C.Thwaites, R.Curley 1985.

CAFFELL SIDE CRAG (268176)

Hairy Mary. 80ft. E2.

5c. Follow Everhard to a hollow flake, continue directly up the wall to rejoin Everhard at a small tree after 120ft. Finish directly up the wall above. D.McDonald, M.Moran. 2/6/85.

Street Walker. 70ft. E2.

Climbs the shattered wall, just right of the vegetated gully in the centre of the crag.

(5c). Climb a groove until a step left can be made onto the arête. Up this and the left wall; then back into the top of the groove. Surmount the overhang and continue up the steep wall until a mantelshelf move leads to easier climbing to the top. D.David, J.Waters. 8/6/85.

BROWN DODD, WATENDLATH (265178)

This is the last crag on the west side of Watendlath Valley overlooking Derwentwater.

Bird Brain. 110ft. E1.

Climbs the pillar and loose overhanging headwall at the right end of the crag. Start behind a silver birch on a ledge up and right of the start of The Buzzard.

(5b). Step left and climb a groove to the left side of a tree, containing a large nest, below the headwall. Climb this, moving first left then right, to a block overhang above the tree. Straight up to the top. Belay 30 feet back.

R.Cassidy, R.Gerrish. 18/5/85.

Bird's Nest Buttress. 110ft. E1.

A companion to Bird Brain; also loose at the top. Start as for Bird Brain.

(5b). Climb straight up the front of the pillar to the right side of the tree. Climb the headwall, moving left above the tree, to a block overhang. Straight up to the top, as for Bird Brain. Belay 30ft. back.

R.Gerrish, R.Cassidy. 18/5/85.

There is another route on the North-east side, on the slabby wall, roughly facing Reecastle Crag.

Anyone For Tennis. 100ft. E1.

Start from an obvious rock step below a steep reddish groove with a prominent "bite" out of the left arête.

5b. Climb the groove via two suspect blocks, exit right onto ledges. Move up to a crack which leads to a bulge. Climb the bulge and groove above, then move left to finish at the highest point of the wall. Belay well back.

R.Cassidy. 4/6/85.

NATIONAL TRUST CRAGS (269195)

Spider Wall. 50ft. V.S.

Start just left of Spider Man in the descent gully.

4c. Climb the wall on excellent holds.

R.Kenyon. July 1985.

One In Six. 100ft. E1.

Starts on the ledge to the left of Naked Edge, below a big groove.

5b. Climb the groove then step left under the overhang into a hanging groove. Continue up this to a large ledge. Climb the fault line to the right of a tree. Step back left and finish up the wide groove.

R.McHaffie, P.Hirst. 8/6/85.

The Naked Edge. 100ft. E2.

Climbs the arête of Catgill Grooves. Start on the large sloping platform. Block belay.

5b. From the right hand end of the large block, pull up onto a sloping ledge and move left onto the arete. Climb the overhang strenuously to a resting place 25ft above and leftwards. Move back right onto the arête and climb directly to the top and tree belay.

P.Hirst, R.McHaffie. 7/5/85.

Vicissitude Regained. 70ft. V.S.

Climb the obvious groove to the overhang. Continue up the overhanging crack to a tree belay.

P.Hirst, R.McHaffie, G.Spensley. 17/11/85.

Ivor the Boneless. 75ft. V.S.

Start as for Vicissitude at the lowest point of the crag.

4c. Ascend the clean ramp up the right edge to tree roots below an overlapping wall. Pull over both overlaps on good holds to a steep 'slab'. Follow the arête to the top. Tree belays.

P.Hirst, R.McHaffie, M.Trickett. 26/10/85.

Bloodaxe. 70ft. H.S.

Start 10ft. left of Wild Boys on top of a shattered pillar with a tree.

Climb the wall to a perched block. Move leftwards into the groove. Follow this to the top and tree belay.

P.Hirst, R.McHaffie. 26/10/85.

Tina Turner. 70ft. M.S.

Start at the obvious clean slab to the left of Cat Ghyll Grooves.

Climb the corner of the slab to the top. Pull up onto the rib. Move left into the groove, then up to a tree belay.

R.McHaffie. 23/11/85.

Bat Out Of Hell. 50ft. E1.

The climb starts 20ft. right of the Wild Boys, across the wide gully.

5c. Up the steep smooth wall to a good hold under a bulge. Swing up left then follow the crackline to the top.

R.McHaffie, P.Hirst. May 1985.

I Need A Hero. 50ft. E1.

Start from the top of a split boulder.

5b. Climb the leftward slanting crack on side pulls to a bulge. Make an awkward move left, pull onto the wall above. Move right into the groove, then past a tree to the top. Tree belay.

R.McHaffie, P.Hirst. 26/10/85.

SHEPHERD'S CRAG

Wild Side. 40ft. E3.

Starts as for Black Sheep.

5c. Climb the initial moves of Black Sheep until a rising traverse leftward past an in situ peg runner gains the finishing groove of Thin Air.

J. Dunne. 1985.

CRAG BEHIND BORROWDALE HOTEL

Fight With A Beech Tree. 55ft. H.V.S.

Climbs the groove in the second bay. Start behind the central oak tree.

5a. Go up the groove trending slightly left to the top then move right to a small beech tree. Move through this and up the overhang on the right to a mossy slab.

T.J.Robinson, S.Banks. 24/6/85.

GRANGE CRAGS (258117)

Forty yards left of Veterans Buttress at a slightly higher level is another even smaller buttress.

Dihedral Wall. 60ft. H.V.S.

Starts at a shattered crack at the left side of the buttress.

(5a). Climb the crack onto a pinnacle. Step up and traverse the ramp, rightwards, below the top bulge and finish up the arête on the right.

S.Millar, R.Allen. 19/6/85.

The Shield. 50ft. E1.

Starts 10ft. right of Dihedral Wall.

(5b). Climb the wall direct to the ramp of Dihedral Wall. Pull round the bulge above, leftwards, to finish on good holds.

S.Millar, T. Stephenson. 3/7/85.

The Nose. 40ft. H.V.S.

Start just right of the arête.

(5a). Up left to gain the arête and follow it to the top. Alternatively the arête can be gained from the left-hand side (5c).

S.Millar, R.Allen. 18/6/85.

North America Wall. 35ft. E1.

The wall just right of The Nose.

(5b). Follow the crack for a few feet to a good runner. Swing left onto the wall and climb it direct to the top.

S.Millar, R.Allen. 19/6/85.

QUAYFOOT BUTTRESS

The In Between. 60ft. E1.

Climbs the righthand side of the arête of Loitering With Intent, starting at the tree belay of the Crypt, second pitch.

5c. Follow The Crypt to a good hold on the right, then step down and left to the arête. Pull over a small overlap to a hold above. Continue directly up the rib.

C.Downer, C.Bacon. 30/7/85.

WODEN'S FACE

Loki. 60ft. V.S.

Starts 15ft. right of Woden's Cheek in a small bay.

4c. Ascend a broken corner to a flake/pinnacle, move slightly left and climb the open groove and obvious crack line above.

F. and R.Southell, T.Thompson. 11/9/84.

LONG BAND CRAG (282126)

The Sadist. 100ft. E2.

Climbs the lichenous slabby wall right of The Professional. Start 20ft. to its right at a pointed block.

5c. Climb a shallow groove to gain a slab, then traverse delicately left up a ramp to gain the groove of The Professional. Up this, then follow the rightward slanting crack (where The Professional traverses left) to the top.

R.Wightman, K.Long, A.Phizacklea. 26/10/85.

EAGLE CRAG (277122)

Animotion. 150ft. E2.

Climbs the wall between Daedalus and The Cleft Direct. Start as for Daedalus.

1. 40ft. (5a). Up to below the chimney, then rightwards to a large ledge.

2. 60ft. (5c). Step down left onto the wall, and climb it on good holds and pull out left onto a slab. Move back right to gain a small ledge on The Cleft Direct; continue straight up to easier ground, then right to belay as for Daedalus.

3. 50ft. (5a). Pitch 3 of Daedalus.

C.Downer, D.Scott, A.Hall. 13/6/85.

BLEAK HOW CRAG (274122)

Pop Goes the Asteroid. 100ft. E2.

Start just right of Brush Off.

(5c). Climb directly up the slab, over two tiny overlaps, to better holds. Move right and up, passing the right end of a vegetated ledge, to finish as for Footloose.

C.Dale (solo). April 1985.

Seconds Out. 100ft. H.V.S.

Start 5 feet right of Brush Off at a thin crack.

(5a). Climb the crack to an overlap, step left and pull over on good holds. Climb more easily, (trying to keep left of Footloose), towards the vegetated ledge above. Pass the right end of this and finish as for Footloose.

C.Downer (solo). 29/5/85.

The Boj Eliminate. E2.

Climbs the area between Bleak How Buttress and the Reiver. Start to the left of Bleak How Buttress, behind some trees.

5b. Climb a corner and wide crack to a spike runner at the lefthand side of the slab of Bleak How Buttress. Climb the groove then move right to a slab and up to a steep wall. (A high side runner was placed by traversing into Bleak How Buttress). Continue up the wall to a good hold, move up and rightwards into the final groove of The Reiver. Move back left into another groove and up this moving right to finish.

S.Reid and L.Steer. 20/6/85.

RAVEN CRAG, COMBE GHYLL (248114)

Crystal Slabs. 140ft. M.V.S.

Starts slightly left of Slab Route.

Climb up a 'spikey' groove, then up a shallow scoop to a light-coloured slab below a wall. Step up and right then traverse left to a good hold. Continue directly up on easier ground.

P.Hirst, E.Hirst. 1/6/85.

Birds of Prey. 220ft. E1.

Start at a leftward-facing groove 10ft. left of Savage Amusement.

1. 100ft. Climb the leftward-facing groove and clean slabs above. Nut belays under overhang.

2. 120ft. 5b. From the belay move left into a left-facing corner, swing out right onto a sloping ledge. Climb the overhang with difficulty, then follow the crack to a slab, and then the top. Nut belays.

R.McHaffie, P.Hirst. 31/5/85.

Classic Rock. 250ft. E2.

The climb starts below the slender gangway of Pendulum.

1. 100ft. 4c. Follow the groove until forced onto the left wall, then back right to the corner. Climb up to a ledge, then up the right-hand wall on doubtful flakes, traverse right 10ft. to a stance and belay.

2. 150ft. 5c. Traverse back into the corner and continue until stopped by the overhang. Move leftwards on undercuts to an open groove. Step left into bottom of groove, move up and enter chimney with difficulty. Ascend the chimney, step left then up to a resting place. Step right and continue up the groove with difficulty to the top. Belay to left of light-coloured square-cut corner.

R.McHaffie, P.Hirst (alts). 11/5/85.

Savage Amusement. 220ft. E2/3.

Climbs the obvious continuation of Classic Rock where that route escapes left.

1. 100ft. 4c. Pitch 1 of Classic Rock.
2. 120ft. 5c. From the belay climb easily to below the overhanging corner, bridge up to a good handhold on the left wall. Attain a standing position on the handhold and precariously bridge or lay back onto the ledge on the right. Follow the crack above moving leftwards after the bulge to below a crack which is followed to a large ledge. Possible belay or continue to top.
C.Downer, P.Hirst. 30/6/85.

THORNYTHWAITE KNOTS, COMBE GHYLL

No More Heroes. 120ft. H.V.S.
Starts 20ft. left of Red Shift at an obvious deep groove.
1. 80ft. 4c. Climb the slab in the corner (with an overhanging back wall) to the bulge. Move round the bulge into a groove. Continue up this to a stance. Nut belays.
2. 40ft. 5a. The overhang groove leads to some slabs.
R.McHaffie, P.Hirst (alt. leads). 10/7/85.

Red Shift. 130ft. E3.
From the lowest point of the crag, behind two rowan trees. A holly tree grows 20ft. above these.
5c. Climb the corner for 30ft. above these. Step right and up the corner above until below the obvious steep groove (the pod). Climb the groove (crux), exit left, then continue directly to the top.
P. Hirst, R.McHaffie. 3/7/85.

Phantom of the Opera. 100ft. V.S.
Starts at the right-hand end of the crag.
4c. Climb the left-facing groove in the arête. Move right at the top onto a gangway. Flake belay.
R.McHaffie. 24/11/85.

HANGING STONE (228120)

This is the buttress overlooking Seathwaite Farm on the northern ridge of Base Brown.

Puritan. 60ft. H.V.S.
Start 20ft. right of the tree-filled gully on the left of the crag at an obvious break in the overhang above a small sapling.
(5a). Pull through the break to a 'sawn-off tree stump'! Step left, and over a small bulge onto a slab. Move back right; then straight up to finish just left of a large perched block.
C.Downer, J.White. 6/5/85.

Shake Down. 60ft. H.V.S.
Start as for Puritan.
(5a). Pull through the break and move rightwards to below a chimney/groove. Up this to finish over two large perched blocks at the top. Care!
C.Downer, J.White. 6/5/85.

Loose Connections. 80ft. H.V.S.
Start 20ft. right of Shake Down below a loose corner above the overhangs. Care needed with rock.
(5a). Pull over the overhang and continue up the corner into a flake crack. Follow this, steeply, to a grass ledge. From this, step across the wall on the right and up a short crack to finish.
C.Downer, A. Hall. 9/5/85.

Joker Man. 80ft. E1.

Good climbing up the obvious rightward-slanting slabby groove. Start as for Loose Connections.

(5b). Pull over the overhang, keeping out of the corner. Move rightwards on sloping holds which lead into the groove. Follow this to a steep finish.

C.Downer, A.Hall. 7/5/85.

Skimmerhorne. 80ft. E2.

A very pleasant route which attempts to climb the obvious knife-edge arête on the right of the crag. Start from an embedded rock below the arête.

(5c). Using holds on the right wall, pull up and round onto the left wall. Traverse left on small holds, then pull round onto the slab. Trend up rightwards to good holds on the arête; stand on these, then up to another good hold on the arête. Finish up a short layback crack behind a flake.

C.Downer, A.Hall. 9/5/85.

Stan the Man. 60ft. V.S.

The corner at the right-hand end of the crag.

(4c). Climb the corner direct, exiting left at the top.

A. Hall, C.Downer. 7/5/85.

STEEL KNOTTS (247164)

Ambling Ant. 80ft. M.V.S.

Start right of Route One.

Climb the obvious corner crack. Move up left to a ledge. Finish up the wall above.

R.Kenyon, T.Price, L.Jordan. 20/10/85.

GOAT CRAG-North (265165)

Silly Billy. 70ft. V.D.

Start just left of Billy Goat Bluff.

Climb the rib and shallow groove to a slabby area above. Easy scrambling to the top.

D.Armstrong. 19/10/85.

Billy Goat Bluff. 70ft. H.V.S.

Start 60ft. left of The Kremlin.

5a. Climb the smooth rib, keeping to the right wall.

R.Kenyon. 29/9/85.

Legless Lizard. 170ft. E5.

A link pitch from Athanor to The Thieving Magpie, which climbs the wall and twisting crack through the orange bulges 15ft. left of Footless Crow.

1. 90ft. 6b. Climb Footless Crow to the niche, step up left to a good foothold then straight up the wall to a small ledge just right of a crack. Climb the wall and bulge right of the crack to gain a good flake hold. Up leftwards over the bulge to a chockstone. Move right and up a flake crack to a small ledge. (Just right of the belay at the top of pitch 3 of Praying Mantis.)

2. 80ft. 5b. Finish directly over the bulge and up the slab above as for Thieving Magpie.

D.Dinwoodie, D.Hawthorn. 8/8/85.

LOWER KNITTING HOW (245169)

Ripping Yarn. 100ft. E2.

The steep delicate corner gives a sustained route. Start from the grassy ledge below the corner.

5c. Up the corner to a ledge just below the top, then pull up right into a slanting slabby groove which is followed to a tree belay on the rib at the top.
D.Armstrong, P.Whillance. 3/5/84.

Woolly Jumper. 80ft. E5.
A sustained pitch up the right-hand crack on the smooth impending wall.
6b. Gain and follow the crack past two peg runners, pulling up rightwards at the top. Scramble up to a tree belay.
D.Armstrong, A.Murray. 6/6/85.

LANGDALE

PAVEY ARK (286080)

Rock Around the Clock. 135ft. E3.
Start at the left hand side of the Brackenclock slab at a flake.
1. 45ft. 6a. Climb a short corner until holds lead left to a small ledge. Step right and climb the slab direct to belay on Brackenclock.
2. 70ft. 5c. Move slightly right and pull through the bulge at an obvious finger-slot, straight up the triangular wall and pull leftwards up a rib to belay at the top of pitch 3 of Brackenclock.
3. 20ft. 5b. Climb the centre of the slab on the right passing an overlap on its right side just below the top. Finish as for Brackenclock.
M.Dale, R.Brookes. 26/6/85.

CRINKLE GILL (257049)

Lying above Oxendale and reached by a 50 minute walk from Steel End Farm. Turn left at the Band and follow the beck up into the gill.

THE SOUTH GULLY WALL

This appears on the left as one walks into the gill. The routes are described from left to right.

Private Investigations. 80ft. E2.
5b. The stepped groove on the lower left hand side of the gully wall.
J.White, B.Birkett. 3/6/85.

Naked Edge. 80ft. E4.
6a. Climb the slim groove in the overhanging nose just right of Private Investigations.
B.Birkett, P.Cornforth. 16/6/85.

Private Dancer. 80ft. E4.
6a. Climb the groove and steep crack right of the overhanging nose.
B.Birkett, J. White. 3/6/85.

Genital Touch. 80ft. E4/5.
6a. Climb the series of slanting cleaned grooves right of Private Dancer.
P.Cornforth, B.Birkett. 14/6/85.

Crimes of Quality. 80ft. E1.
5a. Climb the obvious slab starting up the gill from Genital Touch.
J.White, P.Cornforth, B.Birkett. 14/6/85.

Private Eye. 140ft. E4.
   6a. Takes the striking corner groove left of the area of overhangs at the right hand end
of the gully wall.
B.Birkett, J.White. 14/6/85.

Private Affair. 140ft. S.
   Takes the obvious weakness right of the area of overhangs.
B.Birkett (solo). 3/6/85.

THE NORTH GULLY WALL

   The steep buttress on the north wall higher up the gill from the South Gully routes.

Bitter Days. 120ft. E5.
   6b. Takes the line of niches and grooves on the right hand side of the buttress.
B.Birkett. 4/7/85.

Cold Nights. 120ft. E2.
   5c. Climb the corner, wall and diagonal crack to the left of Bitter Days.
B.Birkett. 4/7/85.

BLEA CRAG, EASEDALE (301079)

No Flange for the Poor. 90ft. E1.
   Start as for No Rest.
   Climb the wall of No Rest to sloping ledges. Move left to a ledge below Simon Says.
Climb the left arête of Simon Says direct.
M.Dale. Solo. 15/6/85.

RAVEN CRAG GRASMERE

   This is the crag on the flank of Helm Crag opposite the Travellers Rest Inn.

Climbs of Quality. 80ft. E1.
   5b. The steep pod/crack line left of the green ramp is climbed to the tree. Abseil
descent.
R.Graham, A. Phizacklea. 24/3/85.

LOUGHRIGG MINES, RYDAL WATER

   Climbs the rock around the largest cave with the pool.

Scary Monsters. 150ft.
   5b/c. Start at the right-hand side of the cave. Climb a short slab to a corner. Move left
under the overlap, then move up to a ring peg. Continue left on undercuts (crux), then
move easily left to a sapling below an overhang. An awkward move left leads to a ledge
(runners). Descend slightly across the lip of the cave, or continue up the groove.
C.Dale. April 1985.

SCAFELL, DOW AND ESKDALE

GATE CRAG ESKDALE (185999)

These two routes are on a buttress immediately to the left of the start of Left Hand
Groove.

Waving At Trains. 70ft. V.S.
Starts behind a large tree at a weeping groove.

4c. Climb the groove to a ledge on the right. Up the overhung corner to a slab. Finish more easily up a groove. Belay well back.

J.D.Wilson, A.Wilson. 4/6/85.

Off The Rails. 70ft. E1.
Start just left of Waving At Trains, behind a small groove.

5b. Climb to the top of the pinnacle. Up left to a hanging flake. Use this to traverse right a few feet, then straight up the wall above. Belay as for Waving At Trains.

J.D.Wilson, A.Wilson. 14/6/85.

The Golden Bow. 130ft. E2.
5b. Start up Hybrid to the overhang, traverse left underneath the overhang, up a short groove to the arête. Follow this to the top.

Peter Strong, Dave Hinton. August 1984.

Rock Aid. 70ft. E4.
This route is on a buttress about 50 yards left of Track of the Cat and Niche.

6a. Climb up to a right-sloping gangway and then up to a rest under a small overlap. Make hard moves up and left until an awkward escape left can be made onto the arête. Belay.

D.Hall, D.Hinton. 25/7/85.

The next two routes are on a shield-shaped buttress to the left of and at right-angles to the previous routes.

Air Attack. 40ft. E2.
Take a line up the right-hand side of the shield. Start from a large tree and scramble up to a downward-pointing spike.

5c. Bridge delicately up between the wall and spike. Move up to reasonable footholds on the wall. Follow some discontinuous cracks to an awkward exit at the top.

D.Hinton, A. Wilson. 3/7/85.

An Esperanto Degree. 40ft. E1.
Takes the left-hand side of the shield. Start as for Air Attack.

5b. Climb the left-hand edge of the buttress overlooking a dirty gully, until a move out right can be made onto the face. Climb up to a small overlap. Over this leftwards to the top.

D.Hinton, A.Harrison. 11/9/84.

The next two routes are on an isolated buttress about 100 yards left of the main area, which contains one previously recorded route, Trial Rib.

The Niche. 60ft. E3.
This route takes the obvious feature of this buttress, a triangular niche just under half way up and to the left of Trial Rib. Gain a belay ledge by climbing up the arête a short way (V.Diff) and traverse to about 15ft. below and slightly to the right of the niche. Peg belay.

6a. Enter the niche from the left-hand side (poorly protected), and continue out of it to the top of the crag via a crack.

D.Hall, P.Strong. June 1985.

Track Of The Cat. 70ft. E4.
Takes a line to the left of The Niche. Belay as for that route.

6a. Climb the first few feet of The Niche to a poor runner, then traverse delicately left on side pulls to a good hold and runners. Climb directly up the wall on long reaches to an awkward step onto a sloping ledge. Move right to easier ground and belay.
D.Hall, D.Hinton. 3/7/85.

THE QUARRY ESKDALE (164003)

This quarry appears in the Great Gable guide, 1977.

Rubble Run. 120ft. E2.
Climbs a groove to the left of Moria. Start below white stained rock. The bottom of this route is very loose.
5a. Climb the white rock to a narrow groove. Up this strenuously.

HERON CRAG, ESKDALE (222030)

Much of a Mouthful. 130ft. E1.
A direct start to Minor Sixty Niner.
5b. Start up Steerpike and continue up the arête on its right-hand side to join Minor Sixty Niner. Follow this to the top.
Brian Davidson, Andy Smith. 27/7/85.

YEW CRAG, ESKDALE (220018)

Mission Impossible. 100ft. E2.
Starts 10ft. left of Broken Arrow and ascends the steep clean buttress and obvious sentry box above.
1. 45ft. 5c. Climb the wall easily leftwards to gain a high runner then pull right into the scoop/depression. Step left and follow the wall above direct to the left hand end of the large sloping ledge. Horizontal crack belay at the point of arrival.
2. 55ft. 5c. Gain the overhanging sentry box by a desperate move from either left or right (small runners on left). Then climb direct to the top.
K.Phizacklea, J.Daly. Pitch 1 — 25/2/85, Pitch 2 — 2/3/85.

Steppin' Out. 100ft. H.V.S.
Starts 15ft. left of Broken Arrow beneath the holly tree.
5b. Climb the easy groove to the holly tree, pull up right to the base of a short corner crack, climb it on the right hand side and make an awkward move back left to a ledge beneath the obvious corner groove. Climb the strenuous groove pulling out right at the top. Easier rocks leads to the top.
J.Daly, K.Phizaklea. 9/3/85.

DUDDON VALLEY-(DUNNERDALE)
WALLOWBARROW GORGE (224966)

Tales from the Riverbank. 130ft. E1.
Start a few feet right of the Cornflake block at the obvious crack.
1. 30ft. 5a. Climb the overhanging crack to a ledge.
2. 60ft. 5b. Climb the slabby wall on the right direct to a ledge. Follow the overhanging crack in the wall on the left to a belay in the Cornflake groove.
3. 40ft. 5c. Gain the overhung ledge above and to the right by a thin crack. Easier rocks on the left lead to the top. Tree belay well back.
D.Geere, K.Phizacklea, J.Daly (*Alt*) K.Garstang. 16/12/84.

Nebraska. 120ft. H.V.S.
Start 10ft. to the left of the Cornflake block at a wide rightward-slanting crack.
1. 70ft. 5a. Climb the crack for 10ft. and follow the easy slab to a tree. The corner in the steep wall above leads to a large ledge.
2. 50ft. 4c. Climb the steep corner to the top.
D.Geere, K.Phizacklea (*Alt*) J.Daly. 5/1/85.

In the Mood. 100ft. H.V.S.
Start as for Nebraska.
5b. Climb the slab left of the crack to ledges beneath an undercut groove. Pull into the groove above and follow it to a ledge. The leftward-slanting crack in the undercut arête leads to a large ledge. Tree belay. Scrambling up and right leads to the descent path.
K.Phizacklea, D.Geere, J.Daly. 5/1/85.

Wild Prairie. 100ft. V.S.
Start as for Weetabix, 25ft. left of the Cornflake block, beneath a slab.
4c. Climb the slab easily to a ledge. Follow the groove to the horizontal break and the flake crack in the wall above to a large ledge. Tree belay. Scrambling up and right leads to the descent path.
D.Geere, K.Phizacklea. 3/1/85.

Hostile Territory. 100ft. E1.
Start 20ft. up and right of the Cornflake block at the left-hand side of a steep slab.
5b/c. Climb the slab direct and the short groove above to a ledge. Short walls on the rib, left of the chimney, lead to the final impending wall. Follow a thin vertical crack to a small square-cut overhang, swing up and left to an abrupt finish.
J.Daly, D.Geere, K.Phizacklea. 26/1/85.

Backtrackin'. 100ft. S.
Start as for Hostile Territory.
Climb the slab rightwards to a ledge. Follow the chimney/groove line on the left, finishing up a steep wall.
D.Geere, K.Phizacklea, J.Daly. 12/1/85.

Crossflow. 185ft. V.S.
A rising girdle of Lower Cornflake Buttress. Start as for Weetabix.
1. 70ft. 4b. Climb the easy slab to the oak, gain the hand traverse line above and follow this rightwards to a ledge (as for pitch 1 of Weetabix).
2. 40ft. 4c/5a. Climb the steep corner for 20ft., traverse right and step round the arête to belay in the niche of Cornflake.
3. 75ft. 4c. Traverse rightwards to the chimney of Backtrackin, climb this for 10ft. then move right towards the arête, slabby at first. Climb the crack in the short wall to gain the slab above, step right and follow the easy angled arête to the top.
J.Daly, K.Phizacklea, M.Gibson. 2/2/85.

Finger Poppin'. 130ft. H.V.S.
Start by the tree, 25ft. left of Cracklin' Brant.
1. 50ft. 5a. Climb the impending wall to gain the ledge on the right, then follow the fist wide crack above to easier ground. The short crack above leads to a tree below the large flake of Cornflake.
2. 80ft. 5b/c. Climb the thin crack in the front face of the flake, move left, and from the tip of the flake pull up leftwards to gain the slabby wall above. Up to a short corner, and finish up the slabs on the right.
J.Daly, K.Phizacklea. 6/1/85.

BURNT CRAG DUNNERDALE (243990)

The Burnt Ones. 60ft. E4.
  This route takes the open corner 15 yards right of S.P.C. Start below the right-hand end of a large sloping ledge about 20ft. up the crag.
  6b. Climb directly up to a ledge below the steep open corner. A strenuous move up this leads to a left-facing flake. Use this to step up leftwards to a thin crack, follow this to the top.
G.Smith, D.Hinton. 6/7/85.

Out of the Ashes. E5.
  6b. Climb the crack just right of Double Trouble to finish up Innocenti.
M.Radtke, A.Ledgeway, I.Cooksey.

Waking The Witch. E4.
  6a. Climb the groove right of Innocenti.
M.Radtke, A.Ledgeway.

  There is another little buttress approximately 150 yards left of Burnt Crag.

The Rhetoric of Meritocracy. E4.
  6b. Climb the steep central wall.
A.Towse. P.Short.

Twilight Wall. V.S.
  4b. Climb the left side of the wall.
A.Towse.

  Another 100 yards left is another little crag with a stone wall running up to its base.

Arpeggio. S.
  Climb above the stone wall.
A. and K.Towse.

Natural Progression. E2.
  5c. Climb the wall to the left to a crack at the top.
A. and K.Towse.

MART CRAG CONISTON (305988)

Clean Sweep. 125ft. E1.
  Takes the obvious corner halfway up to the centre of the crag. The climb is on clean rock (in sharp contrast to surrounding routes), and starts six feet left of Caravan Slab, below a steep blunt rib.
1. 40ft. 5a. Climb the steep rib and short V-groove to the peg belay of Diamond Buttress.
2. 45ft. 5b/c. The steep corner behind the belay is climbed with some difficulty to a large ledge. (Small wires for protection).
3. 40ft. 4b. The short slab and corner groove lead to the top.
K.Phizacklea, J.Daly. 28/4/85.

BUTTERMERE AND EASTERN CRAGS

BUTTERMERE

GREEN CRAG (201131)

Berlin Bunker Blues. 250ft. E1.
Climbs the wall between Thorgrim and Paper Tiger. Start at a holly tree.
1. 120ft. Climb the groove to the right of Thorgrim moving out right after 40ft. Trend left to a large ledge. Block belay.
2. 130ft. 5b. Step right and ascend the block to a narrow ledge below a thin flake. Climb the flake and step left to an edge. Up this to ledges below a steep wall. Pull up over a bulge onto good holds, then up the cracked wall, step left to blocks. Continue up the steep final wall. Peg belay.
D.Hellier, G.Taylor. 8/5/85.

THIRLMERE

RAVEN CRAG (304188)

Gates of Delirium — Direct Start. 70ft. E5.
Start at the foot of Gates of Delirium.
6a. Arrange nuts above in a shallow groove, traverse the wall leftward to reach a more prominent groove. Move up the arête, then make long reaches up and right to improving holds and a rest on Gates of Delirium near the end of the traverse. Step back right and use a loose chockstone to climb the bulge. Up layback flakes to exit left into the groove of Gates.
D.Dinwoodie, C.McLean. 12/8/85.

Close to the Edge — Direct Start. 50ft. E5.
Start as for the Medlar.
6b. Climb up the groove of Medlar to gain nut runners. Step back down and move right onto the rib using a low side pull. Pull up the rib to gain a good letter-box hold, then move up right to join the Gates of Delirium near the end of the traverse.
D.Dinwoodie, C.Ord. 1985.

ULLSWATER

GOWBARROW CRAG, MIDDLE BUTTRESS (414206)
The roof to the left of **Whistler** has been climbed before at E2 5b, **Valicide.**

GOWBARROW CRAG

By Pass. 70ft. H.V.S.
A variation pitch to the girdle traverse, starting from the oak belay above pitch 1.
Traverse left to Susan, step left and continue traversing the Mossy Slab into Gowbarrow Buttress. Climb the crack for about 10ft., move left round a rib and continue traversing to the oak belay.
B.Rogers, S.Scott. 26/10/85.

YEW CRAG

Automan. 150ft. H.V.S.
Starts at an obvious groove containing yew trees.
1. 60ft. 4b. Gain the groove from the right and layback up a large pinnacle moving left at the top and passing outside of a yew tree to belay on a higher yew tree.
2. 90ft. 5a. Up the wall to the groove trending slightly left. Step right and climb directly to a hanging corner. Move up on good holds to the top.
P.Hirst, R.McHaffie, N.Robinson. 31/12/84.

Tom Thumb. 50ft. S.
Starts at the obvious corner jamming crack at the far left of the crag.
Climb the corner then the short wall.
R.McHaffie. 1985.

Brass Monkey. 150ft. H.V.S.
Start 40ft. right of Automan.
1. 30ft. 4a. Climb into the triangular niche then swing round the left rib to a ledge and tree belay.
2. 120ft. 5a. Climb into the overhanging groove above and climb it, with a short detour onto the slab on the right. Spike belay 6ft. left of finish.
P.Hirst, R.McHaffie. 10/2/85.

MARTINDALE

UPPER THRANG CRAG (431177)

Simple Solution. E3.
Start at the stacked pinnacle between Desperate Remedies and Microcosm.
5c. From the top of the pinnacle climb up the wall until forced right then move up and back left to ledges. Climb the short groove to gain a standing position on the shoulder on the left. Follow the diagonal crack right to gain the groove above at the large spike. Continue up the groove to the top.
R.Smith, J.Earl. 15/6/85.

Stern Test. 80ft. E5.
The impressive arête between Bomber Wall and Responsibility. Scramble up to a ledge and large flake beneath the arête.
6b. Climbs directly up the arête to a peg runner. A long reach or awkward moves enable the horizontal break and a second peg runner to be reached. Move up to a good rest at the large foothold on the arête. A couple of thin moves up the left side of the arête leads to an overlap and easier climbing to large spike belays and the top.
J.Earl, R.Smith. 15/6/85.

Gouttes d'Eau. 80ft. E3.
5c. The arête right of Responsibility is climbed on its left side.
R.Smith, J.Earl. 15/6/85.

THRANG CRAG — FARM BUTTRESS

Norman The Undead Direct. E2.
5b. From the fence post climb straight up to the break, move up and right to gain the bottom of the final crack.
J.Earl, R.Smith. 18/5/85.

The Chain Gang. E4.
6a. The groove and thin crack left of Friend Beyond. Climb the groove to the peg, move around the arête, then up and right to gain the cracks.
R.Smith, J.Earl. 18/5/85.

Poule De Luxe. 50ft. E3.
6a. Start at the right side of the left-hand face. Climb straight up on small holds to join Norman The Undead. Follow this to a small niche. Move boldly up on layaways until a reach right brings good holds. Go up to an awkward finish.
S.Howe, J.Beveridge. 10/6/85.

The Archers. 100ft. E3.
A left to right girdle of the crag.
6a. Climb the wall immediately left of the fencepost to below the final crack of Norman The Undead. Move right past the peg on Chain Gang to gain the hollow flake on Friends. Reach up to a good hold just above the flake then stretch right (P.R.) to the arête. Delicately move across and slightly down to the ledge right of the crack. Finish up Human Shows.
A.Moss, A.Birtwistle. 15/6/85.

THRESHTHWAITE COVE

RAVEN CRAG (419112)

Baby Driver. E3.
The groove and orange wall left of Grand Prix.
5c. 20ft. left of Grand Prix are two obvious grooves. Climb the right-hand one to the horizontal fault and go through the overhangs at the obvious weakness to a peg on the left. Move right and up to faint flakes which are climbed to Grand Prix. Move back left to a peg and continue left to an undercling which enables the diagonal crack and then the top to be reached. Belay 30ft. up on left.
R.Smith, J.Earl.

Cabriolet. 140ft. E4.
Follows the rightward-slanting crack just above and parallel to the crack of Redex which terminates at the large obvious roof between the upper grooves of GTX and Redex.
1. 80ft. 5b. Follow the crack rightward crossing the horizontal fault line until a step right can be made at the tree. Belay on the right.
2. 60ft. 6a. Climb up to gain a good handhold on the large flake beneath the roof. Use the large undercling right of the flake to initiate difficult moves across and round the lip of the roof to gain ledges above. Climb straight up the rib above and move left at the top to a crack. Nut belays, two spikes up and right.
R.Smith, J.Earl (alt leads). 7/6/85.

Silverstone. 135ft. E4.

Climbs the faint groove right of High Performance's first pitch and the white groove right of its top groove.

1. 75ft. 5b. Climb the faint groove on good holds to the spike at its top. Move right and climb the short diagonal groove to the horizontal fault. Climb the largest scoop in the band above to belay below the white groove. Good thread up and right.

2. 60ft. 6a/b. Make an awkward move on the sloping ledge to gain the groove right of High Performance, which is climbed to a good ledge at two thirds height. Continue up the groove (crux) to the top.

R.Smith, J.Earl. 7/6/85.

Chicane. 140ft. E3.

1. 80ft. 5c. Start at the white groove immediately left of the descent route at the right-hand side of the crag. Climb the groove, which curves left at the top, to a ledge. Follow the cracks diagonally right to the diagonal grass ledge. Straight up the slabs via the faint groove directly above. Belay beneath the groove immediately left of the right-hand arete.

2. 60ft. 5c. Move up to a thread left of the groove, traverse right on the obvious fault and move up to a large flat hold in the groove. An awkward move off this leads to a niche. Climb the crack on the left to a large ledge. From the higher ledge on the right one move leads to pleasant slabs and the top.

J.Earl, R.Smith. 7/6/85.

SWINDALE

FANG BUTTRESS (515127)

Bloodhound Left Hand Finish. 100ft. E1.

5b. Follow the normal route to a sloping ledge. From the left end of this pull into a short corner, up this, then the right-hand of two cracks.

Steve Howe, Ian Walker. May 1985.

One Small Step. E1.

A direct finish to One Step Beyond.

5b. Climb Dogleg Crack until above the roof. Traverse down across the lip of the roof to a good hold, then up to a peg runner. Continue straight up to the top.

S.Howe.

GREAT GABLE

Eagle's Nest Ridge Super Direct.

5a/b. From the top of the Direct, climb a fine crack on the left for 30ft. then up easy slabs to the foot of a gendarme. Move down to a ledge on the left. Climb the overhanging crack. Loose rock near the top.

J.Morgan, P.Johnson. 13/10/85.

IN MEMORIAM

R.Cook 1935-1986
F.M.Coventry 1922-1986
Mrs. E.Hervey 1959-1986
Miss Gladys Kitchener 1928-1985
G.H.Mackereth. 1929-1986
W.G.Pape 1921-1986
E.C.Pollitt 1933-1984
Miss E.Wells 1923-1985
M.H.Wilson 1921-1986
A.E.Wormell 1942-1985

GLADYS KITCHENER, 1928-1985

Older members of the Club will remember Gladys as one of the regular devotees of the Whitsuntide meets at Thornythwaite. Her tent was to be found alongside the lane crossing the meadow behind the barn. During the warm Spring evenings it was the focus for tea and gossip. While following her career as a teacher of English she lived for many years in Bishop's Stortford, and divided her leisure time between the Lake District, Scotland and the Alps, walking and climbing extensively. When the Club's slides were in my care she was a frequent borrower, and took particular pleasure in introducing senior scholars at Felixstowe College to the mountain landscape.

She was a devout church-goer, and her strong religious convictions found expression in her constant concern for the poor and the oppressed, and the victims of war and injustice. These qualities, and her intense love of the hill country, are reflected in her poetry. She published two books of poems under the name of Greta Rowell, one in 1938, and a second larger edition, containing later work, in 1977. We corresponded regularly, and from her letters emerged her strongly-held views on a variety of issues, her often abrasive sense of humour, and her compassion for the aged and under-privileged. She was in many ways a perfectionist, and the neat disposal of her camping gear in and around her tent was an object lesson. Having learned the basic skills in the sport from those who set the early standards, she was severely critical of the modern rock gymnasts and their aprons of metal aids and bags of chalk. The appearance amid the soft greens and greys of the fellsides of the vivid colours of today's fashionable outfits, she saw as an outrageous disfigurement.

She retired in 1959 to live quietly in Keswick until the Autumn of 1984 when advancing years forced her to give up her home. What hurt her most in making this decision was having to part with her piano. Her maps and journals she gave to the Club. Her subsequent letters described a series of disagreeable experiences in various establishments purporting to provide shelter for the aged and infirm. These experiences, though upsetting, only served to sharpen her critical faculty and sense of humour, and she expressed deep concern when writing of the commercialisation and turmoil passing for creative activity which has invaded the District, Grasmere (where she stayed briefly) and Keswick in particular.

Happily, she found an oasis of quiet and seclusion near Skelwith Fold from which she was able to enjoy short walks, and recapture the tranquility she so greatly valued. In her last letter to me, written only five days before her death, she noted the cutting of the hay and the shearing of the sheep, adding that her room was bright with honeysuckle and spiraea.

Gladys died peacefully on 2 September 1985 in her eighty-seventh year. Members of her family living in the South arranged a memorial service at Holy Trinity Church, Queen's Square, Bath, and an obituary appeared in the February edition of *Cumbria*. At her request the Keswick Mountain Rescue Team undertook the scattering of her ashes on Great Gable. It was natural that she should choose the exact place — where the gully bounding Westmorland Crags meets the summit plateau. Gladys was a remarkable lady, and it was a privilege to be her friend.

F.H.F. Simpson

EDGAR CAMPBELL POLLITT (1933-1984)

I do not think that Edgar ever got over the accidental death, whilst they were on a training walk in the Alps in August 1951, of his climbing friend and distant relative Laurence Pollitt. They had climbed together for very many years — Laurence a brilliant rock-climber and Edgar a steady and strong man on their guideless climbs in the Alps. They were regular attenders at Club Meets, particularly Easter and Whitsuntide, before and after the 1939/45 War. Edgar continued to join our 'bachelor' Easter Party at Wasdale for many years after 1951, but I do not think he ever climbed in the Alps again and some of the attraction of the rocks seemed to be missing. He married late in life and dropped out of climbing; taking more seriously to golf, a pursuit which he shared with his wife Kay. Be coincidence and not accident they passed away in the same hospital within three days of each other.

Edgar was in the design department of a Chorley linoleum manufacturer and his many friends will remember his lino-cut Christmas Cards — always of mountain scenes.

You could not have had a better climbing companion.

Charles Pickles

REVIEWS

BOOKS

BAILEY, ADRIAN. Lakeland Rock . . . .
BARRY, JOHN. The Great Climbing Adventure . . . .
BENNET, D.(Ed.). The Munros . . . .
CALVERT, HARRY. Smythe's Mountain's . . . .
POUCHER, W.A. Lakeland Fells . . . .'. . . . .
SHIPTON, ERIC. The Six Mountain Travel Books . . . .
TILMAN, H.W. The Seven Mountain Travel Books . . . .
UNSWORTH, WALT. Classic Walks of the World . . . .
WORDSWORTH, W. The Illustrated Wordsworth's Guide to the Lakes . . . .

JOURNALS

U.K. Journals . . . .
Overseas Journals . . . .

Correction

In the last issue of the **Journal,** *no. 69, pp 164-5, the review of the SMC Central Highlands and Western Highlands Guides attributed to Dave Miller was in fact written by David Rhodes. We apologise for this error. Ed.*

Lakeland Rock: classic climbs with Chris Bonington. By Adrian Bailey. 251pp. Illus. Sparkford, Somerset: Oxford Illustrated Press. 1985. £8.95.

Lakeland Rock capitalizes on the Border TV/Channel 4 television series of the same name adding more flesh to the pictorial bones. Adrian Bailey has done a most competent job in tracing the evolution of the sport from dank gully to holdless wall and profiling the pioneers. The legendary O.G.Jones, he writes, showed his indifference to pain, fear or frostbite by dipping his fingers in boiling glue not as a forerunner of chalk but as a remedy for frostbite. Bill Peascod's repeat of Eagle Front in Birkness, some forty years after he established the route, and Don Whillans on his own early classic Dovedale Groove rank as classic TV footage, particularly since both climbers sadly died of heart attacks soon afterwards.

Lakeland Rock the book uses a broader canvas than the television series and is a useful insight into the history of climbing in The Lake District.

R. Faux

The Great Climbing Adventure. By John Barry. 251pp. Illus. Sparkford, Somerset. Oxford Illustrated Press. 1985. £8.95.

This is not, as the title suggests, a re-run of famous mountaineering conquests but an autobiographical account of one man's rich and remarkably chaotic climbing career. John Barry was a climbing specialist in the Royal Marines who later became director of the National Centre for Mountain Activities at Plas y Brenin in North Wales; a Bootneck with civilian tendencies. He acknowledges that the military are regarded as an odd-ball breed by the wider climbing fraternity. Perhaps the suspicion is that they treat the hills as a surrogate battlefield with prudence subborned to a stiff upper lip.

Certainly the officer Barry has a gritty obsession with climbing. When goals are not achieved he senses the failure keenly and though this determination to win might be the grist that wins battles, it does not make him in the least degree a blimp. He emerges much more in the mould of Whillans than General Bruce, distrusting or rejecting many of the impressions that others have of particular mountains or climbs. He condemns much of mountaineering literature as marvellously mundane, spectacularly awful or plain daft and then boldly adds this own contribution. That is typical of the man.

The fact that there was no literature available about the Southern Alps of New Zealand meant that on his first serious mountain, Mount Cook, his own view of the climb was uncluttered by those of other people. In this state of sweet ignorance and in spite of losing one crampon, he and Dave Nicholls reached the summit but were forced to spend a night out on the retreat; Nicholls comfortable in a Michelin-proportioned duvet, Barry in an agricultural poly bag (the only protection he could muster), "the incongruous smell of fertilizer rising on feeble body heat to freeze in the nostrils." It is the incongruous face of moutaineering which clearly appeals to him and gives this book an hilarious edge. There is Barry's clear admiration for the marine officer who, having showered awesome hospitality on his guests until one of them crashed to the floor unconscious, took off the victim's shoes, nailed them to the floor, replaced the feet in the shoes and awaited results.

"He rose unsteadily and uncertainly to his feet, wobbled, terribly transfixed, and crashed down again. An expression of bleary-eyed bewilderment gave way to one of wild-eyed anxiety as the implications of his apparent paralysis and loss of motor coordination sunk in." Fortunately he took the joke in good humour.

John Barry seems to prefer expeditions with a few amusing wrinkles that make a better story. His lead of Carnage at Malham is one example. Emerging from the strenuous last pitch he was confronted by the feet of two utterly naked bodies *in flagrante delicto* on the grass at the cliff edge. Strength in hand and arm were fleeting fast, it was a long way to his last runner and, glancing down, he saw his second was rolling a ciggy, a two-handed job. A polite peel was out of the question so in the best military tradition over the top he went.

There are more serious moments; blown from his holds by an apocalyptic gust of wind on the west ridge of Gauri Sankar he fell 200 feet and survived. Other close scrapes caused either by bad luck, impetuosity, cornices collapsing or powder-filled gullies avalanching leave him with a firm platform from which to judge the value of it all. "If we choose this game and its dangers," he says, "we should not complain if we, our friends or others of the same persuasion fall victim to 'the fell clutch of circumstance'."

An excellent book this, written with honesty and breathless gusto leaving only small stances between chapters.

R. Faux

The Munros The Scottish Mountaineering Club Hillwalkers' Guide — ed. Donald Bennet. Scottish Mountaineering Trust. £10.95.

The Munros is a guidebook to the Scottish hills over three thousand feet. Despite this somewhat antiquated measurement the Munro hills retain an appeal to British hillwalkers well described by Hamish Brown in the introduction.

The book is divided into areas; within these areas each range is described as a day's outing by well known mountaineers such as Donald Bennet, Hamish Brown, Malcolm Slesser and Adam Watson. Each description contains useful access and route length information accompanied by appropriate photographs as well as the well executed maps by James Renny which are such a feature of the Munros Tables book. One small quibble however is that whilst the route descriptions are for summer conditions a great many of the photographs show the hills in their winter glory when conditions are much more severe.

This apart, the book is well produced and would be an ideal companion volume to the Munro Tables for the committed. For other Scottish mountain lovers it is a good reference book, superbly illustrated, which is very good value in its hardback form.

Richard Morgan

Smythe's Mountains: the climbs of F.S.Smythe. By Harry Calvert. 233pp. Illus. Victor Gollancz. 1985. £14.95.

This, the author claims, is not a biography of Smythe: it is a companion volume for those who have enjoyed Smythe's own books. My Calvert has gathered together the information to produce a comprehensive account of all Smythe's mountaineering life, and is certainly to be commended for his industry and enthusiasm. Smythe the man still remains a rather remote and private figure; no attempt is made to reveal the inner man, beyond a few interesting vignettes and brief conjectures. What is made clear is his stature as a mountaineer. He held his own in a small elite world of high mountaineering in spite of being regarded by some as something of a parvenu. In addition, this account of his climbing and ski-touring convinces one, in a way his own writing never quite did, at least for me personally, of the sincerity and simple ardour of his love of the hills.

Where one has some knowledge of the terrain in question, Mr Calvert's painstaking accounts of Smythe's climbs are very interesting and readable, but they can become harder going when this is not the case, and more sketch-maps would be a help. As it is, to digest the book fully one needs to have a large number of maps to hand.

Smythe's Mountains makes a good contribution to the sum of knowledge of mountaineering achievement, and it does a considerable service to the memory of a great mountaineer.

Tom Price

Lakeland Fells. By W.A.Poucher. 203pp. Illus. Constable. 1985. £12.95.

One wonders sometimes if there can be room for another book of Lakeland photographs — but if so then this is it. Here are 100 entrancing pictures from Mardale to Wasdale guaranteed to start you reminiscing and packing your rucksack.

Mr Poucher's skill and artistry in photographing the delectable mountains are rightly famous and this latest dazzling sequence can only increase our admiration. Incidentally it was interesting to learn from the cover that his talents have combined to give Mr Poucher *two* successful careers, the other being 30 years as Yardley's chief perfumer.

His choice of viewpoints and composition together with his appreciation of lighting, cloud effects and seasonal colouring have produced an enviable cornucopia of lovely pictures. They are presented in well produced large format as part of a series. What a pity the finest are cut in two by their double page spread!

The text, though minimal does contain useful suggestions for the elderly, for the tough young enthusiast, and of course for the photographer.

Browsing through the pages of this attractive book one realises that here we are given the fruit of year upon year of happy days wandering in the mountains. 'My book' said

Wordsworth of his Guide to the Lakes, 'could not have been written without much experience.' This beautiful volume of Mr Poucher's colour photographs is also the crown of 'much experience' *and* it goes without saying, much love of Lakeland Fells. It will certainly give great pleasure to many people.

Margaret Thompson

The Six Mountain-Travel Books. By Eric Shipton; intro. by Jim Perrin. 800pp. Illus. Diadem. 1985. £16.95.

"2 shirts (Tilman only took one)"

The item is part of a short list of equipment deemed necessary for one man for 5 months travel in the Karakoram. The journeys undertaken were of epic size, achieved an enormous amount of invaluable survey work and mapping, but were accomplished with the minimum of participants and organisation. This was how Eric Shipton preferred to travel, to explore and to climb in the uncharted high moutain regions which fascinated him.

At times the amount of geographical detail may be tedious and to follow the progress, continual reference to the maps is necessary but the tremendous and overwhelming scale of features, the difficulties which they posed and the complexities of these regions are forcefully conveyed. He was immensely interested in the structure of the ranges which he described fully but concisely. The hefty weight of this material is balanced by descriptive passages which bring to life the exquisite beauty of his surroundings in so many different places, and reveal his sensitivity and total appreciation of some of the most remote mountain areas.

Equally important are the people encountered: the rhythm of their lives; their seasonal movements and responses to their hostile environments. Food was bought whenever possible from villagers or groups of herdsmen and the variety or monotony of their diet depended on the terrain, climate and the availability of produce. He felt it important to live and travel in these areas, on the terms which the geography imposed.

His outstanding journeys of exploration occurred in the 1930's and are described in *Nanda Devi, Blank on the Map* and are included in the autobiography *Upon That Mountain.* The third book also deals with the material concerning Shipton's great involvement with the history of the climbing of Everest, and this theme is continued in *The Mount Everest Reconnaissance Expedition 1951.* The contribution which he made to the eventual success is undeniably important, but he seemed to obtain as much pleasure from climbing surrounding peaks from which he was able to sort out the intricacies of Everest's structure and from seeing, for the first time, the feasibility of a route up the Khumu Ice Fall to the South Col, as from attempting a climb on Everest as a member of a large conquest group.

His terms of office as Consul-General in Kashgar and Kunming in the Sinkiang region of China provided him with the opportunites to travel and explore part of the more northerly regions of Central Asia in the simple manner that pleased him most. *Mountain of Tartary* recounts some of these journeys, (including the means of getting there) some of which were accomplished with Tilman in 1947 and 1948.

Following the great disappointments and upheavals in his mountaineering career and in his personal life in the 1950's, Eric Shipton again pursued his vision of seeking the secrets of a distant horizon, sorting out the detail of a complex region, drawing in the fine lines of ridges in relation to summits and glacier systems, and as far as possible being self-reliant in a remote region, and he turned his attention to Patagonia in the 1960's.

Both the book which resulted from these travels, *Land of Tempest*, and *Mountains of Tartary* express in many ways the immense personal satisfaction which he derived from this mode of living and pass on to kindred spirits some of that vast richness.

There are many passages in this collection of books which illustrate his mountain-travel philosophy, and which display his enthusiasm for this endless quest and his warmth of personality and humour. Most revealing is one from *Blank on the Map*, that is also quoted in the introduction by Jim Perrin,

"....we settled down on a comfortable bed of sand, and watched the approach of night transform the wild desert mountains into phantoms of soft unreality. How satisfying it was to be travelling with such simplicity. I lay awaiting the approach of sleep, watching the constellations swing across the sky. Did I sleep that night — or was I caught up for a moment into the ceaseless rhythm of space?"

Jo Light

The Seven Mountain Travel Books. By H.W. Tilman, intro. by Jim Perrin. 896pp. Illus. Diadem. 1983. £12.95.

Although this is a single volume, as the title suggests it includes seven of Tilman's books and represents tremendous value at £12.95.

The seven books in the volume are *Snow on the Equator, The Ascent of Nanda Devi, When Men and Mountains Meet, Everest 1938, Two Mountains and a River, China to Chitral* and *Nepal Himalaya*. Despite having been condensed into one volume, the text is clearly printed and the line drawings and maps are well re-produced. Some of the photographs are very contrasty and as a result they have lost their depth so that scale and distance merge. They are also in two main groups in the book so that it is not always easy to relate them to the narrative. Combining the seven titles in one volume however enables the reader to break-off easily and also saves considerable shelf space.

But what of the author? It is almost impossible to add anything to what has already been written of the man and his exploits. He became a legend in his lifetime. He fought in both world wars and won medals in each. In January, 1916, before his eighteenth birthday, he was on the Western Front at a time when the life expectancy of a young gunnery officer was about ten days. He miraculously survived to fight again at Dunkirk decades later. He commanded a battery at Alamein and at the age of forty five he was parachuted behind enemy lines to fight with the partisans in Albania and Northern Italy.

Between the two wars and after he organised and took part in several major mountaineering expeditions. He hated large numbers, loathed the idea of sponsorship and pioneered the concept of lightweight two-man expeditions completely self-contained.

In *Snow on the Equator* Tilman describes his transition from coffee planter in East Africa to mountaineer. After climbing on Mount Kenya, Kilimanjaro and Ruwenzori and prospecting for gold near Lake Victoria, he cycled 3,000 miles across Africa on a bicycle.

The *Ascent of Nanda Devi* is a classic of mountaineering literature. The success of lightweight expeditions led Tilman to being appointed the leader of THE 1938 EVEREST EXPEDITION. His experiences in both wars are profoundly dealt with in *Where Men and Mountains Meet*. After the war there were explorations in China, Nepal, Sinkiang and Kashmir. All these expeditions consisted of very small self-contained units. Mustagh Ata and other important Himalayan peaks were attempted and these post-war journeys come together in *Two Mountains and River, China to Chitral* and *Nepal Himalaya*.

In addition to all these he sailed three Bristol Channel Pilot Cutters to the most inhospitable oceans of the Arctic and Antarctic in pursuit of unclimbed mountains.

As a writer he was a master craftsman and together with the fascination of their content in these seven books, is the added bonus of the author's literary style.

Tilman was probably the best expedition writer of his time and arguably the finest mountaineer-explorer of this century. His life was always in the grip of a captivating fascination that held him in its spell even as he sailed south on his last voyage in his eightieth year.

W.A. Comstive

Classic Walks of the World. By Walt Unsworth. 160pp. Illus. Oxford Illustrated Press. 1985. £14.95.

This book describes seventeen excellent walks of varying length and difficulty from all over the world. The shortest takes three days and longest forty-four, but most can be done in a normal vacation period of two to three weeks. One walk is in Britain (the Pennine Way), six in Europe, one in Africa, four in the Himalayas, one in North America, two in South America, one in Japan, and one in New Zealand. At one time it would have been unthinkable for the average walker to venture further afield than Europe for a holiday, but now that more and more go to the Himalays and the Americas, I suppose it will not be long before even Japan and New Zealand will enter into 'where shall we go this year?' conversations.

All are mountain walks requiring a degree of fitness and experience, but they cater for all tastes. Some can only be done by back-packing and are very strenuous, especially the Concordia Trek in Kashmir which can also be extremely dangerous. (The Braldu gorge, reached in the second day of this walk is where Pat Fearneough was killed.) Another tough walk is the John Muir Trail in California, and nearer home the Pyrenean High Level Route is a serious and demanding route which attempts to keep to the frontier-watershed between France and Spain.

The only walk in the book which I can claim to have done in its entirety is the very beautiful Via delle Bocchette in the Brenta Dolomites. This is a three day walk along spectacular narrow ledges (not all that narrow — about a yard, and protected by hand rails), and up various ladders and other devices of the *via ferrate* in some sensational places. Overnight stops at comfortable huts with good food add to the pleasure of this route. Other walks, along with many other Club members, I have walked in parts, and look forward to re-visiting. These are the Tour de la Vanoise, The Tour de Mont Blanc and the GR20 in Corsica.

This book will have most appeal for the dedicated long distance walker. Naturally it does not give all the necessary detail for these walks, but references are given to all the appropriate maps and guide books. Secondly, it gives food for thought to walkers like myself who enjoy walking in high, mountainous and wild places but prefer to do so without being weighed down by a heavy pack. Thirdly, it can give pleasure to the armchair traveller who can do all the walks by simply turning the pages.

J.Parker

The Illustrated Wordsworth's Guide to the Lake District. ed. by Peter Bicknell. 208pp. Illus. Exeter. Webb & Bower. 1985. £12.95.

When Wordsworth's *Guide to the Lake District* was re-issued some years ago, in paperback but with the same rather elegant type-face as was used in the first edition, I thought it was a good idea. But it is entirely surpassed by Peter Bicknell's handsome publication the *Illustrated Wordsworth's Guide*, which in my view epitomises what has made the Lake District the gem of English upland landscape and the embodiment of what is romantic and picturesque.

Wordsworth's comments are interesting, both historically and in their own right, but we have got used to a terser and livelier prose in the twentieth century. His text is made much more readable by the wealth of illustrations, most of them taken from prints and paintings of about Wordsworth's own time, with full and interesting captions. They create a mood in which Wordsworth's prose seems more appropriate. The colour reproductions, though rather small, are rich and striking, and though there are a few photographs as well, these in my opinion only go to show how superior a drawing or a painting is to a photograph in conveying the atmosphere of a place. The watercolours of Francis Towne are particularly attractive.

Nowadays one could fill a library with books about the Lake District. If I had to limit myself to three or four, this would be one of them. Even the price is right.

Tom Price

JOURNALS

The Alpine Journal, 1985.

To anyone interested in the contemporary developments and advances in mountaineering, this journal would seem a good enough reason in itself to consider joining The Alpine Club. The high quality of the printing and presentation almost took my breath away when I first picked up the volume.

Just dipping into it one fact became at once obvious: this is not really a book for your top level technical crag climber. Only the article "North American Assortment" would please the cragrat and this mainly because of some excellent colour photographs taken in Colorado; the text also includes a few excellent alpine climbs in Canada. There is also an account of South African rock climbing by Michael Scott and a very interesting study: "South Pembroke Hazards" by Rod Brown and Mike Browell which points to some of the weaknesses in coastal limestone which affect climbing safety.

This is the way I read the book, just dipping in wherever a title attracted my attention and I was hardly ever disappointed and frequently surprised.

I happened to read "Dear Dad" by Peter Mould quite early and was absolutely gripped by this open and frank description of an ascent of the Eiger North Face which, like so many others, encountered unexpected problems in the Exit Cracks.

"A Sortie on Broad Peak" by Kurt Diemberger is, in my opinion, a brilliant piece of writing, containing flash-backs to the death of Herman Buhl and the harrowing story of the author's and his partner Julie Tullis' narrow escape from avalanche on the same mountain. The following chapter "Broad Peak climbed in one day" by Krzysztof Wielicki, although recording an amazing feat of endurance, reads more like a railway timetable.

The style of climbing epitomized by the piece by Diemberger is the style recorded by most of the articles in this journal: small scale Alpine type expeditions to relatively remote ranges in the world. There is an excellent and succint article by Doug Scott, entitled "Multi Peak — Alpine Style" which really brings home the remoteness, danger and psychological problems encountered when tackling giants such as Makalu in this style.

According to Edward E.Vaill in his piece entitled "Mountaineering in China", "one hundred years of first ascents remain". But I think I was more amazed at the chapter: "North America 1984", by Bob Milward, to find that the scope for mountain exploration in Canada is extensive and that possibly hundreds of mountains remain untouched. Two people, John Clarke and John Baldwin climbed 20 new peaks in a 29 day ski tour in 1984. The problems are access and the current concentration of interest in the higher ranges of the third world.

The only piece which disappointed me was "Fortunat Enderlin — Letters to a client" by Diane Tyson. Unfortunately (for me, anyway) the letters are in German.

There are, however, over forty different articles, so it was pretty remarkable to find only one which annoyed me. I found the rest interesting and a few absolutely fascinating.

Jim Sutcliffe

Cambridge University Mountaineering Club Journal, 1985.

In the introduction to the Journal the Editor says that the Club has a considerable reputation to live up to and it is now difficult for the Club to be at the forefront of the climbing scene when hard rock climbing is the prerogative of the dedicated unemployed and the unexplored ranges are no more. The Editor sadly admits that the Journal is evidence of this sad decline.

In the Journal, however, one finds that the Club is still quite active albeit with most of the articles about climbing in the British Isle. In years gone by the University Clubs were the basis of the British climbing scene; but now the mountains are accessible to a great many more people and the role of the University Clubs has diminished, however they are still a breeding ground for climbers for the future. Climbers must start somewhere and although initially, as with other clubs, there is a reluctance by club members to take out and train these freshers, after a few outings the freshers become part of the club and in time may become the leading lights of the club.

The Journal gives an indication of the members' activities which varies from traditional ascents in the Lakes, Wales and Scotland through to more esoteric gems such as Cherry Hinton Chalk Pit, a new climbing, mecca near Cambridge and also winter ascents of the Lakeland rock climbs of Engineers Slab and Moss Ghyll Groove — the photo of Brian Davison on Engineers Slab looks most peculiar. The same climber can be seen in more traditional climbing garb on White Wall at Millstone.

For the more domestic reader Mrs Wainwright's Trangia Tips for making Welsh Cakes should be of interest.

I liked the captions for the photos — Two snow coated climbers are "Pete realises he is alone with a lunatic"; someone atop a sea stack is "Bert posing on an obscure Scottish sea stack" and the upturned and rather bent looking Club minibus is "the CSU minibus, having failed to make the traverse of the A604/A1 junction" — that's what weekend trips are about.

Overseas we are treated to a selection, amongst others, of articles giving warnings of "Five Alpine Hazards", ascents of "Route Minor" not to mention "Route Major" and details of expeditions to the Hoggar region of Morocco and an insight into exhaustion and dejection with a near success in Pakistan. It is good to see the Club members making full use of their 14 weeks summer vacation.

As with all printed matter nowadays costs are cut and this is shown by the type setting and some dreadfully reproduced photos especially the one on the cover. The journal is not up to standard of the hard back "Bibles" of years past but indicates that the University, which is 300 (?-200) miles from the nearest mountain and 3 hours from the nearest decent crag still has a club which is very much active in the climbing scene.

R.Kenyon

M.A.M. Journal, 1983/84.

The Editorial comments at the beginning of the Journal could similarly be attributed to the members of the FRCC in that certain acts such as portering loads through the Khumbu Icefall, obtaining Directorship of the ISM and the joining of the ACG could have a shortening effect on one's life expectancy, whereas obtaining the Editorship of the M.A.M. Journal or membership of the FRCC should ensure a long life. The Editorial comments on the structural problems of Glandena, and indicates the moves towards a new hut which are well advanced. The Journal is the produce of a well established and active club covering a wide spread of mountaineering activity.

The joys of climbing are mixed with tragedy — memories of Scottish rock with blow by blow accounts of the Etive classics and a very sad tale of an attempt on a sea stack. An article on Gower opens up this mini crag land with its now abundant collection of hard routes sufficent to attract climbers who are en route to Pembroke. An insight is given to the easier routes of Lundy and "100 Best Abseils in the Verdon" gives one details of what not to do in the limestone mecca.

Further afield, an article by Rick Allen on the Scottish Garhwal Himalayan Expedition, 1982, indicates the usual hard work necessary in the Himalayas, eventually rewarded by a solo ascent of Kirti Stambh. I am not sure whether it was intentional, but the final few paragraphs, after all but Rick Allen had retreated and he continued solo, appeared on the following page, so that there seemed to be a change, on turning that page, from a struggling group to a freedom unleashed, leading to what must have been a memorable solo moment on the summit.

A series of Canadian articles give an insight into the Rockies in which a photo on the North Face of Mt. Edith Cavell looks really stunning. Enlightening articles on Mt. Kenya and Morocco are padded out by infillers (very useful for Editors). Overall a well-balanced Journal.

R.Kenyon

Scottish Mountaineering Club Journals, 1984-85. Nos. 125 and 126.

These two journals contain the account of a sojourn, in 1898, at the Ben Nevis observatory during its main operational period (1883-1900). These are well worth reading and give a dramatic picture of weather and living conditions, summer and winter, in that elevated spot. Having myself once lived in Fort William and worked on the slopes of the Ben and adjacent hills I can vouch for the severity of the weather described.

The usual well-documented accounts of Scottish mountain accidents and the tables of 20-year statistics make for sober reading and bear witness to the importance of good judgement of route, conditions and timing when climbing in the Highlands. A fine batch of new climbs is included in both journals as is an interesting account of a walk across

Scotland and a useful description of some good (and bad) boulder 'howfs' near crags in Arran.

The obituary of George Roger in the 1983 journal is a fitting tribute to 'that well kent and much loved figure' — the words of Tom Weir. George was well known to many FRCC members and he epitomised what Scottish climbing is all about.

Two excellent journals in keeping with the best traditions of the SMC.

H.S. Thompson

The American Alpine Journal, 1984.

Anyone who climbed anything of significance in 1984 has their effort recorded in this 400-page tome published by the American Alpine Club. Its thickness testifies to the astonishing number of expeditions from all over the world to mountain areas anywhere in the world. Doug Scott describes an attempt to traverse Makalu which turned from a family outing (eleven climbers plus wives and children) into a close encounter with the limits of endurance for Scott, Stephen Sustad and Jean Afanassieff.

Within this thorough picture of the world mountain scene is one curious chapter "Taping for Hand and Fist Jam Cracks" which rather turns the viewpoint from telescope to microscope. Not many people known how to tape properly, according to the Journal. Illustrations show how this should be done, transferring the sliding stress from the loose skin to the solid bones of the wrist. It avoids lacerations that take a week to heal even if they don't get infected and reduces bloodstains on the rock. I'm back to fell walking.

R. Faux

The New Zealand Alpine Journal, 1984.

The Journal makes pleasant and indeed inspiring reading. It covers a very wide range of moutaineering activity from high mountaineering in distant lands to the doings of the local crag-rats. What is particularly attractive about it is the way it captures and communicates the fun and excitement of climbing and the exuberance of the people that do it. Perhaps this is because the population is small enough to enable a national publication to have some of the characteristics of a good club journal. And there's nothing stuffy about the Kiwis' approach to climbing.

Tom Price

OFFICERS OF THE CLUB

1985-86

President	D.G.Roberts
Vice-Presidents	D.Miller
	B.A.Butcher
Secretary	P.L.O'Neill
Assistant Secretary	R.Lyon
Treasurer	K.D.Andrews
Assistant Treasurer	J.R.Coates
Editor of Journal	A.G.Cram
Chronicler	J.L.Sutcliffe
Guide Books Editor	D.Miller

Librarian	Mrs. M.J.Parker
Assistant Librarian	P.Fleming
Dinner Secretary	W.A.Comstive
Meets Secretary	S.M.Porteus
Huts Secretary	W.E.Smith
Hut Wardens	T.Parker, W.G.C.Lamb, R.Atkins, D.Rhodes, S.R.Charlton
Elected Members of Committee	R.Kenyon, Mrs. J.Light, T.Pickles, R.Precious, Miss M.Roberts, S.Roberts, C.Shone, Mrs. M.Shone, T.Sullivan, A.J.Wardropper, P.Whillance, Mrs. V.Young

Meets 1986

	Date	Venue	Leader
	Jan 11/12	*Beetham Cottage*	Bill Smith
CD	*Jan 25/26*	*Salving House*	Chris & Ron Kenyon
	Feb 8/9	*Raw Head*	Stan Roberts
	Feb 22/23	*Salving House*	Mike McKenzie, Geoff Oliver
	March 8/9	*Black Rock Cottage, Glencoe*	Audrey & Jim Sutcliffe
	March 22/29	*Tignes/Val d'Isere, France (skiing)*	Joyce Cosby & John Wild
	March 23/27	*CIC Hut, Ben Nevis*	Stephen Porteus
	March 29/31		
	Easter	*Brackenclose*	Norma & Roy Precious
	April 12/13	*Glandena Joint Meet M.A.M.*	John Loy & Roy Townsend
C	*April 19/20*	*Birkness*	George Lamb
M	*April 26/27*	*Beetham Cottage*	Tom Parker
	Bank Hol.		
	May 3/5	*Rawhead Joint Meet C.C.*	Kay & Stuart Charlton
	May 3/10	*Balmacara Hotel, Loch Alsh*	Joyce Cosby & Ron Brotherton
	May 17/18	*Birkness Cycle Touring*	Jo Light & John Wild
	Bank Hol.		
	May 24/26	*Pembroke (camping)*	Bill Lounds
	May 24/31	*Roybridge (camping)*	Dick Morgan
M	*June 7/8*	*Birkness*	George Lamb
C	*June 21/22*	*Rawhead*	Kath & Alan Wardropper
D	*June 28/29*	*Brackenclose Needle Centenary*	John Wilkinson
D	*July 5/6*	*Sun Hotel, Coniston*	Harry Ironfield
	July 19/20	*Birkness*	John Girdley
	Aug 2/3	*Beetham Cottage*	Francis Falkingham
	Aug 16/17	*Rawhead: University Invitation Meet*	Paddy Gaunt
	Bank Hol.		
	Aug 23/25	*Wales (camping)*	Paul Selley
CD	*Sept 6/7*	*Brackenclose*	Vice Presidents
M	*Sept 20/21*	*Rawhead*	David Rhodes
M	*Sept 27/28*	*Brackenclose*	Reg Atkins
	Sept 27/28	*Derbyshire*	Brian Griffiths & David Cobley
M	*Oct 4/5*	*Salving House*	Stuart Charlton
	Oct 3/5	*Brackenclose London Section*	Hattie Harris
	Oct 18/19	*Eden Valley*	Ron Kenyon
D	*Nov 1/2*	*AGM & Dinner*	The President
	Nov 8/9	*Brackenclose*	Jane Taylor
CD	*Nov 29/30*	*Salving House*	June Parker & Jill Aldersley
	Dec 13/14	*Birkness*	Nelson Clark
	Dec 31/Jan 1	*New Year Meet*	The President

C = Committee Meeting   D = Dinner   M = Maintenance Meet

F I S H E R

WE ARE PLEASED TO
WELCOME FELLOW CLUB
MEMBERS TO HELP YOU
IN YOUR REQUIREMENTS
FOR THE HILLS AND ALL
THE LATEST "ILLICIT
AIDS" FOR ROCK
CLIMBING.

KESWICK

KARRIMOR

RUCSACS

FOOTWEAR

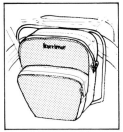
CYCLE BAGS

SLEEPING BAGS

SALEWA ALPINE GEAR

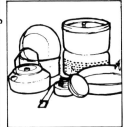
TRANGIA STOVES

SKIS & ACCESSORIES

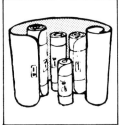
KARRIMAT

CLOTHING

EQUIPMENT *for* ADVENTURE

Karrimor International Limited, Avenue Parade, Accrington, Lancashire BB5 6PR, England.

THE CLIMBERS' SHOP

CLIMBING, CAMPING & SKIING EQUIPMENT SPECIALISTS

AMBLESIDE

OVER THE YEARS THE CLIMBERS' SHOP HAS ESTABLISHED ITSELF AS ONE OF THE FOREMOST SUPPLIERS OF CLIMBING & MOUNTAINEERING EQUIPMENT. WE OFFER THE MOST COMPREHENSIVE RANGE IN THE LAKE DISTRICT. OUR STAFF ARE ALL EXPERIENCED ENTHUSIASTS, ACTIVE IN MOUNTAIN SPORTS.

* BOOTS BY SCARPA, ZAMBERLAN, KOFLACH ETC.
* WATERPROOFS FROM BERGHAUS, PHOENIX, HENRI LLOYD, MOUNTAIN RANGE, MOUNTAIN METHOD.
* SPECIALIST CLOTHING FROM MOUNTAIN EQUIPMENT, JAVLIN, HELLY HANSEN, ULTIMATE.
* CLIMBING HARDWARE BY TROLL, CLOG, WILD COUNTRY, SALEWA, SNOWDON MOULDINGS, EDELWEISS, BEAL, EDELRID, MOUNTAIN TECHNOLOGY.
* SACS BY LOWE, KARRIMOR, BERGHAUS.
* SLEEPING BAGS FROM CARAVAN, RAB, MOUNTAIN EQUIPMENT.
* PLUS SKI HARDWARE & CLOTHING, CAMPING EQUIPMENT & ACCESSORIES, GUIDEBOOKS, MAPS ETC.

The Climbers' Shop
Compston Corner, Ambleside, Cumbria
Tel. Ambleside 32297